Twenty Year
Spoof and Bluff

Carlton

Alpha Editions

This edition published in 2024

ISBN : 9789362513366

Design and Setting By
Alpha Editions
www.alphaedis.com
Email - info@alphaedis.com

As per information held with us this book is in Public Domain. This book is a reproduction of an important historical work. Alpha Editions uses the best technology to reproduce historical work in the same manner it was first published to preserve its original nature. Any marks or number seen are left intentionally to preserve its true form.

Contents

PREFACE ....- 1 -
CHAPTER I EARLY EXPERIENCES ....- 2 -
CHAPTER II I POSE AS A SHOWMAN ....- 13 -
CHAPTER III WITH THE GYPSIES.......................- 23 -
CHAPTER IV THE TRICK THAT FAILED ....- 31 -
CHAPTER V CLIMBING TO FAME AND FORTUNE ....- 41 -
CHAPTER VI PLAYING IN HUNLAND................- 55 -
CHAPTER VII AUSTRALIAN EXPERIENCES.....- 69 -
CHAPTER VIII MELBOURNE TO LONDON ....- 82 -
CHAPTER IX SOME AMERICAN EXPERIENCES ....- 93 -
CHAPTER X MORE AMERICAN EXPERIENCES............- 104 -
CHAPTER XI PANTOMIME SPOOFS AND JOKES..........- 114 -
CHAPTER XII AFRICA AND THE ORIENT ......- 128 -
CHAPTER XIII WHEEZES AND GAGS ....- 142 -
CHAPTER XIV THE BIGGEST NEWSPAPER SPOOF ON RECORD ....- 158 -
CHAPTER XV HOW THE BIG SPOOF WAS WORKED ..- 167 -
CHAPTER XVI TELEPATHIC AND MESMERIC SPOOFS ....- 178 -
CHAPTER XVII SHARPS AND FLATS...............- 190 -
CHAPTER XVIII FLOTSAM AND JETSAM ......- 205 -
CHAPTER XIX IN EGYPT IN WAR-TIME ....- 218 -

PREFACE

IT has been said that any man of mature age could write at least one interesting book, if he confined himself to relating his own experiences.

Well, that is what I have done. This is primarily the story of my life, interspersed with various anecdotes, "wheezes," and "gags," pertaining to a profession concerning the real inside of which the public is mostly ignorant.

Like Topsy, the book "growed." An incident recalled here, a story remembered there, has been jotted down at haphazard as the mood seized me.

I may add that the incidents recorded in Chapters XIV. and XV., as also the human telescope story in Chapter XIII., first saw the light in the *Strand Magazine*, to the Editor of which periodical I am indebted for permission to reproduce them here.

CHAPTER I
EARLY EXPERIENCES

Work as a telegraph messenger boy—First attempts at "public" entertainment—Small but appreciative audiences—I introduce the cycle to the Post Office—Christmas-boxing on my own—I am rewarded with the "Order of the Sack"—Hard times—A home-made conjuring outfit—On tramp to Southend—Busking on the sands—Wrathful "niggers"—"Stage" fright—"Best clear, kid"—I clear—On the road back to London—Hunger and thirst—Four shows for fourpence—A "welcome" home—No food in the house and the brokers in—"Covering the spot"—Jimmy Jennings—I win watches—Beat a game and gain a friend—"A quick way of making money"—Learning to be a street patterer—Tricks of the showman's trade—Nearly a riot—Jimmy grows anxious—Good-bye to London once more—A new pitch—And the beginning of a new life.

MY first experience as a public conjuror and card manipulator dates back somewhere about five-and-twenty years. Sheer necessity drove me to it. A slim, shy youth of sixteen, or thereabouts, I was out of a job at the time, with no prospect, so far as I could see, of getting into one.

This was awkward, because I was practically the sole support of my widowed mother, who was a cripple, and four young sisters. So, as a last resort, I determined to tramp down to some seaside town, and try and earn a little money busking on the sands.

As a boy I had worked for a while as a telegraph messenger, one of those blind-alley occupations that lead nowhere, and I had frequently watched peripatetic conjurors giving their shows at street corners and elsewhere. These exhibitions had always had a great fascination for me, and I presently started to try and copy their tricks.

It was difficult at first, for I had no one to teach or advise me, but I persevered, and was able in time to do quite a variety of simple stock tricks with cards, coins, etc. My audiences were small but appreciative, consisting as they did of my fellow telegraph messengers attached to the old Buckingham Gate Post Office in the Buckingham Palace Road—long since done away with—where I was then stationed. Afterwards I was sent to the Castelnau Post Office, Barnes, which was situated at a chemist's shop.

Here I had plenty of spare time on my hands, telegrams being comparatively few and far between. The distances I had to travel to deliver them, however, were often considerable, and this gave me an idea. I was at the time the proud possessor of an ancient solid-tyred bicycle. This I requisitioned in order to cover the ground more quickly, a complete novelty in those days, when cycles for post-office work were not even thought of.

My "boss," the sub-postmaster, was particularly struck with the innovation, and he wrote to the Postmaster-General about it, with the unexpected, and to me very gratifying result, that I received from the Department an extra allowance of three shillings and sixpence a week for the upkeep, etc., of my machine. Afterwards the practice received general official sanction, and in time became well-nigh universal. But I can, I believe, truthfully lay claim to having been its originator, and I was certainly the first telegraph messenger-boy to ride a cycle for the Post Office in an official capacity.

From Barnes I was sent to Battersea, where our family had also gone to live, and it was here that my too-enterprising spirit led to the severance of my connection with the Post Office Service. It came about in this way. When Christmas came round I was given a temporary job as auxiliary postman. We boys used to hear the regular postmen talk a lot about their Christmas-boxes and the fine harvest of tips they expected to reap, and I did not see why, as I was doing my share of the work, I should not share in the pickings.

So, very early on Boxing Day morning, before the regular postman had started out to "box his walk," I went round and collected the gratuities, or at all events a considerable portion of them. I didn't say I was the postman, but simply knocked and asked for a Christmas box, and being a tall youth the money was mostly handed over to me without demur. Later on, of course, when the regular postman called round, there was an awful row, and I was called upon to resign; a polite way of investing me with the "order of the sack." In this dilemma, as narrated above, I purposed turning to account my knowledge of conjuring in order to earn a livelihood, or try to.

As a preliminary I went and begged the lid of a cheese-box from a near-by shop. This I covered with a bit of old cloth my mother gave me, and trimmed it round with a yard or so of penny-threefarthing ball fringe. Next I set my transmogrified cheese-box lid on top of three thin bamboo canes, arranged tripod-wise, and behold I was in possession of quite a pretty little table, such as street conjurors affect.

Next I procured a rabbit—all conjurors had to have a rabbit in those days—and some balls and tins for what is called the cup-and-ball trick, together with a pack of cards, and a few other simple paraphernalia, not forgetting half-a-dozen pennies—in conjuring parlance "a pile of megs"—for palming and working disappearing coin tricks. Thus equipped, I set out. I had been told that Southend was the best place to go to, and as I had no money to pay my fare I had to walk there, carrying my poor little "props" with me.

It was weary work. The long dusty road seemed endless. Several times I was tempted to go into a public-house and try and do a show. But directly I set up my little table, my nerve forsook me, and out I came again. When night fell I chopped some wood for a farmer's wife, who gave me in return a glass of milk and a crust of bread and cheese and permission to sleep in the barn.

Eventually I reached Southend, hungry, thirsty, and footsore. Also I was penniless, having been forced to part with my six coppers in order to keep myself in food on the road, thereby spoiling my best tricks. All day long I prowled about, watching the buskers at work on the beach, but never being able to pluck up sufficient courage to make a start myself.

I had managed to get a room by promising to pay at the end of the week, but after the first morning, when I ate a breakfast that I am afraid astonished and frightened my landlady, I was denied further board unless I paid something on account, which, of course, I was unable to do. For three days I prowled around, living as best I could, watching with hungry eyes the picnic parties on the beach, and greedily devouring the scraps they left after they took their departure. I never felt so famished in all my life before.

On the morning of the fourth day, a Bank Holiday, a letter came from my mother. She wrote that she had got the brokers in, that my little sisters were crying for bread, and would I please send her some money? That did it. I felt that it was now or never. And, marching down to the beach, I set up my little table, and soon had quite a respectable audience—respectable in point of size that is to say—gathered round me.

Then again the fatal shyness came over me; stage fright in its first, worst, and most terrible form—only there was no stage. My legs shook under me, my knees knocked together, my tongue felt as if glued to the roof of my mouth. I almost think I would have made a bolt for it once more, but for the fact that the crowd hemmed me in on every side.

Ten minutes passed by. My audience began to show unmistakable signs of impatience. "Get a move on, kid!" they cried; "start your bloomin' show." Thus adjured I began. But just as I was in the middle of my first trick, there was a commotion on the outskirts of the crowd, people jostling and shoving, pushing and being pushed, and a moment or two later four burly nigger minstrels burst through to where I was. I got a punch on the back of my neck that sent me sprawling, and when I scrambled to my feet I was just in time to see my poor little cheese-box table go flying seaward, propelled by a vigorous kick from the biggest and burliest of the niggers.

I was too weak from hunger to even try to retaliate, too flabbergasted at the unexpected, and as it seemed to me unprovoked and unwarrantable, attack to attempt to expostulate even. I just stood stock-still, open-mouthed and trembling, while the leader of the buskers asked me, in language the reverse of polite, what in thunder I meant by taking their pitch, for which they paid, and which nobody else therefore had the right to occupy?

There was some further talk, and then I learnt for the first time that the sands at Southend belonged to the corporation, and that buskers were not allowed to perform there without permission, and without paying for the privilege. Naturally I was terribly downhearted at this, and I suppose I showed it, for after the niggers had given their show they clubbed round amongst themselves, and handed me two shillings. "Best clear out, youngster," they told me, not unkindly. "You can't do anything here without capital."

Their advice seemed good advice. So that very day I started to tramp back to London. I had retrieved my table, and although I had been compelled to sell my rabbit in order to buy food during my stay in Southend, I still had with me my pack of cards, and one or two other trifles. With these, on the way back, I gave four shows at as many separate "pubs." One of these shows netted me fourpence, the other three yielded nothing. I reached home after a week's absence, weak, weary, and ill, to find a welcome of words waiting for me, and that was all. There was not a morsel of food in the house, not even the proverbial crust, and the broker's man had cleared out most of the furniture.

For these reasons I am not likely ever to forget my first "provincial tour." That night I cried myself to sleep, the hunger gnawed at my vitals, and I don't believe there was an unhappier lad in England than I was just then.

Next morning I felt a little better; but not much. However, it was, I reflected, no good sitting down and repining, and I started out to look for work. After a while I got a job as potman and under-barman at seven shillings a week in a public-house in the Battersea Park Road.

One day a travelling conjuror came into the saloon bar, and did a few tricks with coins. The proprietor was greatly interested in the show, and the next day, when he and I were having dinner together in a little recess behind the bar, he remarked:

"Clever chap that conjuror who was here yesterday. Those coin tricks of his were wonderful."

"Oh!" I replied, "I didn't think very much of them. Why I could do better than that myself. Look here!" And I took a penny from my pocket, and palming it from one hand to the other I made it disappear before his eyes.

To my unbounded surprise my employer promptly jumped up, his face crimson with rage. "You young rascal!" he cried. "That's quite enough for me. I've been missing money from the till for quite a long while now. Out you go!" And, suiting the action to his words, he seized me by the scruff of the neck and the seat of my trousers, and threw me out of the house on to the pavement.

When I got home and told my story, my mother was naturally very much upset, and she went round and expostulated with the landlord; but all to no purpose. He insisted that money had been missed, and that I must be the thief, as there was nobody else who could have taken it except the head barman, and he had been with them a long while and was quite above suspicion.

This individual, who slept in the same room as myself, was, I may add, a very great pet of the landlady, who was firmly convinced that he could do nothing wrong.

Yet he was the thief all the while, as it turned out; for some little time afterwards, and while I was away in the country, he was convicted and sentenced to three months' imprisonment, the stolen money having been found in his box. My mother sent me a copy of the local paper with the account of the police-court proceedings.

Some few years later I had succeeded in making a name for myself. I was at the Palace Theatre in Shaftesbury Avenue, and my name was blazoned in letters a foot long on the buses, and on all the hoardings in London. It was a hot day, and I felt thirsty. I turned into a little "pub" in Wellington Street, Strand. There behind the bar was my old "boss."

I had grown a lot in the intervening years, and he didn't know me; but I knew him directly.

Over a whisky-and-soda we got into conversation, and presently he asked me who I was.

"My name is Carlton," I said, "I'm at the Palace Theatre this week."

"Oh yes," he replied, "of course. I saw you the other evening. Wonderful good show, yours."

"Glad you like it," I said. "But say—do you remember the day when you took me by the scruff of my neck and threw me out of your old place in the Battersea Park Road, after accusing me of stealing money from the till; money that your wife's favourite boy afterwards got three months for stealing? Do you remember that—eh?"

The landlord looked surprised. So did his wife, who was behind the bar with him at the time. But they would neither of them admit that they remembered anything about the affair.

Of course they did, though; only they would not acknowledge it. Possibly they thought I might bring an action against them, even after the lapse of all that time, for wrongful dismissal and defamation of character.

But to resume the thread of my story. At the time I was thrown out of the "pub," and out of work at the same time, we used to live in the neighbourhood of Clapham Junction, in a turning off the Falcon Road.

There was a man at a pitch near here who earned his living at a game called "covering the spot." On a table covered with white oil-cloth he had painted several round red spots, each about as big as a plate. The player was given five tin discs, for which he paid a penny, and his aim was to drop these on one of the spots so as to completely cover it, leaving not even a peep of the red showing. If he succeeded in doing this he got a watch, which the proprietor of the game, if the winner so willed it, would buy back again for three shillings and sixpence.

It was rather a fascinating game to watch, and having nothing else in particular to do I stood and watched it for a long while. He was a splendid patterer, was the proprietor, and he was simply raking in the pennies like dirt all the while. The game was new then.

"Money for nothing!" was one of his stock phrases he kept shouting out. So it was "money for nothing," but he was the man who got the money, I noticed. "If you don't speculate, you can't accumulate," was another of his gags. "This, gentlemen, is a scientific game of skill. Span your tins and drop them on. Try it! Try it! Try it! Cover the red, and carry off a watch. Hide the red you win; show the red you lose. Come along, gents! Come along! Come along! Faint heart never won fair lady!" And so on, and so on. And in between his patter, at intervals, he would himself "cover the red" with the five discs to demonstrate how easily it could be done.

I kept watching him closely, and I saw there was a knack in it. A man who had tried twenty or thirty times, but without success, was turning away. On the impulse of the moment I spoke to him. "I can do it," I said. "Lend me a penny and let me try; we'll go halves if I win."

The man looked at me rather dubiously. "Why don't you risk your own money?" he asked. "Because I haven't got any," I replied. "Oh well, in that case here you are," he said; and he handed me a penny.

I dropped the discs one by one, carefully, methodically, slowly, and—I covered the red. A great shout went up from the crowd. Everybody was delighted, including the proprietor. He wanted somebody to win occasionally, but not too often, and he made a tremendous fuss.

"Hi! Hi! Hi!" he cried. "The boy's won a watch. Come along, you sports, now. Come and do likewise. Don't let a lad like this beat you."

He handed me the watch, and I gave it back to him, receiving in return three-and-sixpence. This, he explained, was because the law would not allow him to give a money prize direct. It was my first experience of how simple a thing it is to get round an inconvenient legal enactment, though not my last one by any means.

After sharing the cash with the "capitalist" who had financed my venture, I still had of course one shilling and ninepence left, and I invested a penny of this on my own account in another five discs.

Again I won. Things were getting lively. The crowd cheered louder than ever. I was more than cheerful. The proprietor tried his best to look cheerful also, but there was a glint of anxiety in his eyes.

For the third time I tried my luck, but this time I just failed. Or so, at least, the proprietor asserted. Producing a pin, he inserted the point between two of the discs without moving either of them, thereby proving to his satisfaction, if not quite to mine, that the red was not completely covered. Here was a new trick of the trade, I reflected; no smallest patch of red was visible, but the pin's point showed apparently that it existed, therefore I had lost.

"Try! Try! Try again!" shouted the showman. "Faint heart never won fair lady."

I took his advice, and this time I succeeded once more. This made three wins in four tries. "Clever lad!" cried the crowd. But the proprietor looked glum. He leaned over the table and implored me in a stage whisper to go away.

I went, taking with me my eight shillings and sixpence winnings. That night the family sat down to a real, slap-up hot supper of tripe and onions, the first square meal that any of us had eaten for many a long day.

As for me, I was in high glee. I had, I considered, hit on a quick and easy way of making money. Next evening I sauntered down to where the showman had his pitch, and directly he had got his table set up I marched in, and soon won another watch.

This was too much for the proprietor. He called me on one side.

"Look here," he said, "you're too hot for me. Come and have a drink."

We adjourned to the "Queen Victoria" public-house, and he called for a large rum for himself. I had a "small lemon."

Over our drinks we discussed business, or rather he did. His name, he informed me, was Jimmy Jennings.

"I have been in the business for years," he went on, "but I've never run up against a smarter lad than you are at the game. You're hot stuff, and no mistake. Tell you what now. There's room for a couple of stalls at my pitch. Will you work for me if I put another one up for you to take charge of? I'll pay you five shillings a night, and ten per cent. on the takings. What do you say?"

Naturally, I was quite agreeable, and the following day, true to his promise, Jimmy had a table fixed up all ready for me to start. Being pretty well known in the neighbourhood I soon had plenty of customers, and raked in a good lot of money. Here, too, I first learnt to do the showman's patter, for Jimmy, as I have already intimated, was a splendid patterer, and I, being all the time at the next stall to him, naturally picked up the art from him, almost without effort on my part.

Also I learnt many tricks of the showman's trade, more especially as regards the particular stunt we were working. I was shown, for instance, that although the five red spots on the tables looked to be all exactly of one size, they were not so in reality. As regards four of them, although they could just be covered by the discs, the task was so exceedingly difficult a one as to be almost impossible of achievement. The fifth spot, however, was slightly smaller than the others, and the feat of covering it, therefore, was comparatively easy.

But as it was impossible to detect the smaller spot without actually measuring it, the chances were five to one against any player, picking his spot at haphazard, as of course he invariably did, choosing the easiest one. When either of us performed the feat for the benefit of the onlookers, however, we naturally always used the small spot. It was due to my sharpness in detecting this fact—though not until after long watching—coupled with a natural dexterity and quickness of hand, that had enabled me to win the watches in the first instance.

I might also mention that the flares which we used to illuminate our stalls—we did not usually start performing until after dark—were so arranged as to throw the light slantwise to our side of the table where the smaller spot was. This enabled us, if we performed the trick quickly—and this we invariably did—to leave a little bit of red showing without the audience being able to detect the fact. This was both handy and necessary, for even when working on the smaller spot, and notwithstanding all our acquired dexterity, we were neither of us so clever at it as to be able to bring off the trick with certainty every time.

And one had to be very careful, and exercise plenty of tact. The main thing was to keep the crowd in a good humour. That is where the art of the patterer comes in. We should have stood but a poor chance without it. Even as it was there were rows. One of the worst was on my account. A man in the audience asserted that I was standing on a box, and that that was why I was able to perform the trick. "Let me come round your side of the table and mount your box," he cried, "and I'll do it as easily as you can."

In vain I assured him that I was not standing on a box, that it was only my unusual height—6 ft. 2½ ins.—that made it appear to him as if I were. He protested, began to get obstreperous, tried to force his way round. The crowd took sides, for and against: mostly against. There was something approaching a free fight, and we were afraid the stalls would be mobbed and wrecked. However, a policeman appeared on the scene, and things quieted down after a bit.

But Jimmy looked thoughtful that night after we had closed down.

"Look here, laddie," he said presently, "this pitch is getting a bit too hot. Tonbridge Fair opens next week. We'll pack up and open there."

Which we did.

So closed one chapter of my life. The next one was to open amongst far different surroundings.

CHAPTER II
I POSE AS A SHOWMAN

Practising conjuring—Why I rarely play cards—The great Maskelyne and Cooke box trick—I make a trick box of my own—The "Flying Lady" who flew—away—In partnership with Gypsy Brown—My life with the show folk—I begin to make money—The kings of the fair grounds—Caravan life and cookery—The Romany people and their ways—Gypsy Brown cheats me—How the "bluers" work—Fights in the Fair Ground—The etiquette of the showmen—In a boxing booth—Taking on all comers—A rough life—"Do a slang to get a pitch"—The tricks of the travelling boxing-booth proprietors—A gypsy duel with cocoanut balls.

DURING the period when I was working for Jimmy Jennings at his "covering the spot" stall I had lots of spare time on my hands, for of course we only occupied our pitches for comparatively short intervals of an evening, and then only on certain days of the week, Saturday being always one.

This leisure I utilised mostly in practising conjuring tricks, and in card manipulation. In the beginning I used to use old tram and omnibus tickets for the latter purpose, and found them very useful, for being much smaller than ordinary playing cards they were of course more easily palmed or otherwise manipulated, while at the same time they afforded excellent practice to a comparative tyro, as I then was.

I may mention that at that time I rarely handled the cards themselves, and still more rarely played a card game. Nor do I now, at least not for money; and the same rule holds good, I have observed, with most professional conjurors and card-manipulators.

The reason of this self-denying ordinance is, of course, not very far to seek. Take my own case for example! If I should play cards for money, and win, although I have as much right to win as any other player taking part in the game, there is always the risk that the others—even one's own friends—may think I have utilised my professional skill in order to take an unfair advantage of them; in other words that I have cheated them. While should I lose, people are apt to say: "Well, Carlton is not so smart with the pasteboards as we thought him to be, after all; the man's a bit of a mug." So that's why I very rarely play.

It was, too, during my term of "apprenticeship" with Jimmy, if I may so term it, that I first became interested in the great Maskelyne and Cooke box trick. These two gentlemen were showing, at the Egyptian Hall, Piccadilly, a trick which consisted in a man being corded up in a locked box, and from which he freed himself in a few seconds.

At each performance they offered £500 to anyone who could make a similar box, and successfully duplicate the trick. Two young men, clever mechanics they were, set to work, and eventually succeeded in making a box and performing the trick. I, being at the time a lithe and supple youth, was placed inside the box at the trial exhibition, and I released myself and appeared outside in three seconds.

I should add that after I was placed in the box, it was locked, and then enveloped completely in a canvas cover, which was sealed and corded, as Messrs. Maskelyne and Cooke had stipulated. Notwithstanding this they declined to pay the promised £500, and the case came into the Queen's Bench, and was eventually carried through the Court of Appeal right up to the House of Lords.

Messrs. Maskelyne and Cooke lost, and the two young men who had made the box got their £500, but of course I received none of the money. Nevertheless, I have mentioned the incident because it was indirectly the cause of my getting my first real boost up in my present profession. But of this more anon.

Suffice it for the present to say that I had learnt all there was to know about that particular box trick. And not only that. I had set to work on my own initiative, without saying a word to anyone, and had made a similar trick box of my own, and in regard to which, moreover, being a youth of an experimental and inventive turn of mind, I had introduced one or two notable improvements; or at least so I regarded them, and so, as a matter of fact, they eventually turned out. The reason for my mentioning this here will appear presently.

On arriving at Tonbridge Fair Ground I became acquainted with a big gypsy named Brown, a typical Romany lad, or diddyki, as these people call themselves in their own dialect.

He had a booth in which he was giving a show with a so-called "Flying Lady." She had been working at other fairs with him on the basis of half the takings, but at Tonbridge, greatly to Brown's disgust and disappointment, she failed to put in an appearance. The flying lady had in fact flown—away.

In this dilemma Brown suggested that I should take her place for a week, which I did, and this resulted eventually in my performing my box trick at his booth. I had, I should state, rehearsed the trick many times with a performer who called himself "Lieutenant Doctor Lynn, Junior," and who was a son of the one-time famous conjuror, Dr. Lynn. He it was who presented the trick for the two young men mentioned above who successfully sued Messrs. Maskelyne and Cooke. I was, therefore, absolutely part perfect in the act, and with the improvements I had made in my box I felt confident that I could hold my own with anybody in the business.

CARLTON—ON

At Faversham Fair Ground, to which we went from Tonbridge, I arranged with Brown to share his booth, he paying the rent for the ground, or the "tobee" as the fair folk call it, each to have half the takings. I was also to help him by pattering outside the show, and performing card tricks, in order to attract the people, and by interesting them induce them to come inside: in showman's parlance "doing a slang to get a pitch." This arrangement was certainly a by no means unfavourable one for him, but he was not satisfied, as I shall have occasion to show hereafter.

Prior to our opening at Faversham I had cut some paper letters, and stuck them on a big, bright ultramarine blue banner, advertising my show as follows:

CARLTON PHILPS

in a facsimile of the famous
Box Trick
that won £500 in the House of Lords.

This act went with a rush from first to last, and this was where I began to make money. It was a novel experience to me, and need I say it was as pleasant as it was novel. I was now able to send home a substantial sum each week to my mother and sisters, put by a little against a rainy day, and still have enough left over for my personal needs, which, however, I may add, were at that time of quite modest dimensions.

To go back a little, I should explain that the roundabout people are the kings, so to speak, of the fair grounds; and it is these usually who arrange for the pitches in advance, and pay the "dinari for the tobee" (i.e. money for the ground) in a lump sum to whoever owns the land, afterwards sub-letting it to the smaller showmen, the amount of the rent paid by these latter varying with the size and position of their individual pitches. The name of the roundabout firm who rented the fair grounds at Tonbridge and Faversham was Messrs. Hastings and Wayman, now well-known travelling showmen in Wales.

I got very friendly both with Mr. Hastings and Mr. Wayman. Though wealthy men as show folk go, and very smart at a deal, they were poor scholars, and I used to assist them in making up their accounts. I also, at their request, acted as their advance agent in so far as I used to go on ahead and arrange for the renting of the tobee.

In this way I got my first insight into the life of the road as led by the Romany folk. It was, I have no hesitation in saying, the happiest time of my life. When on the move I lived in one of their waggons—caravans ordinary people call them, but to the gypsies they are always waggons—and to travel slowly along through the beautiful English country lanes behind the sleek, well-fed horses, was a revelation in restfulness to a bred and born Cockney lad like myself.

We almost lived on the country. Our dogs brought us in rabbits and to spare. Even pheasants for the pot were not lacking. For this I make neither apology nor excuse. The true gypsy regards all fur and feather that runs or flies as his by divine right, and the word "poaching" has for him literally no significance whatever. When we pulled up at set of sun by some wayside brook the odour of cooking was always quickly wafted on the breeze—and such cooking!

It was on one of these journeys that I first tasted that famous Romany dainty, a hedgehog rolled whole in clay, and baked in the hot ashes. Believe me it is a dish fit for a king; tasty, succulent, juicy, and possessing a delicious flavour—gamy but not too gamy—that is all its own. We also used to cook birds, and even rump steaks, after the same fashion, and very toothsome I found them. Of course care must be taken to select the right kind of clay for an envelope, and it is also advisable to pick out the worms from it before using it.

Heaven knows how long I might have continued leading this kind of life had it not been for an untoward incident that happened later on, and to which I shall refer presently. I might have even continued the vagrant gypsy existence that fitted in so well with my tastes and inclinations, and become in time almost one of themselves. As it was, after only a comparatively short spell of it, I was becoming half a Romany, using their dialect, and falling by degrees, and almost unconsciously, into their ways of thought and methods of expression.

However, as I have already said, my career as an amateur gypsy was destined to be cut short sooner than I had bargained for. I was, of course, never really one of themselves. All the gypsy show folk are related to one another more or less, either by marriage or descent, and although they will show friendship to an outsider on occasion, they never fully trust any such, or admit them to a real, close intimacy. My trouble with them began, as so many other troubles begin, over money matters.

My show, as I have said, was unusually successful, and for some time it had been borne in upon me that I was not getting my fair share of the takings. I mentioned my suspicions—they were in fact much more than mere suspicions—to Mr. Wayman, and he was very much upset and annoyed about it. At the same time he warned me that it would be as well to avoid if possible having any open quarrel with Brown, who had the reputation of being a violent man, and who would be certain, if trouble arose between us, to have all the other gypsies on his side irrespective of the rights or wrongs of the matter in dispute.

This of course was all very well in its way, and I quite recognised how excellent was his advice, and how kind and well-meaning was the man himself in giving it. But then, on the other hand, I did not see why I should go on being cheated, nor did I intend to, if I could help it. So one day between the shows I quietly slipped off up to London, without saying a word to anybody, and bought an automatic pocket register; one of those tiny affairs, not much bigger than a watch, which you can hold behind you, or keep hidden in your pocket if need be, and tick off with one hand the number of people passing in or out of the building.

That night when we came to settle up, I found, as I had surmised, that Brown was cheating me. His count of the number of patrons visiting my show was somewhere about fifty below that registered by my machine; and which, by the way, he did not know I possessed. Nor did I enlighten him even now on this latter point, merely remarking that I thought he must be mistaken as to the number, for I had kept count, and I made it fifty more than he did, which, at a penny each for admission, and reckoning half the takings as mine, made my share 2s. 1d. more than he was going to pay me.

"Oh, that can't be," objected Brown. "I'm sure my figure is the correct one. Perhaps you counted the 'bluers.'"

In order that the reader may be able to appreciate the full significance of this remark, and also understand how little Brown thought, or affected to think, of my intelligence, I ought here to explain the meaning of the word "bluer"; a term perfectly familiar to all the great host of peripatetic showmen, roundabout proprietors, owners of cocoanut shies, and the like, but unknown probably to the generality of people outside these professions.

Literally, then, to "blue," in the Romany dialect, means to push or shove, and a bluer, therefore, means a pushful, forceful individual, one who shoves and elbows his way to the front.

Bluers work on fair grounds in gangs of from four to six or eight. They hang about the outskirts of the crowd that gathers round the show where, we will say, the fat lady is on exhibition, or the tattooed man; and at the proper moment, that is to say when the showman has finished his harangue and is inviting all and sundry to "walk up—walk up—walk up," the bluers start to elbow their way to the front from the rear, pay their pennies with assumed eagerness, and enter the show. The crowd, once the lead is set, follows like a flock of sheep, and the trick is done.

Afterwards the bluers spread themselves amongst the crowd outside again and discuss, of course in highly eulogistic terms, the wonders of the particular show they have just visited, before proceeding to another part of the fair ground, there to repeat their performance for the benefit of some other showman. Or they will give a lead at the cocoanut shies, where, being excellent throwers owing to long practice at the game, they invariably down the nuts, thereby encouraging others to try and do likewise.

Bluers are paid a shilling a day by each of the showmen having stands at a fair, and manage to make a very decent living, following the shows round from place to place all over the country, and from year's end to year's end.

Of course each bluer is furnished beforehand with a sufficient stock of pennies each day to pay for admission for himself to the various shows; and, equally of course, these pennies have to be deducted from the gross total of the takings at the close of the day, and allowed for.

The reader will be able to understand now, therefore, how exceedingly nettled and angry I was when Brown accused me of counting in the bluers; because it was obvious that I knew by sight every one of these men, and that I was not going to count them in as ordinary members of the paying public, unless indeed I was trying to cheat him, a course which, needless to say, I neither intended nor desired.

All this I explained to him, but he still persisted in saying that I was mistaken in my count; so, bearing in mind the advice given me by my friend Mr. Wayman, I decided to let the matter drop just then, hoping that he would take the hint, and treat me fairly for the future. Instead, however, matters kept going from bad to worse. Every night he docked me in sums running in the aggregate into quite a lot of money, and I felt very sore about it. Besides, it was very unpleasant in other ways, for the matter was a continual bone of contention between us, leading to constant bickerings and quarrels.

And I wanted no quarrels just then, either with Brown, or with any of the other gypsies. I had had quite enough to go on with already, if the truth must be told. Indeed, before I had been following the fairs a week I had fought no fewer than five pitched battles with the show folk, and their hangers-on the bluers, and others. This, however, was in a sense partly my own fault, and it was also partly due to my ignorance of the unwritten law that govern the working of the fair grounds.

For example, it is the custom for everybody to help in the setting up and taking down of the various shows, roundabouts, cocoanut shies, and so on. The bluers, too, gave a hand in this work without extra remuneration, except that when a fair is finished they are given a lift on the waggons as far as the next town to which the shows are going. Now I, being ignorant of this custom, used to go off on my own somewhere as soon as I had finished putting up or taking down Brown's booth, thereby, of course, giving offence. The others thought I was trying to shirk my obligations to them, whereas nothing was further from my thoughts. I simply did not know.

However, I had been used to taking my own part. Trust a Cockney lad for that! So I was usually able to give a pretty good account of myself. Besides, I got plenty of practice in the fair grounds. When business was slack at our show, I used to go over to a boxing booth in another part of the ground that was kept by one Alf Ball, an ex-champion pugilist, and he put me up to many a pretty wrinkle.

In return I used to help him get an audience by "doing a slang" for him, and would also, on occasion, put on the gloves outside his booth. This meant taking on all comers, and I fought many a hard bout on his account, for being tall and thin, in fact a typical light-weight, people used to pick on me. "I'll have 'em (the gloves) on wi' yon long fellow," a burly rustic would say, and smile confidently to himself in anticipation of an easy victory.

As a matter of fact, however, I always won, although not exactly on my merits. What happened usually was this. Alf would keep a watchful eye on our performance, and if my opponent turned out to be a bit of a bruiser, and "out for a scrap" as we used to say, then the rounds, instead of lasting the regulation three minutes, would be cut down to one minute, or even less. On the other hand, if I was getting the best of a round, then it would be made to last out to perhaps as long as five minutes, or until the chap was finally knocked out.

There were other "tricks of the trade" too, all designed to make sure that the booth's champion won. For instance, all the boxing-gloves looked alike; but that was all. My pair, weighing perhaps fourteen ounces, were of solid leather. The pair lent to my opponent for the bout were padded with horsehair, and as soft as a couple of sofa cushions. With these "dud" gloves he could make little impression on me, while if I got one home with mine it was all over with the other fellow. "By gum, but that thin consumptive-looking chap *can* punch," my discomfited opponent would remark, as he quitted the ring, a sadder and sorer man than when he entered it.

I may add, however, that the gypsies, when fighting between themselves, seldom "fight fair," as the term is understood amongst boxers. They "go for" one another with sticks, feet, hands, stones, anything. One favourite way of settling their differences is by what may be called a duel with cocoanut balls.

Everybody nearly is familiar, of course, with these round, hard wooden balls, and the gypsy keepers of the cocoanut shies are naturally adepts at throwing them. When two of them fall out, and agree to fight after this fashion, two heaps of six or eight balls are placed about twenty yards apart. The "duellists" then stand back to back midway between the two heaps, and at the word "go" from their seconds each makes a quick dash for the heap facing him, gathers up the balls, and then, turning about, he races towards his opponent, throwing one or more balls as he advances.

They do not, however, as a rule advance directly towards one another, but zigzag and circle about, wary as two panthers, and every now and again one or the other of them will let fly a ball with unerring aim, which the other has to dodge, or run the risk of being put out of action, for a blow from one of these missiles, when thrown by a gypsy, is extremely apt to be a knock-out one.

I once indeed saw a man's arm broken in one such encounter, and another gypsy had his skull fractured. The interest of the spectators of these curious duels increases as ball after ball is disposed of, and reaches fever-heat when each combatant has thrown all his balls but one, without any decisive result being attained; for obviously the holder of the last ball, if he is not disabled, has his opponent practically at his mercy. The other can only run, circle, and dodge, in order to try and evade for as long as possible the blow he knows must come sooner or later.

CHAPTER III
WITH THE GYPSIES

I start a show of my own—Gypsy Brown plays me a dirty trick—The hunchback in the box—Bank Holiday at Cheriton Fair—I plan to circumvent Gypsy Brown—And succeed only too well—The crowd wrecks Brown's booth—Pandemonium in the fair ground—The gypsies attack my show—The fate of a peace-maker—My fight with Gypsy Brown—£10 to £1 on my opponent and no takers—A knock-out blow—Gypsy Brown vows revenge—My life in danger—How I outwitted the gypsies—The last of my experiences as a fair-ground showman.

MEANWHILE all this time Brown was steadily robbing me. Again I confided in my friend Mr. Wayman, telling him that I had by this time saved enough money to buy a tent (but not a proper showman's booth) and asking his advice as to starting on my own. He thought it would be a good idea, but again took occasion to warn me against incurring the enmity of Brown, and his many friends and relations.

At this time we were performing at Sheerness on an open space in front of the beach, and having made up my mind to act on Mr. Wayman's advice and chance it, I went to Messrs. Gasson & Sons of Rye, the big military tent-makers, and bought from them a fairly large second-hand army marquee, that I considered would about answer my purpose, at all events for the time being. Then, after our last show at Sheerness, having quite decided to sever all connection with Brown for the future, I made shift to get my box away from his keeping; but unfortunately he was able to retain possession of my banner, and my other "outside props."

Our next destination after Sheerness was Cheriton, outside Folkestone, where there was a big volunteer camp. We arrived here on an August Bank Holiday, which, I should explain, is the showman's day of days. All was bustle and animation. I could not, I reflected, have chosen a more auspicious occasion for my first venture as an independent showman.

Helped by the bluers, and a few others, I soon ran up my marquee, and Mr. Wayman very kindly lent me a lorry for an outside platform. I had previously engaged a big ex-army man named Sam Cliff as doorman, and to take the money, etc. He was a fine-built chap, weighing over fourteen stone, and by his own account a bit of a bruiser. I had also provided myself with another banner, a duplicate of the first one I had made, and which was now in Brown's possession.

"Let him keep it," I kept saying to myself. "Much good may it do him! He'll never dare to use it."

But to my disgust and disappointment this is precisely what he did do. Our two shows, situated almost directly opposite one another, each flaunted an almost identical banner proclaiming to all and sundry that Carlton Philps would give a performance of the famous box trick that won £500 in the House of Lords.

This was, of course, intolerable, and I promptly went over to Mr. Wayman and lodged a complaint. Whilst I was talking to him a little hunchback chap came over to where we were, and asked:

"Are you Mr. Carlton Philps?"

"Yes," I said, "that's me. What do you want?"

"Well, sir," he answered, "I hope you won't be offended, but Mr. Brown has engaged me to do a box trick. He fetched me down from London to do it, and now I find that he is using your banner for my trick."

"Oh," I said, affecting an indifference I was far from feeling, "that's all right. Of course there are box tricks and box tricks. Now what sort of a one is yours, may I ask?"

The hunchback gave me a description of it, from which I gathered that his was a very ordinary show indeed, and far inferior to mine; his box being about four times as big as mine was, and minus the canvas cover. Also his trick was worked by means of a trap-door, whereas mine was independent of any such adjunct. So, after turning the matter over in my mind for a little while, I told him it was all right, and he was to get on with his trick.

Well, by the time the fair ground opened, there were I should think between fifteen and twenty thousand people present. The weather was lovely, the crowd was in excellent spirits, and it looked as if we had a record day in front of us.

Brown was ready before me, and he gave a first show under my banner. "This will never do," I thought. "I've got to queer him right here now, or else he'll queer me."

So, after thinking hard for a second or two, I called to Cliff, and told him to come up outside on the lorry with me, and to bring my box, together with the canvas cover and the rope.

"Now," I said, addressing the crowd, "I want some of you gentlemen to step up here on the platform, put me inside this box after you have examined it, lock it and keep the key, and then put on the canvas cover and cord it up as tightly and securely as you can. Then, when you have done all this, I want you to carry the box, with me in it, inside the tent, and I will escape from it inside of ten seconds. Finally I will guarantee that, as regards this my first performance here, everybody shall get their money back which they have paid for admittance."

"Hurrah!" cried the crowd, and before you could say "Jack Robinson" half a dozen sailors had scrambled up on the lorry, and proceeded to carry out my instructions as to locking me in the box, and roping it up. Afterwards they carried me inside, followed by the rest of the crowd, and I escaped from it, as I had said I would, within the time stipulated.

Then I made them another speech, explaining to them that I was the one and only original Carlton Philps, and showing them my photograph and papers to prove it. "Now," I concluded, "I promised that you should all have your money back, and so you shall—but on one condition. I want each one of you to take the penny my doorkeeper will give you, and go over to the opposition show and see fair play. I ask you to rope the other man up in the same way as you roped me, using the same precautions. Then see whether he will be able to get out as I have done."

"Hurrah!" shouted the crowd once more. And off they went, sailors and all, their pennies clutched tight in their hands, making a bee-line for Brown's booth. Then I began to get frightened. Cliff, too, looked serious. But, as I pointed out to him, it was no good worrying ourselves. What had to be, must be. Our business now was with our own show.

By this time the fair was in full swing. The roundabouts were going merrily, the steam organs were at full blast, and I had just begun to gather another crowd round me when I suddenly noticed the central pole of Brown's booth began to wobble to and fro in a most alarming manner. I could plainly hear, too, angry shouts, and cries of derision, coming from the interior, and almost immediately the entire canvas edifice collapsed with a crash.

"Good Lord! That's done it!" cried Cliff. "Now we're in for it. The gypsies will never forget or forgive us for this day's work."

I began to think the same, for I quite realised what had happened. The sailors had roped the hunchback in the box, and he had been unable to get out. In revenge the crowd, led by the sailors, had wrecked the show.

However, I reflected, this was primarily Brown's concern, not mine, and I went on with my preparations for my own show. My marquee was about half full of people, and more swarming in every minute, when the expected happened. Brown, his huge face crimson with anger, and bellowing like a bull, came charging across from the ruins of his booth, followed by a score or so members of his tribe, all of them obviously bent on mischief.

Nor did they come unarmed. Some carried iron tent pegs, others long cudgels, and one big, brawny ruffian swung aloft a heavy iron-shod oak capstan bar, used in the roundabout business. I also noticed, and this caused me most misgiving, that several had round wooden balls taken from the cocoanut-shy boxes. These are very dangerous missiles indeed in the hand of the gypsies, for they can throw them, owing to long practice, as straight as a rifle-shot. Many a time had I seen men stretched senseless by a well-directed shot from one of them, as narrated in the previous chapter, and I had no wish to repeat the experiment in my own person.

However, there was neither time nor opportunity to do much thinking. Calling to Cliff to follow me, I scrambled on the lorry, and with a loaded revolver in one hand, which was ordinarily used in my show business, and a heavy stake hammer in the other, I awaited the onset of the gypsies. These surged round my lorry, a veritable sea of savage humanity, shouting curses and execrations, and swearing that they would have my life.

Sticking my revolver in my belt, I swung the heavy hammer aloft, and threatened to dash out the brains of the first man who tried to climb up on the lorry. This made them pause. Not that they were not plucky. There was, I doubt not, many a brave lad amongst them. But none was so brave or so foolhardy as to wish to court certain death.

By this time pandemonium reigned in the fair ground. All the shows emptied, the roundabouts stopped, the cocoanut shies were deserted, and everybody, showmen and public alike, came surging round my tent. At this moment Sam Cliff, first throwing away a wooden stake he had armed himself with, very pluckily leapt down amongst the gypsies, and tried to parley with their leader. But hardly had he uttered two words, when Brown, mad with rage, rushed at him and knocked him senseless with a terrific blow in the face.

Poor Cliff was not expecting this. In fact he was purposely holding his hands down by his sides at the time to show that his intentions were peaceful. But Brown seemed to think he had done a very clever and plucky thing in "outing" him for the time being, and elated by his success, he came straight for my lorry, and made as if to climb up on it. I raised my hammer aloft, and in my temper I should most certainly have used it. But the crowd, fearing a tragedy, pulled him back.

Meanwhile Messrs. Hastings and Wayman, the managers, were talking to the other gypsies, and trying to pacify them, pointing out to them that they were wasting the best hours of the best day of the year; that while they were quarrelling, money was being turned away, and that people were even now commencing to leave the fair ground, fearing a riot. "Yes, and as for the others," put in Mr. Hastings, addressing Brown and me, "they're mostly climbing on the roundabouts and tents, and damaging my property. Let's to business, before it is too late."

By this time I began to see that there was only one way out of it. "I'll fight Brown now," I cried, "if the crowd will make a ring, and see to it that I get fair play."

"We'll see to that, never fear," yelled the crowd; and in a few seconds a big ring was formed, and Brown, taking his place in the centre of it, stripped himself to the waist. His huge hairy chest heaved with excitement, and I noted, not without inward misgiving, his powerful biceps, his brawny bull-like neck, and the closely cropped, bullet-like head of the fighter by instinct and profession.

When I came to strip in my turn, a great roar of laughter went up from the multitude, and no wonder. I was lean and lanky, and my skin, by contrast with his, appeared soft as velvet, and in colour and sheen not unlike to old ivory. "The lad's beat before he begins," said one man in the forefront of the crowd, and who looked like a professional pugilist; "I'll lay £10 to £1 on the big 'un," and he looked round inquiringly. But alas! in all that crowd there were no takers. I don't blame them.

Directly I stepped into the ring Brown made a rush at me, his great arms whirling aloft like the sails of a windmill. I stopped him with a straight left on the nose, and down he went. He scrambled to his feet, and came for me again, bellowing with rage. This time I caught him in the eye with my right, more by luck than by judgment, and he tripped and fell over a tuft of grass.

Now in a rough-and-tumble fight such as this was the strict rules of the prize ring are, it is well understood, not exactly enforced. You may not kick of course, and you may not hit a man when he is completely down, and that is about all. Everything else almost is considered fair, or at all events legitimate. So when Brown, having partially recovered himself, raised himself on one knee, I considered that my turn had come, and making a dive at him, and stooping down myself, I upper-cut him under the chin, and down he went again flat on his back.

Moreover, greatly to my relief, this time he elected to stay down. He wasn't knocked out by any means, but he had had enough. The other gypsies picked him up, and took him away. The crowd dispersed. The roundabouts were restarted, the shows reopened, and all the fun of the fair was soon in full swing once more. Only Brown's one-time beautiful booth remained lying where it had fallen, a tangled heap of rent canvas and broken cordage. Brown himself spent the rest of the day presiding at a cocoanut-shy, and nursing a bad black eye.

Every now and again he would turn and shoot a malevolent look in my direction, nor did it need this to tell me that my trouble with him was only now beginning. All day long, too, the other gypsies kept coming up to my show in order to tell me of what was in store for me later. "Brown," they said, "swears he'll kill you to-night, and he's a man of his word."

"Tell Brown," I retorted, showing them my revolver loaded in all six chambers with ball cartridge, "that I'll certainly shoot dead any man I catch prowling round my marquee after the fair closes down."

This, I may add, was a bit of sheer bluff, designed to throw them off the scent. I used to sleep in my marquee, there was nowhere else to sleep in fact, and I knew full well that I could not keep awake all the night long, and that once asleep it would be easy for one of them to creep under the canvas and brain me with a stake hammer. True, Cliff and I might have taken it in turns to keep awake and on guard, one watching while the other slept; but even this, I reflected, would only be postponing the evil day, or rather night. I knew too well the fierce, vindictive nature of the gypsies, to imagine for one moment that Brown and his tribe were going to forgo their revenge altogether.

No! I had another plan worked out in my mind, and soon after it was dark I proceeded to put it into execution, with the help of Mr. Wayman in whom I had confided.

He had slipped off to the station at my request, and had ascertained that a fast train left for London at 10.20 p.m. The fair ground closed at 11 p.m. Shortly before ten o'clock struck a man with a barrow, whom I had engaged beforehand, took his position, silently and without being observed, in a lane at the back of my tent.

Then I started the usual patter on the lorry outside in order to collect an audience. I could see that the gypsies were watching me. Possibly they had some suspicion of my intentions. But anyhow I outwitted them.

We got the crowd inside all right, but these people did not get their money back, nor did they see the show; for, instead of giving it, Cliff and I made some excuse to the audience for a brief delay, as we put it, and quietly slipped away out under the tent at the back, bearing with us my box, which I had already packed with our joint personal belongings. To hoist it on to the barrow was the work of a moment. Then we trundled it off to the station. We had, of course, to leave the marquee behind us, but as Mr. Wayman had promised me to look after it, and sell it for me as soon as he got a fair offer for it, this did not trouble me much.

As luck would have it, the train was on time. And as it steamed out of the station, bearing our two selves with it, I was just in time to wave my hand derisively at Brown and a lot of the other gypsies, who, having found out too late the trick I had served them, came charging pell-mell up the lane, cursing and shouting, with the object of trying to cut off our retreat.

So ended my first, last, and only experience as a fair-ground showman. I never went back to the business again; nor, if the truth be told, had I ever the least desire to do so.

CHAPTER IV
THE TRICK THAT FAILED

Back in London—At the Westminster Aquarium—"The Pro.'s Casual Ward"—Zæo's Maze—"Oriental beauties from the Far East-End of London"—"Fake" side-shows—A "fasting lady's" prodigious appetite—A lively subject for a coffin—I sell conjuring tricks to visitors—"Uncle" Ritchie—An audience of one—Annie Luker, the champion lady high diver—I find myself barred from the Aquarium—The mysterious voice in the maze—Mr. Ritchie investigates—And Mr. Wieland scores—Penny-gaffing in London—Working the shops—Sham hypnotism—How to eat coal and candles—And drink paraffin oil—The box trick again—Venice in Newcastle—I offer a £1000 prize—The trick that failed—My first engagement in a regular "hall"—My absent-minded partner.

RETURNING to London after my exciting experiences at Cheriton Fair Ground, I got into rather low water financially, and was glad to accept an engagement at thirty shillings a week at the Royal Aquarium, Westminster.

This famous place of amusement used to be known irreverently in the profession as the "Pro.'s Casual Ward," on account of the very meagre salaries ruling there. At the time I went there it was the custom of the management to pay in cash those artistes who were in receipt of anything under £2 a week. Those drawing over that amount were paid by cheque, which they had to cross the road to the bank to cash. Very few crossed the road.

My engagement, however, was not with the Aquarium people direct, but with Mr. Harry Wieland, the husband of Zæo, a once famous gymnast. She was the lady who used to be shot out of a catapult, and perform other sensational feats in mid-air, and concerning whose performance, or rather, to be strictly accurate, the poster advertising it, which was the first poster to appear on the hoardings of a lady in tights, so tremendous a controversy raged in the public Press and elsewhere during the spring and summer of 1890.

At the time I went to the Aquarium, however, Zæo had ceased to perform as a gymnast, and was engaged in running a profitable side-show known as "Zæo's Maze," and which consisted mainly of a lot of mirrors arranged at different angles. There was also run in conjunction with the maze what we called a Turkish Harem, the forerunner of the similar type of exhibition afterwards made popular by the proprietors of "Constantinople in London" at Olympia.

My job was to act as doorman and attendant at this exhibition, and by my patter, etc., to induce the public to enter. "Pass in, ladies and gentlemen!" I would cry. "Pass in and see the wondrous hall of mirrors, and the bevy of dark-eyed Oriental beauties from the Far, Far East-End of London."

This sort of thing served to put the crowd in a good humour, and in they would troop. The maze was a sufficiently puzzling place to be in, owing to the arrangement of the mirrors, fifty-two in number. But by swinging a certain double one round I was able, when I deemed it expedient to do so, to close the exit altogether, so that it was impossible for anybody inside to get out until I chose to let them. Many a sixpence and shilling used I to receive for showing bewildered wanderers round and round, how to escape from the trap I myself had set for them.

Also, visitors were not permitted to take sticks or umbrellas inside the maze, for fear they might poke the mirrors. I took charge of these for them, and the fees I received from this source still further swelled my income. It needed some swelling, I may add, to transform it into a living wage, for I only got thirty shillings a week from Mr. Wieland, and in return for this sum, in addition to all my other work, I had to clean the mirrors, so it will be readily apparent that my job was no sinecure.

Most of the Aquarium side-shows at this time were more or less of the "fake" variety. I remember, for instance, a "fasting lady" who came there. She was of quite Amazonian proportions when she first put in an appearance, but when she left she was as thin as a lath. Afterwards, however, I helped to clear out the room she had occupied during her forty days'—I think it was—"fast."

Then the mystery, such as it was, was solved. We found sufficient horsehair padding to stuff a good-sized sofa, and then leave enough over for a couple of armchairs. There were also a lot of thin pieces of old iron, weighing in the aggregate pretty nearly half a hundredweight, and these she had evidently used for the purpose of concealing about her person under her clothes, when she was weighed prior to beginning her "fast." Furthermore, in a certain dark corner was a huge pile of empty tins, that had once contained "bully" beef, salmon, sardines, chicken, vegetables of almost all sorts, baked beans, and various other toothsome comestibles. I came to the conclusion there and then that I would not have minded "fasting" for forty days on the same diet as did that lady.

Another "fake" show was performed by a girl who was supposed to be in a trance in her coffin. She was called "The Sleeping Beauty." As a matter of fact she was not sleeping, nor was she beautiful. The coffin in which she reposed was tilted at an angle, and muslin drapery was hung over it. Through this she was able to see when a visitor, or visitors, were ushered into the room, and she would then go "off" into her trance. At all other times she was as lively as a kitten.

Quite near the maze was another side-show run by a conjuror calling himself Professor Field. This was a genuine show so far as it went, although Field, in my estimation at all events, was not much of a conjuror. His business consisted in performing certain tricks, and afterwards selling the "secret" of them, together with the simple apparatus necessary to perform them, to anyone who was prepared to pay him half-a-guinea for the same.

Now as it happened, soon after I came there, this gentleman joined partnership with another conjuror named Carlton, the show being run under the title of Field, Carlton & Co. This gave me an idea. If these people could give lessons in conjuring for money, I didn't see why I shouldn't do the same.

So when I got a likely-looking visitor inside the maze I used to show him some tricks, and offer to sell them to him at half-a-crown apiece, at the same time pointing out to him that I was the one and only original Carlton, and that the same tricks sold by the Field & Carlton firm outside—which I was careful to add was not connected with me—would cost him half-a-guinea each. I did a fairly lucrative business, and in a little while my total earnings, including the standing thirty shillings weekly paid me by Mr. Wieland, averaged £7 or £8 a week.

But of course it was only a matter of time before Messrs. Field & Carlton got to know that I was undercutting them; and, not unnaturally, they were very angry about it. Off they went to "Uncle" Josiah Ritchie, the Aquarium manager, and lodged a complaint, pointing out that they paid a big rent for their pitch, and that all the while I, who paid nothing whatever, was stealing their business.

The result was that I was had up on the carpet, and somewhat severely reprimanded, being made to promise not to sell any more tricks. As some sort of a set-off against this, however, Mr. Ritchie gave me the job to go up on the central stage and "announce" Miss Annie Luker, a young lady who used to do a sensational dive from the roof of the Aquarium into a tank sunk in the floor.

But to this arrangement, after a little while, Mr. Wieland objected. He said that he paid me to look after his wife's side-show, and that while I was up on the central stage pattering for Annie Luker I was neglecting his interests. This was of course true, for obviously I could not be in two places at once; but it struck me as being primarily a matter for adjustment between Ritchie and Wieland, and I left it to them to settle.

The result of this arrangement was that what happened to me was something like what happened to the earthenware pot in the fable when it came into collision with the two iron pots. After a particularly busy Bank Holiday, when I did my best to divide my allegiance between Wieland and Zæo on the one hand, and Ritchie and Annie Luker on the other, I lost my job. I didn't get any notice either. When I presented myself at the stage entrance to the Aquarium next morning as usual, I was told by the doorkeeper there that he had orders not to admit me.

"Uncle" Ritchie, by the way, was something of an autocrat in his dealings with the artistes, and his other employees; and especially was he keen on seeing that he got his money's worth out of them. I remember that while I was at the Aquarium, the first turn there used to be a man named Willis, who was also a conjuror. He had to appear three times each day, an hour's turn, for thirty shillings a week, and his first turn was from 10 to 11 a.m., when the place opened, and when as a rule there were very few of the general public present.

Nevertheless Mr. Ritchie always insisted on his giving his full hour's show, even although it was to a beggarly array of empty benches, and he even used to make a practice of seating himself in front of the conjuror and ticking off each item on his programme in order to be sure that the unhappy man missed no single one of his tricks; and this, too, on wet mornings, or off days, when possibly he (Ritchie) was the sole "audience." A more irritating or depressing experience for a performer than this, I should imagine, it would be impossible to conceive.

Occasionally though "Uncle" met his match. For instance, he used to be fond of prowling about the building at the times when it was supposed to be closed to the public, in order to see if he could find anything amiss; and on one of these occasions he heard, or rather he thought he heard, human voices proceeding from the interior of the maze.

This, of course, was strictly against all rules and regulations, for the interior of the side-show was at such times in pitch darkness. Mr. Ritchie was on the alert immediately.

"Send for Mr. Wieland," he commanded.

"There's somebody inside your maze," he said when that gentleman presently appeared on the scene in obedience to his summons.

"Nonsense!" was the reply. "How can there be anybody in there? I locked the maze up myself at closing time, and nobody has had possession of the key since."

"Well," persisted Mr. Ritchie, "I'll swear I heard voices there anyhow, and I'm going to search the place."

This he started to do, and as a preliminary, directly he got inside, he struck a match.

"Here! None of that, Mr. Ritchie, if you please," cried Wieland. "To strike a light in there is against your own orders. Besides, if you burn my show down, what redress have I got?"

Ritchie, although inwardly fuming with rage, had to recognise the reasonableness of this, and he contented himself with groping about in the dark, and calling to the supposed intruder to come out.

For a while there was no response. Then suddenly, from the innermost recesses of the maze, a hoarse voice shouted: "Get out yourself. Who are you?"

"I'm Mr. Josiah Ritchie, the manager of the Aquarium," answered "Uncle" wrathfully, "and I order you to come out immediately."

"Oh, you go to hell," was the polite rejoinder; whereat Ritchie came outside hurriedly, his face aflame with rage.

"There you are," he cried, addressing Wieland. "I told you there was someone in there," and he called a messenger boy, and ordered him to fetch the Aquarium policeman and fireman.

The lad started on his errand, but before he had gone many yards Wieland intervened, and called him back.

At this Ritchie, not unnaturally, was more furious than ever. Stamping his foot, he asked how dare Wieland countermand his order?

"Well," answered the latter quite suavely, "I called the boy back in your own interest. If the policeman and fireman are sent into the maze to lug out the individual you think is inside there, the only result will be to make you the laughing-stock of everybody about the place."

"Wait a minute, and I will show you," he resumed. And going inside, Mr. Wieland presently returned with a big cage, in which was a red and green talking parrot.

Tableau!

After I got the "sack" from the Aquarium I started on my own, working a conjuring show at various empty shops in and round London. That is to say, I would bargain for the temporary tenancy of any likely-looking shop in a main thoroughfare that chanced to be vacant, and having secured it, I would then proceed to give a more or less continuous performance, charging a penny for admission.

My show consisted in a combination of conjuring and (alleged) hypnotism. With me as assistant I had a thin consumptive-looking youth, by name Freddie Andrews, whom I used to pretend to mesmerise, and he would then, on my commanding him to do so, drink paraffin oil with apparent gusto, eat with relish lighted candles and chunks of coal, and perform other similar antics.

This part of the show, I may state at once, was a fake. The upper part of the candle, which the lad ate, was carved out of an apple, and fitted with a wick made from an almond, and soaked in brandy to make it burn. The particular portion of the chunk of coal devoured by him was merely chocolate, deftly affixed to the genuine coal by myself at the moment of its being handed to him. While the paraffin oil was just plain water, poured into a bottle round the neck of which an oily paraffin rag was wrapped to make it smell when it was handed round amongst the audience for inspection.

Well, I was working a place on these lines in the Edgware Road one day towards the close of the year 1901, in the basement of a shop in which was a waxwork exhibition run by Mr. Louis Tussaud, when a man I knew slightly came to me in a great state of exhilaration and excitement. He had, he told me, secured a £35 a week contract for seven weeks for a conjuring and illusion turn at an entertainment called "Venice in Newcastle," and which was to open at the Drill Hall there shortly before Christmas.

The bother of it was, he explained, that he knew nothing whatever of conjuring or illusions. He was under no illusion about that himself at all events. He had, he said, answered the advertisement in the *Era* newspaper at haphazard, setting forth his (purely imaginative) qualifications as an A1 wizard at great length, and very much to his surprise he had secured the contract. "Now," he concluded, "what am I to do about it?"

"Do about it?" I exclaimed. "Why go whacks with me in the £35, and well fix up the turn between us."

"But," he objected, somewhat doubtfully, "the ordinary stock card tricks, etc., won't do, except perhaps as a stop-gap. We must have at least one really slap-up, first-class illusion."

"Right ho!" I replied, struck by a sudden happy thought. "I know! We'll run the great Maskelyne and Cooke box trick. I know all about how it is done, and what's more I've got at home a facsimile of the box that was used in the great £500 prize case."

There was some further talk, but in the end we came to terms as I had suggested, share and share alike.

Then, however, a new difficulty arose. Neither of us was able to muster the fares to Newcastle. Eventually, however, struck by another happy thought, I journeyed down to Ratcliffe Docks, and there I found a captain of a tramp coasting steamer, who happened to be bound for Newcastle, and who agreed to take the pair of us for fifteen shillings. These we managed to scrape together, and in due course arrived at our destination, penniless but hopeful. Our sole luggage consisted of my precious box, in which was packed our wardrobes.

The show was to open on December 21st, and I spent most of the intervening time coaching my partner in the part he was to take in our "Great £1,000 box trick."

I had christened it this because it sounded well to offer a good, big, thumping reward. Those world-famous wizards, Maskelyne and Cooke, had offered £500 to anyone who guessed the secret of their trick. We doubled the prize, making the winning of it, however, conditional on the winner escaping from the box.

CARLTON AND ONE OF HIS SATELLITES AT THE THEATRICAL GARDEN PARTY, LONDON, 1919

My partner demurred somewhat to this; but, as I pointed out to him, we might as well offer a reward of one thousand pounds as one thousand shillings. We hadn't, as a matter of fact, got one thousand pence. So what did it matter? "Besides," I added consolingly, "no one in the audience will ever succeed in getting out of my box. The thing is impossible."

This, I may add, was the literal truth; for, in order to make assurance doubly sure, I had hit upon the expedient of having two keys made. One of these simply locked and unlocked the box, allowing the lid to be raised. The other one not only locked the box, but it also locked, at the same time, the mechanism actuating the secret panel by which I was enabled to get out of it. If the first key were used it was possible for anybody inside who knew of the existence of the panel, and how it was worked, to escape from the box's interior. But if the second key were used, the individual inside was as securely imprisoned as he would be if sealed up in a living tomb.

Well, the eventful day came round at last. The town had been well "billed" beforehand, and the hall was packed with curious spectators, all of them eager to see for themselves the wonderful box trick, and try and unravel the mystery of it.

We produced the box, and called up the usual volunteer committee of inspection, while I expatiated at length on our generous and unprecedented offer of "£1,000 in hard cash" to any lady or gentleman who succeeded in escaping from its interior. A good many, I may add, tried. But of course none succeeded. I saw to that.

Following these preliminaries, the box was placed open on a table in the centre of the stage, and a threefold screen on legs was drawn round the back and two sides, leaving the front facing the audience exposed to view, and also allowing of a clear view underneath the table. This was so that I could get inside the box, and be corded up in it, in full view of the spectators, after which a curtain, falling only as low as the top of the table, was to be drawn across the front by my partner, who was to fire a pistol as a signal for me to emerge.

This was literally all he had to do; just draw the curtain tight, shutting the box from view, and then fire his pistol. But he didn't do it. He fired the pistol all right, it is true, but in his flurry and excitement he forgot to draw the curtain.

As a result I popped up out of the box in full view of the audience, and every man, woman, and child in the building saw at a glance exactly how I did it. I never felt so small in all my life. I wanted the ground to open and swallow me up. If there had been a convenient hole anywhere near I would have crawled into it. As it was I sidled off the stage, followed by the jeers and laughter of several thousand people.

My partner was there before me. So was the manager of the hall. He was furious. "Get out of my sight, you two!" he cried, "and don't let me ever see either of you again."

We went. What I said to my partner when we got outside would not look well in print. Suffice it to say that my language was neither kind nor complimentary.

Next morning I went round to the theatre to claim my box. The manager was there. To my surprise he was quite civil, even courteous.

"Carlton," he said, "I've been thinking over last night's business, and I realise that it wasn't your fault. The box trick, of course, is dead as mutton. We should never dare to show it again. But you can, if you like, stay on and give an ordinary conjuring and card trick turn. I'll pay you £5 a week. What do you say?"

Needless to say I promptly closed with the offer. It was my first regular engagement at a proper hall, and to me at the time the terms seemed sufficiently liberal; as indeed, under the circumstances, they were.

For seven weeks I performed there, and was lucky enough to amuse and please my audience. What became of my absent-minded partner I haven't the remotest idea. I never saw him again.

CHAPTER V
CLIMBING TO FAME AND FORTUNE

I give an impromptu show at the Palace Theatre—"Chuck him out!"—I seek out Mr. Wieland again—At the Crystal Palace—I adopt my present make-up—"The Human Hairpin"—Charlie Coborn and "Two Lovely Black Eyes"—I do a trial turn at the Bedford Music-hall—Billed as a star turn at the Alhambra and Palace Theatres—And at the "Flea Pit," Hoxton—My reception there—I work the Alhambra, Palace, Middlesex, Metropolitan, and Cambridge together—A record for those days—A Press "spoof"—Continental engagements—Paris, Milan—An overdose of Chianti—And its results—The night life of Milan—A blood-curdling adventure—Murder most foul—Callous passers-by.

ON my return to Town from Newcastle, and remembering how well my show went there, I really did begin to think that I was "some conjuror," as our American friends have it, and I started to look round for a regular London engagement.

Meanwhile I used to visit the galleries of the music-halls where conjurors were performing, in order to observe their ways and methods, and collect such information as I could. On these occasions I used invariably to carry a pack of cards with me, and one day while I was seated in the gallery at the Palace Theatre, Shaftesbury Avenue, a conjuror and card manipulator came on and did a number of tricks, with every one of which I was perfectly familiar.

Acting on the impulse of the moment, directly he had finished his turn, I rose from my seat—I was in the front row of the gallery—and facing about, and drawing my pack of cards from my pocket, I exclaimed: "I can do those tricks; just watch me."

Instantly there was a big commotion. Some of the people resented the interruption, and there were loud cries of "Sit down!" "Shut up!" "Chuck him out!" etc. Others among the audience, however, rather welcomed my action, and took my part, applauding and laughing. Meanwhile the next turn was spoilt, and Mr. Charles Morton, the manager, sent an attendant to request me to leave, which of course I did. But I had achieved what I set out to do, by giving what I suppose was the only unauthorised show ever performed in public at the Palace. Little did I dream as I took my departure, and still less,

I suppose, did Mr. Morton dream, that I was afterwards to fill at this same Palace Theatre no fewer than forty-seven different engagements, ranging in length from one to eight weeks, and thereby establishing a record, so far as this particular house is concerned.

My next step was to seek out my old Aquarium "boss," Mr. Wieland, who was now running a variety agency in conjunction with Messrs. Oliver and Holmes in Cranbourne Street, Leicester Square. I told him I was the biggest card manipulator that ever was, and asked him for an engagement. Mr. Wieland was considerably impressed by my cheek; but not otherwise, I gathered. Anyhow I didn't succeed in talking him into booking me.

There followed more wearisome running round from one agent to another, none of whom would listen to me, until in the end I managed to secure, but off my own bat, a trial show in a Café Chantant company then performing at the Crystal Palace under the management of Mr. Humphrey E. Brammall. It was then that I first adopted my present make-up, and I have never altered it since, except that during the first two or three weeks I used to wear a long hairy wig, and whiten my face like a clown's.

At that time the regulation stage costume for all professional conjurors consisted of ordinary evening dress, and the general opinion amongst the audiences was that this attire in some way assisted the conjuring performance; that the performer, in fact, had "something up his sleeve," both figuratively and literally. This gave me the idea of dressing myself throughout in black tights, so that people could see that there was no concealment possible.

This was really the only end I had in view in adopting this particular costume. I most certainly never contemplated making my turn a comic one. Consequently when I went on for my trial show at the Crystal Palace, and at which I appeared in these tights for the first time, I was considerably embarrassed because the audience roared with laughter all through my performance, and I quitted the stage half believing that I had made a mess of it. However, all the other performers saying how funny I looked, and what a splendid patterer I was, and Charlie Coborn, who was singing "Two Lovely Black

Eyes" there at the time, being especially enthusiastic about me, caused me to pluck up courage, and I began to think that, after all, I was perhaps going to be a success there at all events.

My surmise turned out correct. Next week I topped the bill there at £3 a week, being billed as "Carlton Philps, the World's Premier Card Manipulator." Following this I secured an engagement at the Hippodrome, Brighton, then under the same management. This was a combined circus and stage, and I did my show in the ring.

Returning to London, I again sought out Mr. Wieland, and told him of the hit I had made. He was not greatly impressed even then, however; he merely said, "All right, my lad, go over there in the corner, and let's see what you can do."

Now my show needs now, and it needed then, a regular audience in order to make it go properly. I did my best, but I could see that Mr. Wieland thought precious little of my business. In fact he said as much. Agents are not very particular as regards the feelings of unknown artistes, and Mr. Wieland, although one of the best-natured men in the world, was no exception to the rule. However his assistant, a gentleman named Altree, was more cordial. He seemed to think that there might be something in my show that was not readily apparent in the drab surroundings of a variety agent's office; and eventually he got me a trial turn at the Bedford Music Hall, Camden Town, promising at the same time to come down and see it for himself, which he did. As a result he went back to Mr. Wieland, and reported to him that mine was one of the best "acts" he had ever seen.

Still that gentleman was frankly incredulous, and he said so when I again waited on him at his office on the following day. As luck would have it, however, while I was talking to him a telephone message came through from the Alhambra Theatre, Leicester Square, saying that their star turn, Miss Ida Renè, was indisposed, and would Mr. Wieland please send someone that evening to take her place?

Promptly I saw my chance, and as promptly I "butted in."

"Send me?" I said.

Mr. Wieland stared at me in amazement; too flabbergasted at my audacity for a few moments to speak. When he found his voice, it was to rate me soundly for my impertinence. Did I realise, he asked, that they wanted a star turn?

"Well, I am a star turn," I replied, "or, at any rate, I've been one. Topped the bill at the Palace, you know!"

"Palace?" snorted Wieland.

"Crystal Palace!" I corrected.

"Oh!" snorted the great man again, and wilted me with a look.

But now Mr. Altree joined in the conversation.

"Give the lad a chance," he said. "You haven't seen his show. I have. I know. Give him a chance, I say. He'll paralyse 'em."

Well, there was a lot more argument; but the upshot of it was that I went on that evening at the Alhambra, and was a big success, exactly as Mr. Altree had predicted. Three or four times I was called before the curtain at the conclusion of my performance, and all the while I was giving my show the whole house was, I could see, pleased and amused. When I quitted the theatre that night I knew that, barring accidents, my future in the profession was assured.

Nor was I unduly optimistic. That Wednesday they were a turn short at the Palace, and the assistant manager there, who had been to the Alhambra and seen my show, asked me to come over there and deputise. So here was I, a new and comparatively unknown performer, appearing at two of the principal West End halls at one and the same time, and that moreover at two establishments then running in opposition to one another. My remuneration for the first week was £4 a week from each, but I got a second week's engagement to follow on, at £8 a week from each. It was dirt cheap, of course, from their point of view. But at that time I did not know my own value, and, anyway, it seemed to me then a quite munificent salary.

While performing at these two halls, too, I was offered an engagement at the Variety, Pitfield Street, Hoxton, then irreverently known as the "Flea Pit," at £4 a week. This came to me through Macdermott's Agency. It was a two-houses-a-night engagement, and I was at the bottom of the bill; a position I was, of course, quite proud of. The contrast with the Alhambra was most striking. There I had a comfortable dressing-room and a refined and cultured audience to play to.

At the Variety I had to go down a spiral staircase to my dressing-room, which was a sort of disused coal-hole, or something of the kind, and which moreover I had to share with a troupe of performing dogs, and about a dozen other artistes. As for the audience, it simply beggared description. Probably there was no rougher one anywhere in London at the time.

It was about this period that I first began to be called "The Human Hairpin." Standing over six feet in height, I was exceedingly thin, weighing less than nine and a half stone, and my all-black stage make-up accentuated my lankiness, which I still further increased by wearing "elevators," and a high, padded wig, so that I looked to be over seven feet. My appearance on the stage at the Variety was the signal for so uproarious a scene as never before or since have I heard or witnessed. The whole house roared and rocked with laughter, and above the indescribable din I distinctly remember hearing a girl's voice from the gallery shriek out; "Blimey, ain't he a coughdrop? Look at 'is blinking legs!" It was the custom here, if the audience did not like a "turn," to throw "fish and chips" at the unfortunate artiste, which they purchased at a shop opposite the theatre.

As for my performance, it had to be given in dumb show. I could not hear myself speak. Yells, cat-calls, shrieks filled the air. I went away disgusted, but of course I had to return and do my show again at the second house. This was the same scene over again, only more so. Never had I imagined such a pandemonium of noise.

Next day I went round to Macdermott's Agency, told the manager there I was a ghastly failure at the Variety, that the audience simply wouldn't listen to me, and asked to be released from my engagement. "Oh, nonsense!" he cried. "I can't believe it." And he rang up the manager of the hall. That gentleman telephoned back to say that so far from my having been a failure, he had never heard such laughter in his life, and that I had made a big hit—presumably, I suppose, from the standpoint of the Variety, Hoxton. Anyhow, it wasn't so from my standpoint; and I again asked to be released from my contract. "The audience was laughing *at* me, not *with* me," I explained; "I couldn't hear myself speak."

"My lad," cried the manager angrily, "you're too big for your boots. Because you're appearing at the Alhambra you've got a swelled head on you."

Then it was my turn to get angry. "Look here," I answered, "I'll not go on again at the Variety, and that's the long and short of it. I wouldn't go through again what I went through last night for fifty pounds. I never was so insulted in all my life."

The manager thereupon pointed to a clause in my contract, by which it was stipulated that if for any reason I declined to fulfil my engagement I was to pay him £4 in place of his paying me £4. This meant, of course, a dead loss to me of £8. Nevertheless, I paid the money, and I never went back to the Variety.

Next week was a record. My fame spread among the music-hall managers, and I was offered, and accepted, engagements at the Alhambra, Palace, Middlesex, Metropolitan, and Cambridge, the latter a two-houses-a-night hall. This meant my doing six turns a night, and with a brougham, there being of course no motor-cars in those days. It was a sufficiently arduous task, but I managed it all right, and was, I need hardly say, quite pleased with myself.

It was about this time, too, that I began to taste the joys of life. One evening just as I had finished a late turn at the Palace Theatre, a friend gave me a ticket for a Covent Garden Fancy Dress Ball. There was not time to change into a costume, even if I had had one, so I went just as I was in my stage make-up, and signed the book "Arthur Philps [my real name] as 'Carlton.'"

As a result, and greatly to my surprise, I was awarded first prize for the best comic costume. People came up and congratulated me on what they regarded as my "wonderful impersonation." Others I heard passing such remarks as, "Isn't it like him?" "What a marvellous resemblance!" and so on.

Only Mr. (now Sir Alfred) Butt, the Manager of the Palace, who chanced to be present, was not deceived. "By gad, Carlton," he whispered to me, "you *have* got a nerve!"

And, by the way, talking of Sir Alfred reminds me of a journalistic advertising "stunt" I worked while I was playing at the Palace some time back. In conjunction with a Press man I knew, I arranged to bring off a "fake" rescue on Hungerford Bridge about two o'clock one morning.

At this time there was not a soul on the bridge, but I raced off the Surrey end, and gasped out to a policeman that there were a couple of hooligans up there assaulting an old gentleman. "I've given them a pretty good hiding, officer," I said, "sorry I can't stop"; and I ran off towards Waterloo Station, as though in a hurry to catch a train.

Next day there appeared in most of the London papers an account of the "attempted outrage," with the addition that the old gentleman who had been assaulted was wishful to thank his unknown rescuer, and ask his acceptance of a ten-pound note.

That night, at the Palace, I called Mr. Butt's attention to the account of the affair in one of the evening papers.

"It refers to me," I told him. "I was the rescuer."

"Good lad!" he cried, shaking me by the hand. "But what about the ten pounds?"

"Well," I said, "I don't like taking that. After all I only did my duty in protecting a harmless old man from a couple of ruffians. Suppose I hand over the money to the Music-hall Benevolent Fund?"

Naturally he thought this was very kind and generous of me, and he told several people about it. My Press man also let the story be known, and the result was that I got the reception of my life when I appeared on the stage later on.

It was a splendid "advert.," and cheap at the price—£15: which was what it cost me; £10 of which I had of course to find out of my own pocket for the M.H.B. Fund, and £5 which I handed over to my friend the Press man.

Once fairly launched on my career, the rest was comparatively easy. Nevertheless, there were occasional spells of out of work, known euphemistically in the profession as "resting," and it was during one of these intervals of enforced leisure that I first made acquaintance with the Continent. I had been performing at the Empire, Hastings, with the two Brothers Griffiths, well known in connection with their famous Blondin donkey act, and as they, like me, were out of an engagement, they proposed running over to Paris, in order to take a look round, and see if they could not book an engagement or two there.

"Why don't you come with us?" they asked. "You might succeed in getting an engagement as well, you know."

In saying this, they were, of course, only kidding me. I knew this, too, quite well. But I also made up my mind that if I did go, I would not go for nothing, at all events if I could help it.

However I kept my own counsel as to this, merely remarking that as I was out of an engagement for the time being I might as well "rest" in Paris as anywhere else, and that I would be glad to accompany them; which I did.

Arrived there we took up our quarters at the Hôtel Franklin in the Rue Baulfault, off the Rue la Fayette, then a favourite rendezvous for English artistes staying in Paris. Next morning the Brothers Griffiths went to call on their agents. I went sightseeing.

That night they started kidding me again, and suggested that I should give a trial show at one of the Paris music-halls. I pretended to think they were in earnest, but at the same time I feigned reluctance, pointing out to them—what they knew full well beforehand—that I neither spoke nor understood the French language. However, I said that I would think it over, and they went off in great glee to let the other English "pro.'s" staying there into the secret of the joke they fondly imagined they were going to work off on me.

Meanwhile I got a friendly waiter at the hotel, who understood English, to translate my patter, word for word, into its French equivalent. This I wrote down phonetically, and used to practise it with him on the quiet, and by myself at night after I had retired to my room, until I was fairly perfect in it.

Well, my two friends kept kidding me, asking me how soon I was going to pluck up courage to give my trial show; and at last I said that I would give it if they could arrange the preliminaries for me. To this they promptly agreed, and presently they came to tell me that they had fixed it up through M. Marenelli's agency for me to go on at the matinée at the Olympia Theatre, first turn, that day.

The rest of the morning they spent in going round and telling all the other English artistes then in Paris. Most of these did what are called in the profession "dumb acts," a term which explains itself, and they were all quite sure that the joke was going to be on me, knowing that I relied upon my patter, and that I spoke no French. To tell the honest truth I thought myself that it was odds on them, but I made up my mind to do my best to try and win through, and in order to assist my memory I scribbled in pencil the tags of all my gags on the cuffs of my shirt before going down to the theatre.

Needless to say all my fellow-artistes turned up there to witness the fiasco they had made up their minds they were going to see. Not that they really wished me any harm, or wanted to see me humiliated, but it is our way in the profession to guy one another, and especially do we delight to take it out of a beginner. Well, the curtain rang up, and on I went. I was greeted with a regular tempest of cheers, mostly ironical, I thought. Still, I managed all right at the beginning, though afterwards I had to keep turning first to one shirt cuff, and then to the other, for guidance and inspiration.

This amused the kindly French people immensely, and I soon had my audience in great good humour, and I was rewarded with round after round of hearty, genuine applause. In short, my "turn" was a success, a big success indeed; and when I came off there were no fewer than three managers waiting in the wings to interview me.

Naturally I let them bid against one another for my services, and eventually I closed with the best offer, which came from an Italian, Signor Caroselli. He engaged me to go to the Eden Theatre, Milan, at a salary of one hundred francs a day for seven days a week, approximately £28 a week in our money. Of course I was as ignorant of Italian as I was of French, but I adopted the plan I had found so efficacious in Paris, translating my English into phonetic Italian, and it worked splendidly.

My original engagement with Signor Caroselli was for fifteen days, but I remained working in Milan for eight weeks straight off. During this period I did my show at the Eden in the evening, and at the Villa Giardino—an open-air café chantant—in the afternoon, and also at the Stablini Theatre; and during a part of my engagement I filled the triple bill at all three places, a thing never done before in Milan.

On the very first day of my engagement, however, I nearly came a cropper. It happened in this way. The Eden Theatre was a restaurant in the day time, and even in the evening there were little tables dotted about all over the place where people could come and eat a dinner while listening to the performance. Working at the restaurant there was an Italian waiter who had served for a long time at Pinoli's Restaurant in London, and who started out to help me by teaching me a sufficiency of colloquial Italian for my business.

Well, I got there in the morning, and this waiter told me that the proper thing to eat for dinner was a dish of spaghetti (fine macaroni) washed down with a flask of chianti wine. I followed his advice, and then, feeling tired, and as my turn, a late one, was not until ten-thirty that night, I thought I would go home to my lodgings and rest awhile.

Now in Milan chianti wine is very cheap. It is also, but this is a detail, very potent. When serving it with a meal, it is the custom there to place upon the table a huge flagon of it, holding, I suppose, about a couple of quarts, and which is swung upon a pivot. The diner helps himself to as much as he wants of this by tilting up the flagon, thereby allowing the wine to run out into his glass, and he is charged for as much of it as he drinks, and no more.

But I, of course, knew nothing of all this. I thought the entire flagon was intended for my consumption, and the day being very hot, and myself feeling very thirsty, I drank the lot. The natural result was that when I reached my lodgings I felt horribly drowsy, so calling my landlady I told her to call me at "otto d'ora" (eight o'clock) and lay down to rest feeling quite proud at having been able so soon to air, to even that limited extent, my newly acquired knowledge of Italian.

Alas! I was presently to discover that mine was the pride that goes before a fall, for Italian time is reckoned right round the clock, and I ought by rights to have told her to call me at "venti d'ora" (twenty o'clock), eight o'clock there being in the morning. The result was that I overslept myself, and when I at length awoke, of my own accord, the performance at the theatre was over and done with for that evening.

I was in a terrible fever, and rushed round to find the manager and explain matters. I expected nothing less than instant dismissal, but instead, the manager, when I had explained matters, laughed heartily after the good-natured Italian fashion, as if the being obliged to do without his star turn for his opening performance was one of the best jokes imaginable. Needless to say I took care to be on time the next night. Also I was wary of the chianti for the future.

I thoroughly enjoyed my stay in the beautiful city of Milan, barring one terrible incident, the memory of which is indelibly engraven on my memory; and which I will now proceed to narrate. First, however, I must explain that in order to reach my apartment in the house I lodged in, I had to unlock no fewer than four separate doors. The first of these doors opened from the street into a sort of passage, or corridor, at the end of which was a second locked door giving admittance to a quadrangle. A third door, one of several, and also locked, led from this quadrangle to a common staircase, whence a fourth locked door led to my bedroom. For the purpose of unlocking all these four doors, I was provided with one key only, but that of the most peculiar construction. It was in effect, indeed, four keys in one, being shaped like an iron cross, the four separate arms fitting each its own separate individual lock, and none other.

I should imagine that it would be hard to invent a more bothersome key than this diabolical contrivance, especially to the roysterer returning home late at night, and in the dark. The ordinary single latchkey is sometimes sufficiently puzzling to the late comer at his own home who has dined not wisely but too well. Try and imagine the effect in similar circumstances of a fourfold key, each arm, or barrel, call it what you will, looking exactly alike, but each quite different, in that only one of the four is designed to unlock whichever particular lock you may be at the moment negotiating, the odds being, of course, exactly four to one against your picking out the right barrel in the first instance.

Well, on this particular occasion I don't mind confessing that I was in a fairly blithesome mood. I had in fact been "out with the boys" seeing the night side of life in Milan, and was returning home to my lodgings in the early dawn feeling at peace with all the world, when, on turning the corner of the street where I stayed, I was startled to observe a man walking towards me, and being shadowed, at a distance in rear, by another man, who was carrying in his hand a long, bright-bladed stiletto.

I stopped suddenly, but before I had time to call out, or even to collect my thoughts, the man in the rear suddenly bounded forward and buried his weapon in the other's back, between the shoulders. The stabbed man uttered one single, terrible groan, and sank in a huddled heap to the pavement, right in front of the door leading to the house I was lodging in.

The murderer looked hastily round, listened intently for a moment or two, then stooped to withdraw his knife, and strode off in my direction. My first impulse naturally was to turn and run, but on second thoughts I concluded that as he might not yet have seen me, perhaps my safest plan was to keep straight on as if I had seen nothing.

I therefore started whistling in apparent unconcern; but the assassin evidently suspected me. He allowed me to pass, then wheeled swiftly, as if intending to go for me; whereupon I took to my heels, and he after me.

Luckily I am a good sprinter, and on this occasion I ran like the wind, doubling and turning through the maze of silent and deserted streets for fully ten minutes. Then I stopped and listened. I had thoughts of calling for assistance as I ran, and was even on the point of doing so, when it suddenly occurred to me that I was just as likely to bring upon the scene some other desperado, or desperadoes, friends or accomplices very possibly of my pursuer.

I therefore refrained from giving the alarm, and presently, walking very gingerly, proceeding by devious ways, and keeping a sharp look-out round corners, I reached once more the street where the tragedy occurred. There was the body lying where it had fallen, right in front of the door I had perforce to enter in order to reach my apartment. I tiptoed to the spot. The man was obviously stone dead, and a great pool of blood had by now collected on the pavement, and run in red rivulets to the gutter.

Shivering with fright and apprehension, I stepped over the corpse, and started to unlock the street door. Of course I tried the wrong key, and that not once nor twice. It seemed to me that minutes elapsed while I was fumbling about with that beastly puzzle-key, and all the while I kept nervously glancing back over my shoulder, fearing that the murderer would return. Had he done so I had every reason to suppose that my shrift would be a short one, for obviously the man had come to the conclusion that I had been a witness of his crime, as indeed, of course, I had, and for that very reason he would, I am convinced, have had no hesitation in killing me also.

However, I presently got the door unlocked, and slipped inside, after which I roused the concierge and told him what had happened. But, greatly to my surprise, he refused to take any action.

"It is no concern of ours," he said. "If the poor fellow were only wounded now, signor?" he went on thoughtfully. "Well, we might be of some assistance to him. But he is dead, you say?"

I nodded acquiescence.

"Very well then! In that case best leave matters as they are. The police will no doubt find him later. Also, no doubt, they will come here, seeing that the murdered man is lying outside this house. But as for me, I know nothing. And best for you also, signor," he added significantly, "to know nothing. Police proceedings here in Milan are apt to be long drawn out and troublesome."

So saying, the concierge went back to bed, and I went off upstairs to my room. Sleep, however, for me, was, I need hardly say, out of the question. Softly drawing the curtains aside from the big front windows, which opened, in continental fashion, on a little balcony overlooking the street, I peered out.

There was the body, lying cold and still in the grey dawn. Presently a man roughly garbed, probably a workman on his way to his day's toil, came along on a bicycle. He stopped on seeing the corpse, and dismounted. But after a very cursory examination he mounted again and rode off, shrugging his shoulders as if to intimate that it was no concern of his.

A little later a man drove up in a cart, and he went off and fetched the police. That day our house was invaded by inspectors and detectives, and I, in common with all the other inmates of the building, was subjected to a searching interrogation.

Acting on the advice of my friend the concierge, however, I replied that I knew nothing whatever about the murder; and there, so far as I was concerned, the matter ended.

But I have often wondered since what was the ultimate upshot of it all, and what was the name and the station in life of the unhappy victim.

CHAPTER VI
PLAYING IN HUNLAND

Vienna and the Viennese—Churls by nature and instinct—How I made "There's a Girl in Havana" go down there—Chorus men and waiters—Some innocent tricks of the music-hall trade—In Berlin—Death of my giant—Official boorishness—German sharp practice—I engage a Hun giant—Uncomfortable railway travelling—At Buda-Pesth—More sharp practice—I throw up my engagement and return to England in disgust—Litigation and worry—My case is taken up by the Variety Artistes' Federation—A new "Battle of Prague"—Which I lose—A story of a "misspelled" railway station—Back in Old England—A day's rabbit shooting—The two "Arthur Carltons."

LATER, during my professional wanderings through Europe, I could not but contrast the treatment I received in France and Italy with that meted out to me in Germany and Austria. Our allies, the French and Italians, are gentlemen by instinct; kindly, considerate, and courteous. The Germans I found exactly the reverse, and the Austrians are not much better. Nor are either of them above snatching a mean business advantage from an artiste if they get half a chance to do so.

As an example of their churlishness—I shall come to their sharp practice later—I cannot do better than cite a little incident that occurred in Vienna just before the war. I had been given a two months' engagement at the Apollo Theatre there, and sharing the top of the bill with me was Miss Ethel Levey (now Mrs. Graham-White).

She had never performed there before, and was a trifle nervous. Hers was the turn before mine. She sang her first song, and came off. There was practically dead silence throughout the theatre; she hardly got a single "hand."

Naturally she was very much upset, but by dint of coaxing her I managed to persuade her to go on and sing her second song—"There's a girl in Havana." She sang this first in English, and then in her pretty broken German, which she had specially coached up for the occasion.

Miss Levey is, I need not say, an artiste to her finger-tips, and her singing and acting on this occasion were absolutely faultless. Yet the churlish Viennese would have none of it. There was no applause, or at all events so little as made no odds, and the general tone of the audience was, if not exactly hostile, at least not favourable.

Just try and imagine a London audience at, say, the Empire or the Alhambra, behaving in this fashion to a continental lady artiste of standing and repute on her first appearance! It made me mad. And I made up my mind then and there that they had just got to hear Miss Levey, and not only hear her, but applaud her into the bargain.

To this end I suggested to Mr. Ben Tieber, the manager of the hall, that he should have a sheet put up at the back of the stage with the words of the chorus on it in English and German. This he promised should be done. He also fell in with my suggestion to have the waiters (for on the Continent it is customary for people to dine in the hall) taught the tune and words, and to engage half-a-dozen chorus men, and put them in different parts of the building.

The result was that the next night the song went exceedingly well, and within a week the lilting melody had taken Vienna by storm, and was being sung and whistled in every café, on the streets, in the parks, everywhere in fact. All the same, I can never forgive the churlish Viennese for their first reception of the lady who popularised it there.

My own experience of German manners and customs was a far more serious matter for me. It took place some three years before the war, and when, therefore, our relations with Germany were supposed to be of the best. I had been booked to appear, with my company, at the Winter Gardens, Berlin. In my show was a dwarf, and also a giant. The latter, an American named Bobby Dunlop, was a veritable mountain of flesh, the fattest man in the world. He weighed over forty stone, and as he could not pass his immense bulk through the door of an ordinary railway carriage, he had to be accommodated in the luggage van.

Also he had to be taken from the station to the music-hall on a lorry, drawn by two huge dray-horses, a source of wonderment to the Berlin people, and likewise an excellent advertisement for my show. I remember, too, by the way, that once, when we were performing in London, I had him driven in a similar lorry down the Strand to a tailor's shop there, where they were advertising for sale thirty shilling suits. Bobby marched in and ordered one.

Speaking of giants, one of mine (not Bobby) was an exceptionally bad sailor, and on one occasion, during the crossing of the Bay of Biscay on the voyage out to the Cape, his sufferings from sea-sickness were atrocious.

CARLTON MESMERIZING BOBBY DUNLOP

Aroused by his groans and gurgles one stormy night, I went to his cabin which was next to mine.

"Can't you keep anything on your stomach?" I said sympathetically.

"Only my hands," moaned the poor giant.

Poor Bobby was a jolly fellow—for a giant. Giants are usually more or less irritable and lachrymose. At all events this is my experience of them, and I have had several in my employ in my time. But Bobby was just the reverse of this, always singing and laughing. At least, he was before he came to Berlin. Then a cloud seemed to come over him. His cheerfulness departed. He got homesick. Kept on saying that he didn't like the country, and that he wanted to get back to America.

Consequently I was not greatly surprised when, a few days after we opened in Berlin, my little dwarf came to me pulling a very long face, and said: "Mr. Carlton, Bobby's gone."

I was playing billiards at the time, and intent on my game; so beyond remarking that it was a good job too, I took little notice. I knew, anyhow, that he could not get far without a passport, and that a man of his dimensions could be easily traced, and brought back again.

"But, Mr. Carlton," persisted the little chap, "I mean Bobby's dead."

"What!" I ejaculated; and dropping my cue, I ran off to his lodgings.

It was only too true. The big man was no more. He was, I was informed, sitting on the side of his bed singing "Love me and the world is mine," when he suddenly gave a gasp and expired.

Knowing something from hearsay of the methods of German officialdom I expected trouble. Nor was I disappointed.

For four days I was kept running about from police station to police station, and from one official bureau to another. I answered about a million questions and filled up reams of official forms and papers. The police took possession of all the dead man's effects, and but for the intervention of the American Embassy I should have been unable to recover a number of my "props" which he had in his room.

On the afternoon of the day he died they sent and took the body from his lodgings to the public mortuary. It was about the biggest job of the kind, I suppose, that they had ever undertaken. So heavy was he that he broke the police stretcher, and about a dozen of them had to carry the poor fellow bodily to the mortuary by grabbing hold of him here, there, and everywhere, the best way they could. At his funeral, too, about twelve men had to carry the specially made coffin in relays by means of hooks attached to the bottom. It was rather a gruesome "dead march."

Towards evening of the day he died, tired out and dispirited, I sought the manager of the Winter Gardens, and told him of my loss. I expected sympathy, but I most certainly got none.

"Your giant has dropped down dead, has he?" remarked the manager. "That is a pity, because he is the best part of the show. You will of course now take very much less money to stop on? Is it not so?"

"Not much, I won't!" I retorted hotly; for as a matter of fact the giant had very little to do with my show, which is essentially a one-man turn. He used to walk on at the end of my performance, in order to seat himself on a chair, which broke down under his weight. He then had to pretend to get angry and obstreperous, when the dwarf would march in and persuade him to go quietly after everyone else—including the stage hands—had failed. This always caused a lot of laughter, and constituted a good curtain, but that was about all. It had really nothing to do with my conjuring performance proper.

As a matter of fact, when I went on that night my show went just as well as it had done before, nor was there any falling-off afterwards. Nevertheless, at the end of my month's engagement they stopped half my salary.

This was a serious matter for me, because I was due to appear on the Monday following at the Orpheum Fovarosi Theatre, Buda-Pesth, and what with the expenses connected with my giant's funeral plus a run of ill luck at cards and racing, I didn't have enough money left to pay the railway fares for myself, my company, and my wife and eldest daughter, who were accompanying me. Nor was there any time to get money from my bankers in England. The only thing I could manage, and that with a lot of difficulty, was to borrow just enough, at an exorbitant rate of interest, to pay the second-class fares, leaving us not even sufficient over with which to buy food on our long journey. I should add that I had engaged another giant in Berlin, but he insisted at the last moment on being paid £10 in advance before he would come to Buda-Pesth, and this put the finishing touch on my impecuniosity. My only consolation lay in the fact that the narrow wooden seats of the second-class car incommoded him far more than they did us people of normal size.

However, I did well at Buda-Pesth, and from there I went on to Prague, where I opened on a Sunday. I gave my first performance in the afternoon, everything went with a bang and a flourish from start to finish, and I came off feeling very pleased with myself. A few minutes afterwards a messenger came up to me as I was standing in the wings, and said that the manager wanted to see me in his private office.

Naturally I thought that he wanted to congratulate me. Nothing of the sort. When I arrived there I found all the directors sitting in solemn conclave round a big table, and before I could utter a word a choleric-looking individual, whom I took to be the chairman, burst forth as follows: "Mr. Carlton, your show is rotten. In fact it is not at all the show we bargained for. Where is your other giant?"

"He's dead," I explained. "He died in Berlin, as you very well know, for full accounts of the affair have been published in the papers. But the giant I have now is an even greater draw here than was the original one, for he speaks German, and can therefore make himself easily understood by your audiences, which the other, being an American, could not do."

There was a lot more talk, the upshot of the business being that they wanted to insist on my accepting half the salary I had contracted for. I, however, was in no mood to repeat my Berlin experiences, nor did I intend to. I pointed out to them that my contract said nothing about giants, or, for the matter of that, about dwarfs either. These adjuncts to my show were introduced by myself for my own purposes, and I had a perfect right to dispense with them altogether, if I saw fit to do so.

BOBBY DUNLOP, CARLTON'S AMERICAN "FAT MAN," WHO DROPPED DEAD IN BERLIN

I therefore declined to go on again unless they paid me my money as agreed, and as they refused to do this I packed up my traps, and returned to London. On my arrival I reported the matter to the Variety Artistes' Federation. This is, in effect, our trade union, and amongst other benefits we derive, in return for our subscriptions, is that of free legal advice.

Well, the V.A.F. decided to fight the Prague case through the International Artistes' Lodge, an association which before the war used to protect and look after the interests of our artistes in Germany and Austria, we, in our turn, doing the same by theirs over here. The legal battle was waged long and fiercely in the Austrian courts, but after nine months of litigation their judges decided against us, the result being that I was done out of the sum that I ought by right to have received for my Prague engagement, and the V.A.F. was called upon to pay several hundred pounds in costs. Following these experiences I decided to accept no more engagements in Germany or Austria, nor have I.

I should have mentioned that when I first went to Vienna my wife did not accompany me, but followed me later on; she wiring me the date and hour of her arrival, and asking me to be sure and meet her at the station, which of course I did. Much to my dismay and perplexity, however, when the train drew up at the platform she was nowhere to be seen.

I looked everywhere for her, in the refreshment buffet, in the ladies' waiting-rooms, etc., thinking she might have slipped past me in the crowd. But all in vain. At length, and at the very last moment, it occurred to me to search the train itself; and there sure enough I found her, contentedly playing with our eldest child, then quite a baby.

"Why on earth didn't you get out?" I asked, somewhat angrily I am afraid, as I hustled the pair of them on to the platform just as the train was starting.

"But this isn't Vienna," replied my wife, with a pretty air of perplexity. "It's Wien. Look, there's the name on that big board over there."

Then I understood. The Austrians spell the name of their capital city that way, i.e. Wien, and not as we spell it—Vienna. The mistake was therefore a quite excusable one on the part of an English girl who had never set foot in Austria before.

Nevertheless it was lucky for both of us that I happened to enter her compartment just when I did, for the train she was travelling by was the Trans-Continental Express, and the next stop after quitting Vienna was some three hundred miles down the line towards Constantinople.

By the way, I cannot recommend Vienna as a place of residence for married men who habitually stay out late at night, and who are not over wishful to let their better halves know what hour they return home. And for this reason. A householder in Vienna, or even the occupier of a suite of rooms, or a flat, who is out after eleven o'clock at night, has to put two coins, value about twopence of our money, in a sort of automatic penny-in-the-slot contrivance which is affixed to all the doors in order to obtain admission to his own domicile. And, furthermore, the beastly little tell-tale machine actually registers the time of your arrival.

Soon after my return to England, while I was playing at a certain northern town, I was invited by the Chief Constable to go for a day's rabbit shooting on a big estate some few miles out.

There were about a dozen guns altogether. We motored to the place, and before starting the Chief Constable addressed us somewhat as follows:

"Now, gentlemen, mind this is a rabbit shoot. No pheasants are to be killed under any pretence whatever. Remember, all of you! it's the close season and it's a very great privilege we have been accorded, and it must not be abused."

Of course we all promised to remember, and the shoot commenced. I was given a place on the extreme outside of the covert, where I was hidden from the remainder of the party by the thick undergrowth.

Presently I found myself within a few yards of the Chief Constable. I could see him quite plainly, but he could not see me.

There were lots of pheasants about, and soon I saw the Chief peer cautiously round to see if anybody was looking; then he let drive at a fine cock bird, which he picked up and put in the inside pocket of his shooting jacket.

A little later I also yielded to temptation, and bagged a bird for myself. But before I could pick it up, the Chief Constable burst through the undergrowth in a furious rage, and started to tell me off. A lot of the others, attracted by the noise, gathered round, everybody looking daggers at me.

I felt, I must confess, pretty small, though not nearly so small as I should have felt if I had not known what I did.

Finally the Chief Constable, after one violent explosive volley of objurgation, in the course of which he bade me clear off and never let him see my face again, paused for lack of breath.

Then it was my turn. In his heat and excitement his jacket had become slightly disarranged, and I saw, greatly to my delight, two ends of tail feathers peeping out.

Edging closer to him by degrees, and muttering apologies all the while, I suddenly put out my hand, and with an, "Excuse me, sir, but what are these?" I whipped out the dead pheasant.

Never in my life did I see a man more completely taken aback. His face changed from red to white from white to red again. He stamped up and down. Then he essayed to say something, but a roar of laughter drowned his voice.

Finally, putting the best face he could upon it, he picked up both birds, and cried: "Put 'em in the car, and for God's sake don't tell anybody anything about it."

There is in England a theatre proprietor, the owner of several houses, with the same name as myself—Arthur Carlton. One of his theatres is at Worcester, where also his headquarters are.

This doubling of names has been the cause of some confusion. For instance, once while I was at the Palace Theatre, London, I received through the post a cheque—"Pay Arthur Carlton, Esq., £250." It really ought to have been delivered to him, and after a lapse of three days I received a letter from him beginning "Dear Namesake," inquiring about it. Needless to say I sent it on to him by return of post.

At this time, and for some time afterwards, I had never met him; but one year, when I was playing in pantomime at Newcastle, he wrote to me saying he would like to make my acquaintance, and if I had a week vacant at the close of the pantomime season, would I come down to Worcester and do a turn at his theatre there?

As it happened I did have a week vacant, and I was naturally quite agreeable. Now it is the custom among artistes on the last night of a pantomime engagement to have a bit of a "flare-up," and we did so on this occasion, the champagne circulating freely.

We kept it up late, or rather, to be strictly accurate, early, so that I had to hurry straight from the theatre to catch my train for Worcester, which left at the unearthly hour of two-thirty on Sunday morning.

On the Monday I met my namesake for the first time, and the first words he greeted me with were, "Here's a pretty go," at the same time pointing to a stack of letters about a foot high on the table of his private room at the theatre, all addressed to "Arthur Carlton, Esq."

I had arranged, of course, to have my correspondence forwarded to the theatre in the usual way, never giving a moment's thought to the confusion that would arise. Now we neither of us knew which letters were mine and which were his.

"Well," I said at last, "I've no business that I am ashamed of. You're quite at liberty to open my letters."

"All right!" he answered, and started on the topmost one of the pile. He opened it, glanced at it, then threw it over to me.

"That's yours!" he said.

Something in his manner made me feel uneasy. I grabbed the letter, read the first few lines; then my face fell.

"Dear Mr. Carlton," it ran. "Aren't you ashamed of yourself, running away without paying your bill? And me a poor lone widow, with three little children to support, etc., etc."

The letter was from my late landlady. In my excitement and hurry I had quitted Newcastle without settling up with her for my week's board and lodging, the affair having, I need hardly explain, entirely slipped my memory.

I don't think I ever felt so small in my life. But of course I very quickly explained to my namesake how the mistake had happened, and a cheque to my landlady sufficed to appease that (justly) irate dame.

All the same, I reflected, it was a scurvy trick for Fate to play me.

Shortly after this I was at the Alhambra, Brighton, now a picture palace. Sam Mayo, the "immobile comedian," was also there, and it happened to be the first anniversary of his wedding; so he invited me, and three or four other "pros," to a house he was staying at on the front, with a view to celebrating the occasion. Amongst the company was Malcolm Scott, the well-known female impersonator, and brother of Admiral Sir Percy Scott.

There was champagne galore, and we were all very merry, when at about 2 a.m. I suggested, apparently on the spur of the moment, that we should all go for a bathe in the sea to sober us up. The suggestion was received with acclamation by all present, barring Malcolm; the fact being that it was a put-up job between the rest of us to play a trick on him, though of this he had no suspicion.

The weather was bitterly cold, it being mid-winter; nevertheless, we all proceeded to the sea-front, including Malcolm, who naturally did not care to be the only one to hang back. Then we started to undress, but as none of us had the slightest intention of going into the water, we naturally didn't hurry over the operation. I especially, although I removed my coat, and made great play with my boots, the laces of which refused to come untied. I saw to that.

As a result Malcolm was the first and only one to make the plunge. Immediately, I gathered up his clothes, and ran back into the house with them; while Ernest Lepard, the manager of the Alhambra, who was of the party, went and fetched a policeman whom he knew, and got him to pretend to arrest Malcolm on a charge of infringing the local by-laws by bathing nude on the front.

By this time our victim had come out of the water, and was standing shivering and blue with the cold on the promenade. Likewise, despite the unearthly hour, quite a small crowd had gathered, attracted by the unusual spectacle.

I, for one, beginning to think that the joke had gone far enough, fetched his clothes and asked him to dress himself. Not so, however, Malcolm. Addressing the policeman, he said: "All right, constable, do your duty. You've arrested me like this. Now take me to the station like this."

His insistence naturally put the policeman in a bit of a quandary; and, probably fearing trouble with his superiors, and noting out of the corner of his eye the gathering crowd, he quietly slipped away. Whereupon, to our consternation, Malcolm announced his intention of staying where he was until another policeman came along.

Eventually we had to carry him forcibly back into the house, where he promptly collapsed. He came round after we had poured about half a bottle of neat whisky down his throat, and piled a dozen blankets on top of him before a roaring fire; but I have come to the conclusion since that it was rather a silly joke to play. It might easily have caused the death of our victim.

It was about this time that I started to work an illusion of my own which I called "The Mysterious Cross." It created a big sensation all over the country, topping the bills wherever it was shown; but as I am no believer in the saying about good wine needing no bush, I used a device of my own to further advertise it at all the towns where I showed it. Of which more anon!

The trick consisted in having a wooden cross, to which my sister Olive, who has a very beautiful figure, was bound securely. Only one long rope was used, this being fastened round her waist and neck, and finished off at the wrists, which were extended to the ends of the arms of the cross, the two ends of the rope being then held by two members of the audience.

While the rope was thus being held, she used to vanish from under a curtain that had meanwhile been drawn round her, and my assistant was found, on the curtain being withdrawn, to have taken her place. The whole thing was practically instantaneous, and the illusion has, I may say, baffled some of the biggest experts in the world. I used no mirrors, wires, trick scenery, or trap-doors, one or some or all of which in conjunction form the basis of most illusions of the kind, and the secret has never been found out by anybody to this day.

Now as to the advertising stunt I mentioned! I used to pay a man to rise from his seat amongst the audience on my opening night, and call out to me that he knew quite well how it was done—that I used a trap-door in the stage. Of course I would pretend to be very surprised and indignant, and protest that it was not so. But the man would insist that he was right, and challenge me to prove the contrary by doing the trick openly, without the aid of the enveloping curtain, so that the audience could judge between us.

"No," I would say, "I cannot do that, for this trick is my livelihood, and if I let the people see how it is done, it will be no attraction for the rest of the week and I can never come back here again with it." Then I would go on to say that if the interrupter could come behind the scenes after the show, I would show him privately how it was done.

But, no! The man would insist that what he wanted was a public exposition. He knew there was a concealed trap-door. I had as good as called him a liar. And so on.

By this time the place would be in an uproar. Some few of the audience, possibly, siding with the interrupter, but the bulk of them, almost invariably, being on my side. Then if the manager was a sport, I would have him come on the stage from the wings, by prior arrangement between us, and pretend to whisper a few words in my ear.

Whereupon, on his retirement, I would advance to the footlights and, with a sob in my throat, hold forth somewhat as follows: "Ladies and gentlemen, if I expose this trick now, on my opening night, nobody will come here during the week, and business will be ruined. As I have been publicly challenged, however, I as publicly promise that on Friday night I will perform the trick openly without drawing the curtain, so that everybody will be able to see with their own eyes how it is done, and that I do not use a trap-door on the stage."

The next day, and all through the week, the town would be placarded all over with bills (previously printed) headed "Sensational Challenge to Carlton," and giving particulars of the forthcoming exposure of the "Mysterious Cross" illusion. The result was that Friday, usually the slackest night of the week, saw the theatre packed to suffocation at both houses.

I kept my word, too, and performed the trick openly without the curtain. But so quick were our movements, the whole thing only lasting about two seconds, that even then the audience were quite unable to detect how it was done. They could, however, see that there was no trap door.

So good was this trick, and so great an interest did it arouse, that I used almost invariably to get a return date. On my second visit, however, I could not of course work the same advertising stunt, so I evolved another one, as follows:

I used to announce from the stage that I would give £5 for the best letter written by any member of the audience, after seeing the trick, explaining how it was done. These letters, when received, I used to read out from the stage at subsequent performances, thereby stimulating the public's curiosity and interest. Some of the explanations were very ingenious, but none of the writers ever came anywhere near to guessing the secret of the trick. If no real letters were forthcoming that were sufficiently amusing I used to compose fake ones myself.

However, so as not to leave behind me the impression that I was trying to shirk my obligations to the public, I always used to arrange with somebody to appear on the stage as the winner, and claim and receive the £5. Afterwards my manager would wait for him in the wings and get back £4 of the money, leaving the recipient £1 as the reward of his trouble.

But, alas! one day my man was called away to the telephone at the critical moment, and forgot all about the business of retrieving my fiver. He did his best to find the recipient, hunting high and low, but it was not until late on the following day that he was discovered in a local "pub," surrounded and being complimented by his pals, whom he had been treating—with my money—in the most lordly way conceivable. All he had left of the £5 was a few—a very few—shillings.

I may add that it is difficult for me to explain in print, unless with the aid of elaborate diagrams, precisely how this trick is worked.

CHAPTER VII
AUSTRALIAN EXPERIENCES

Eastward bound on the *Ortona*—Dinners and diners—Spoofing a chief steward—A brush with the master-of-Arms—"Queering" a poker game—Trouble in the smoke-room—We plan revenge—And execute it—Potatoes as ammunition—The cold water cure—The Captain sends for me—I decline to go—Trouble brewing—I run my head into the lion's mouth—And am frog-marched before the captain—A stormy interview—I am threatened to be put in irons—All's well that ends well—A benefit performance at sea—Arrival in Melbourne—A tale of two champions—Rabbit-shooting extraordinary—I bag a laughing jackass—And am hauled before the "beak"—Fined ten shillings and costs—I am glad at having "got the bird"—The "interfering parrot."

OF all my professional engagements outside the United Kingdom I look back upon the days I spent amongst our Australian kinsmen with the greatest pleasure and satisfaction.

I went out on the Orient liner *Ortona*, and my eldest child, a girl, was born while I was upon the voyage, so I had her christened Ortona.

At Colombo the boat was surrounded by divers, who dived for silver coins thrown into the water by the passengers, and very quick and clever at it, too, some of them were.

Finally a one-armed chap offered to dive right under the bottom of the vessel, going in on one side and coming up on the other, for a shilling.

"All right!" we said. In he went, and we all ran over to the other side to see him come up.

Greatly to our surprise there were about twenty one-armed natives there, all treading water, and each calling out loudly that he had done the trick and demanding to be paid.

For a few moments we were utterly at a loss. Then the real one-armed chap bobbed up, and the rest swam away, using both arms.

They had been holding one arm behind them, and in the water, against their black skins, it was invisible to us.

On the Orient boats, both the first and second-class passengers dined *à la carte*, a gastronomic system the advantages of which have always appealed to me. I returned by the P. & O. liner *Moldavia*, and on these boats, so far as regards the second-class passengers at all events, we dined on the table d'hôte principle. This entailed a good deal of waiting between the courses, while if one desired to miss, say, the soup, or the fish course, there was more delay.

Some people are very quick eaters, some are very slow; and our pace at dinner on the *Moldavia* was set by the slowest amongst us. I, being a quick eater, used to jib and fidget at this, and when we got to Colombo I hit upon an expedient that resulted in my at least getting a little bit of my own back.

I should have mentioned that at dinner the serving of each course was ordered by the chief steward, a rather pompous and self-important individual, who used to ring a small gong bell when everybody had completely finished with, say, the soup course, as a signal to serve the fish, and so on throughout the meal. Well, while I was on shore in Colombo, I bought a small but very loud sounding gong bell, similar to the one used by the chief steward, and when we went on board again I fixed it underneath our table.

Most of us there were in the secret of the joke, and so no offence was given, or any inconvenience caused to them, but I am very much afraid that the diners at the other tables were at all events considerably surprised when, half-way through the soup course, the bell suddenly sounded, and the waiters began handing round the fish. Thereupon confusion reigned supreme. The chief steward insisted that he hadn't rang the bell. The waiters insisted that he had, and bore one another out. Shortly afterwards our bell sounded again, and at once the waiters started on the third course, before some of the passengers had hardly tasted their fish. Whereupon the chief steward seemed to go suddenly stark, staring, raving mad, rushing from one group of waiters to the other, storming, expostulating, threatening; while we guilty ones, who were in the conspiracy, had hard work to prevent ourselves from exploding with suppressed laughter.

I think it is Mark Twain, in his *Innocents Abroad*, who finds fault with the self-assertiveness and bumptiousness that is so frequently characteristic of a certain type of ship's officer. I have noticed the same thing myself. On the *Ortona*, for instance, on the way out, I myself got into very hot water owing to my resenting what I chose to regard as a piece of unwarrantable impertinence on the part of the master-at-arms.

This individual is, of course, the chief of police on ship-board, and is endowed with a considerable amount of authority, being answerable to the captain only. Amongst his duties he has to see that the lights are turned out in the public rooms at certain fixed hours, and to this no one can reasonably take exception, provided it is done with a due regard to the convenience of passengers and not in an offensive or irritating manner. For, after all, passengers—even second-class ones—have some rights on board ship. They pay their fares, and are entitled to at least a modicum of courtesy and consideration.

The trouble on the *Ortona* began in the smoke-room at ten o'clock one night. A game of poker was in progress, and there was a "Jack Pot" on the table with a considerable amount of money in it, when the master-at-arms entered, and without saying so much as "By your leave, gentlemen," without in fact uttering a word, turned out the light, leaving us in total darkness.

Naturally this made us mad, and as soon as he had gone, I got up and switched the light on again. Whereupon the master-at-arms returned, and, using a very foul expression, turned the light out for the second time, and this time finally, locking the switch in such fashion that we could not use it.

Amongst the second-class passengers were a score or so of hefty lads going out to Australia to try their luck there, and they resented the action of the ship's officer as strongly as I did. Between us we made up our minds to pay him out.

And we did. For several days and nights on end we made the poor man's life a misery to him. Going down the Red Sea the heat was terrific, and everybody nearly—not even excluding the ladies—slept on deck; although, of course, the fair sex were screened off. This was our opportunity. The master-at-arms, going his rounds at night, used to find himself lassooed by mysterious ropes that issued he knew not whence, and vanished he knew not whither. Cords stretched taut across gangways where no cords by rights ought to have been, tripped him unawares. Once he was greeted with a fusillade of raw potatoes; big, round, hard potatoes that bruised him black and blue.

Then, when we thought that possibly he had learnt his lesson, we let up on him for a couple of days, and allowed him to see that we were willing to call a truce, if he was. But no! He was as bumptious and as disagreeable as ever; more so, in fact, and sought every opportunity he could to annoy and molest us. So we held a cabinet council, and decided unanimously that the situation called for a resumption of hostilities.

That afternoon, as luck would have it, I was walking on the afterpart of the boat, when I spotted a partly open skylight, and peeping down I saw our hated enemy lying below in his bunk fast asleep, his mouth wide open and his face turned skywards. This I concluded was too good a chance to be missed, so calling the others together I hastily informed them of my discovery, and together we concerted a plan of action.

In a few minutes we knew that the bell would ring for tea, and that then there would be nobody about on deck. This was our opportunity. Twelve of us hurried below to our respective cabins, and returned with a full glass of water apiece, carefully hidden about our clothing; then, when the bell rang, we lifted the skylight and emptied all twelve glasses simultaneously through the open space, and on to the sleeper reposing peacefully below.

There followed a terrific spluttering and gurgling, and an angry roar from the bunk. But we did not wait. Each man made a bee-line for his cabin, and deposited the empty tumbler where it belonged, after which we quietly filed into the tea-room and settled ourselves down at table as if nothing had happened.

Somehow or other, however, the master-at-arms must have guessed that I was the ringleader in the plot, for half an hour later I was approached by one of the officers.

"Mr. Carlton," he remarked, in quiet, matter-of-fact tones, "the captain sends his compliments, and he wants to speak to you in his cabin on the first-class upper deck."

"Very kind of him I am sure to desire to make my acquaintance," I replied suavely. "But the desire is not reciprocated. Go and tell the captain so."

Another thirty minutes or so went by. Then the first officer, accompanied by two others, marched up to me. "Mr. Carlton," remarked the spokesman of the deputation, "the captain desires to see you on the first-class upper deck."

"So I've heard," I remarked in assumedly bored tones. "But I've already explained that I don't wish to see the captain. And anyhow, if he wants to speak to me, I'm here. He knows where to find me. Let him come down to me. Certainly I'm not going up to him."

At this they began to turn nasty, explaining to me that the captain was a magistrate on board his own ship, and that his expressed wishes must be taken as being in the nature of commands, to be obeyed implicitly and without question.

"Now are you coming, or are you not?" they concluded.

"No," I repeated doggedly, "I'm not."

"Then," they said, "we shall have to use force, and take you."

"Well," I remarked, pointing to the others, who had by this time come crowding round, "there are about twenty of us in it. If one goes, the lot goes. You'll have to carry us. It takes at least four men to carry a resisting man against his will. That means that you will be obliged to summon certainly not less than eighty sailors to do the job properly. Meanwhile, I suppose, the navigation of the ship can go hang."

They got angrier than ever at this, but judged it wiser, apparently, to make no attempt to molest us, contenting themselves with going off and reporting the matter to the captain. The rest of the day passed uneventfully, somewhat to our surprise, and when the best part of the following morning had elapsed without anything untoward happening, we began to think that we had won hands down.

Towards midday, however, being by then lulled into a false sense of security and completely off my guard, I went as usual to the barber's shop to get a shave. This necessitated my going down to the first-class part of the ship, a fact of which the enemy was, of course, perfectly well aware.

It was the opportunity they had been waiting for. I had hardly settled myself comfortably in the chair, and the barber had just started to lather me, when no fewer than four of the ship's officers appeared at the open door.

"When you've finished your shave, Mr. Carlton," said their leader, "the captain wishes to speak to you on the first-class upper deck."

Now, thought I, they've got me, but at the same time I made up my mind to stave off the evil moment as long as possible. If only one or two of the others would take it into their heads to come down to the shop? But no! Not a soul came near the place. And all the while the four stood guard outside, completely cutting off my escape.

I had a shave. Then I had a hair cut and a shampoo. I had my nails manicured. I bought shirts and collars, of which the barber kept an assortment in stock for the convenience of passengers. I purchased curios, and picture postcards, spending as much time as possible over examining them and choosing them. But still nobody from our part of the ship came down that way, and in the end I had to come out alone and face the music.

"Well," exclaimed the leader of the gang, as they closed round me, "are you coming?"

"No, I'm not," I replied; and as they made a grab for me, I threw myself flat on the deck, and let out a yell like a hyena.

"Help! Help!" I shouted. "Help! Murder! Help!"

Instantly the ship was in an uproar. Passengers and sailors came running from all directions. But the master-at-arms had taken up a strategic position at the top of the staircase leading down from the second-class part of the ship, and none of my friends were able to pass him, and come to my assistance.

Single-handed, of course, I could do nothing. They frog-marched me up on to the upper deck, and deposited me panting and perspiring before the captain in his cabin.

I have never seen an angrier man than he was. He literally boiled over with rage, and for ten minutes he told me off as hard as he could. In the end, however, he was obliged to stop owing to want of breath.

Then it was my turn. I asked him how he dared to treat me in such a manner? What had I done to deserve it?

"You know very well," he shouted in reply. "You threw water over the master-at-arms."

"How do you know?" I asked. "You were not there."

"Silence!" he roared. "I'll have you put in irons."

"How many sets of irons have you got?" I inquired.

"Oh! About six," was his reply.

"You'll want more than that," I said. "There are about twenty of us in it, all big, hefty chaps. We've sworn to stand by one another. Besides," I added soothingly, "I don't think it will look very well in the papers, or do you any good with your employers, when it comes to be published broadcast that you could not maintain discipline aboard your own ship without putting half your passengers in irons."

"But," he spluttered, "this is rank mutiny. I'll put you ashore at the first port of call."

"Where's that?" I asked.

"Fremantle," he replied.

"Well," I retorted, "even if you do, I shan't cry about it. I suppose I can take a train to Melbourne."

"Then you suppose wrong," he snapped. "There is no railway communication whatever between the two places."

All this while the other officers had been standing respectfully at attention, waiting further instructions. The captain now sent them away, and closed the door.

"Take a seat, Mr. Carlton," he said.

I sat down, wondering what was coming next.

"Have a drink?" he inquired, producing a decanter of whisky and a syphon of soda.

"Now you're talking," I said; and we both laughed.

This was the end of the bother. And not only that. Next day the captain came and had dinner with us in the second-class saloon, a thing he had never done before; and we, not to be outdone in generosity, gave a benefit show, half the proceeds of which went to the Seaman's Orphanage, the other half going to the Music-hall Benevolent Fund.

I should add that I had previously explained to the captain during the latter part of our interview in his cabin, exactly how the bother began; and he agreed with me that, although we might have been to blame in regard to the method of our reprisals, the master-at-arms had only himself to thank for the trouble he had brought down on his head, since for him to have used the exceedingly foul expression he did towards us on so very trifling a provocation was absolutely inexcusable.

By the way, while on the subject of disagreeable officials, there used to be a certain ticket-inspector at Waterloo Station who was very particular in regard to clipping each passenger's ticket, and once or twice he made me lose my train while I was searching for mine in various pockets.

So one day I decided that I would get even with him, and I placed a penny under my ticket, holding it in such a way that the coin was invisible to him.

I shall never forget the surprised look on the man's face when he found that his nippers refused to clip my ticket. Try it yourself. Anybody can do it. It is not necessary to be a professional conjuror.

On my arrival at Melbourne I found everybody there singing a song the melody of which was exceedingly catchy, and the words of which concerned themselves with various Australian notables, portraits of whom used to be thrown on a big screen at the Opera House while the song was being sung on the stage by the artiste. One verse of this topical ditty ran as follows:

Australia! Australia! She has her champions too.There's old Bill Squires, and Georgie Towns,They've shown what they can do.In ev'ry land, in ev'ry clime,She's kept her flag unfurled.Now, Australia can hold her ownWith the wide, wide world.

Squires, I should explain, was the champion heavy-weight of Australia. He had beaten everybody there. Not one could stand up against him. And Australia, and the people of Melbourne more especially, were awfully proud of him in consequence. George Towns was, of course, the champion sculler of the world, and also an Australian.

Well, as luck would have it, the latter was beaten just about this time by Dick Arnst, the New Zealander; and the very same week, I am not certain that it was not the very same day, Squires was knocked out in one round in America by Tommy Burns. (The Australian was knocked senseless by almost the first real punch delivered by Burns in the first round, and did not come to for half an hour or so. Then, seeing all the people going home, he concluded he had won, and his first words were: "Well, what do you think of your bloomin' champion now?") This double disappointment greatly upset the Melbourne people. It also completely spoilt the song, which had to be withdrawn, much to the disgust of Harry Rickards, the manager of the Opera House.

Afterwards, just for a lark, I used to go into a hotel bar known as "Under the Earth," situated in Burke Street, and a favourite resort of the sporting element of Melbourne, and start to hum over the song and words to myself. This always led to a scene. "Go home, you long slab of misery," they would yell in unison. "Who do you think you're taking a rise out of?" "Why, what's the matter?" I would ask, in assumed surprise. "Can't a man sing what song he likes in this God-forsaken country?" Sometimes some of the boys there who didn't know me very well began to get really angry, but before things went too far I always made it plain that it was only meant for a harmless bit of "kid" on my part, and a hearty laugh and "drinks round" soon caused peace and harmony to reign once more.

Nevertheless, some of the "boys" felt sufficiently sore about it to want to get even with me, so they invited me to go rabbit shooting. This is a joke that is frequently worked off on a "new chum," rabbits out there being looked upon as vermin. Nobody dreams of shooting them, for sport at all events.

But I, of course, knew nothing of all this. I thought it awfully kind of them, and accepted the offer with alacrity. We motored out into the bush on Saturday night after my show, slept in the car, and when day dawned I found myself surrounded by millions of rabbits. They covered the earth to the horizon as far as the eye could reach; they were gathered in myriads against the wire fences; the car had even run over quite a number of them. And so tame were they, I was able to kick them out of my way. I never saw such a sight before, or imagined any such; no, not in my wildest dreams. The other members of the party were in fits of laughter. "Go on!" they cried. "Have a shot. See if you can hit one."

Of course to shoot them was not sport, in the sense that we in England understand the word. Nevertheless I killed half a dozen or so. I couldn't help it. Then I wandered away from my companions into the bush, looking for something else to shoot that would be really worth while.

Presently I heard a loud "Ha! Ha! Ha!" from somewhere behind me. I wheeled quickly but could see no one. "Some of the boys having a lark with me," I thought, and walked wearily on in the direction whence the sound had seemed to come.

Presently another peal of loud laughter rang out, this time from the bush away off on my right rear. Again I wheeled, and was just in time to catch sight of a bird, about the size of a magpie, flitting from one gum tree to another, and from whose throat the sound had evidently emanated.

I knew then at once what it was, for I had often heard the bird described. The laughing jackass, a big kind of kingfisher peculiar to Australia! It is also known as the cuckaburro, which is probably a corrupt native rendering of the name bestowed upon the bird by the early voyagers from Spain, "burro" being, of course, the colloquial Spanish for "donkey." Yet another name for it amongst Australian backwoodsmen is the "settler's clock," because it invariably starts to utter its peculiar gurgling laugh precisely at dawn and dusk each day.

These birds, by the way, are strictly preserved, it being forbidden to kill them under heavy penalties. One reason for this is that they kill the snakes, which are the pest of the farmers out there. This feat the bird performs by darting upon the reptile and carrying it aloft in its talons, afterwards dropping it on the ground from a considerable height. It then flies down and pecks out the snake's eyes, leaving it, if not already dead, to perish miserably.

But unfortunately I was not aware of this, and I followed the bird up some distance, and eventually shot it. Possibly I should not have been so keen on getting it, for there was nothing strikingly remarkable about it, but for the fact that the wretched thing seemed to my excited imagination to be bent upon mocking me with its irritating raucous laugh. Every time I got within range, and raised my gun to my shoulder, he would emit another loud "Ha! ha! ha!" and fly off to another tree.

These tactics he repeated perhaps a dozen times, and when at last, hot, angry, and thirsty, I succeeded in bagging him, he had led me such a dance that I had not the remotest idea where I was, or in which direction to seek the other members of the party. I was, in fact, bushed; and wild visions of my fate if I did not succeed in attracting the attention of my friends rushed into my throbbing brain.

In vain I "cooeed," and fired off my gun again and again. There was neither answering shout, nor shot, nor any sign of human life or habitation; only all around and about me the waterless, foodless, shadeless bush. I was beginning to get really frightened, for I had fired away my last cartridge, when greatly to my relief I heard in the far distance a faint call, and by "cooee-ing" back, and following the answering sounds, I was at length able to rejoin my friends.

But there was more trouble awaiting me. In shooting the laughing jackass I had committed a crime in the eyes of the Australian sporting people, akin to that perpetrated by a man over here who has the temerity to shoot a fox, and when I returned to Melbourne and emptied my bag proudly on the floor of the "Under the Earth" bar, consternation reigned supreme. My "crime" was explained to me in language more forcible than polite. The rabbits I had shot, and which by this time were exceedingly odoriferous, were the cause of much merriment. I had also shot two or three rosella parrots, and these were passed round, and duly admired. But the laughing jackass was quite another matter.

However, in the end, Mrs. Hill, the genial proprietress of the establishment, consented to smuggle it over the bar, and even went to the length, after a lot of persuasion, of promising to have it stuffed for me. This, I may add, she did, and I have the bird now. But the affair got talked about, and in the end I was summoned before the magistrate for my breach of the Australian game laws.

"Why did you shoot the bird?" asked the "beak" sternly.

"Because he laughed at me," I answered on the impulse of the moment.

At this the Court roared, and the magistrate inquired blandly whether I wasn't used to being laughed at? "Would you shoot me if I laughed at you?" he said, with a twinkle in his eye.

I knew then that I was all right, and was immensely relieved, for I had visions of a heavy fine staring me in the face, or even possibly a term in the local gaol. In the end I was fined ten shillings and the costs, and I of course paid up cheerfully, glad to have been let down so lightly; and glad also, for probably the first and last time in my life, at having "got the bird."

Speaking of birds reminds me that just before leaving Australia I bought a talking parrot from a dealer.

I was strolling through a turning off Burke Street, Melbourne, when my attention was particularly drawn to the bird owing to hearing it repeat two or three times, "Marie! Marie! I love Marie!"

Now Marie happens to be my wife's name, and it at once occurred to me that it would please her very much indeed if I took the parrot home, and when I presented it to her explained to her how I had caught it in the bush, and toiled hard through many weary weeks to teach it to speak these beautiful words, always present of course in my own mind—"I love Marie."

I bought the parrot fairly cheap, the dealer explaining that it spoke no other words. This, I reflected, suited me admirably, and I bore my prize away in triumph, inclosed in a handsome cage.

Directly we embarked for home I gave the parrot in charge of the butcher, telling him to look after it well, and promising to tip him a sovereign for his trouble when we arrived at Southampton. During the voyage I didn't bother much about my purchase, beyond inquiring now and again as to the bird's welfare.

The day before we were due to reach England, however, I went down to have a good look at it. Imagine my horror when I was greeted by it (in addition to its stock phrase "I love Marie") with a perfect flood of the most awfully profane language it is possible to conceive.

The wretched bird simply turned the air blue with a string of full-blooded sailormen's oaths, coupled with certain other phrases that, besides being profane, were shockingly indecent.

Naturally I was furiously angry, but the butcher vehemently protested that he was not to blame. The deck hands and stokers, he explained, were constantly at the bird, teaching it all manner of bad language while his back was turned.

Of course, to introduce the now hopelessly depraved parrot

into a decent household was altogether out of the question, and in the end I turned bird and cage over to the butcher in lieu of the promised tip; an arrangement, I may add, with which he was well content.

CHAPTER VIII
MELBOURNE TO LONDON

The "Under the Earth" bar in Melbourne—A swimming challenge spoof—The Australian Vaudeville Association—My connection therewith—They present me with an Address—At Adelaide—A cheery send-off—I bring to London with me Charlie Griffin, the feather-weight Australian champion—Fix up a match at the London National Sporting Club—I train him myself during a pantomime engagement—He is beaten by Jim Driscoll—But afterwards defeats Joe Bowker—My fight at the National Sporting Club with "Apollo"—All the "pro.'s" present—A great night—I am beaten by "Apollo"—Congratulations all round—Only Mrs. "Carlton" does not approve—Other boxing and sporting yarns.

OUR Australian cousins are fine sportsmen, and they dearly love a joke, even if it is against themselves. When I was performing in Melbourne in 1907 I became very chummy with Jack Trenby, at that time one of the best-known jockeys in Australia, and one day we got talking about swimming. I told him that I rather fancied myself that way, and that I used to swim the hundred yards in sixty-four seconds in the days when the record for the English Championship (held by J. H. Darbyshire) was only one-fifth of a second under the sixty-one seconds.

"Good!" cried Trenby. "There's a chap here named Murphy who thinks he can swim. We'll have a lark with him, and unless I'm greatly mistaken we'll rope in a few others of the 'wide ones' into the bargain."

In those days—it may be so now for aught I know—the sporting element in Melbourne were wont to meet together in the hotel bar known as "Under the Earth," situated in Burke Street, mention of which has been made in the previous chapter. A lot of us used to go swimming in the public baths every morning, and foregather here for a livener and a chat afterwards.

Well, for a whole week I went swimming with the rest, and, acting under Trenby's instructions, I made no end of an exhibition of myself; diving in awkwardly flat on my stomach, and panting and splashing and puffing and blowing after I was in, like a maimed grampus. All the while, however, I pretended to think I was getting on famously, and one day when we were all enjoying our drinks in the "Under the Earth" bar Jack purposely switched the conversation on to swimming, and referred somewhat slightingly to my efforts in that direction.

Thereupon I pretended to get huffed, and offered to swim Murphy the length of the public bath and back again for a five-pound note.

Murphy snapped at the bet like a hungry dog at a bone, and every "bookie" there, and nearly every other man in the bar, rushed at me with their money, imploring me to raise my stakes and let them in. Jack Trenby, I may add, was loudest of all in asking to be given a chance to win my money, and although he must inwardly have been bursting with laughter, he never showed a trace of it on his countenance.

At first I feigned reluctance, but in the end I accepted their bets up to a total of £50, and the money was put up with Mrs. Hill, the proprietress of the hotel, the race being timed to come off at eleven o'clock on the following morning. After a little while, however, I pretended that I was only bluffing, and wanted to call the bets off. "You know, boys," I said, "that I'm no swimmer. You've all seen me at the baths. I'm only a novice. I was just swanking. Tell you what I'll do! Call the bets off, and I'll set up wine for the crowd."

But they only laughed, and told me that I had asked for it, and that I had got to go through with it. They, of course, thought that the £50 was as good as won.

Then, after a while, I changed my cue, and told them the truth. "Look here, boys," I said, "I've been kidding you all for over a week. Take my tip and call the bets off. I'll show you in the morning how easily I can beat Murphy, and for nothing. Why, I can swim the hundred yards within a second or two of the record time. I only wanted to show you all how easily I could have you. I don't want your money."

But no! They wouldn't have it at any price. Not a man there, barring of course Jack Trenby, but imagined that I was bluffing, and though I went up to each one separately and offered to call his individual bet off, not one would agree to it.

Next morning all sporting Melbourne was at the baths. The Press, too, was represented. Murphy had seen to that.

- 83 -

We stripped, and then, turning to the crowd, I made a last appeal.

"Boys," I cried, "I'm going to win—sure. Will you call all bets off?"

"No!" roared everybody in unison; and in we plunged.

Well, I beat Murphy by half a length, and everybody crowded round me, wanting to shake hands, and patted me on the back, saying that it was one of the smartest things ever done in Melbourne. And I dressed, and the crowd escorted me to the White Hart Hotel, where I spent my winnings, or the major part of them at all events, on a dinner for the boys. Alf Squires, who is now the proprietor of the Colonial Bar, Savoy Street, Strand, was the landlord of the "White Hart" at the time, and he did us well and no mistake about it.

It was while I was in Melbourne during this tour that I was instrumental in founding the Australian Vaudeville Association, now a large and flourishing organisation, and on my departure they presented me with an illuminated address on vellum, with the following inscription: "Presented to ARTHUR CARLTON. Sir—We the undersigned members of the Committee of the New South Wales branch of the Australian Vaudeville Association convey to you our sincerest thanks and hearty appreciation for your untiring efforts and valuable assistance to us in our infancy. We extend to you the glad hand of fellowship, and deeply regret your departure from Australia. No pen can describe how grateful we feel for the valuable services you at all times have rendered us, often at great personal inconvenience. You have paved the way for a bright and glorious future for our young association. You leave our native land with the good wishes of every true artist here. In conclusion we trust that your sojourn amongst us has been a pleasant one, and we sincerely hope you will at no distant date pay us another visit, for though thousands of miles may separate us we will always keep you in memory. With every good wish for your future health and prosperity, we beg to remain."

Then followed the signatures of a large number of prominent men in the Profession, all of whom I am proud to call my friends. I was very pleased and touched at the reception of this quite unexpected testimonial, and equally so by the fact that when I quitted Adelaide, en route for England, the famous

"Besses o' th' Barn" band came down to the quay, with their instruments carefully hidden under their coats, and, as the ship made ready to cast off, struck up the air "For he's a jolly good fellow."

While in Melbourne on this occasion I met Charlie Griffin, the feather-weight champion of Australia, and brought him to London, where I arranged with Mr. "Peggy" Bettinson, of the National Sporting Club, London, to match him there against Jim Driscoll for £200 a side and the feather-weight championship of the world. I trained him personally myself in Edinburgh during my pantomime engagement there, and seconded him in the ring, with the assistance of the famous Tommy Burns, then heavy-weight champion of the world. He put up a good fight, and looked like winning, but greatly to my disappointment he was disqualified in the fifteenth round for a foul. However, a little later on, I matched him against Joe Bowker, the ex-bantam-weight champion of the world, for £100 a side and the club purse; and this fight Griffin won, knocking Bowker out—for the first time in his life—in the ninth round.

This leads me up to my own fight at the National Sporting Club, which came off on May 4th, 1914. The beginning of it was this way. Mr. Walter (now Sir Walter) de Frece (husband of Miss Vesta Tilley), and one of the Committee of the N.S.C., is well known in the profession for his love of a joke; and one day, knowing that I rather fancied myself as a fairly good amateur boxer, he offered to put up a silver cup, value 25 guineas, if I would box Mr. William Bankier, better known by his stage title of "Apollo," the Ideal Scottish Athlete.

No doubt Mr. de Frece counted on my declining, for Apollo was supposed to be at that time probably the best all-round athlete in the world. His strength was prodigious. He will be remembered by patrons of the music-halls as the man who used to have placed upon the stage, as an item of his performance, an enormous sack of flour. This he used to challenge anyone in the audience to remove, offering £50 to whoever succeeded. Nobody ever did, although many tried, but at the end of each performance Apollo would lift it, and carry it off the stage, apparently with the most perfect ease.

When I add to this that his weight in training was 15 st. 10 lb. as against my 11 st. 10 lb., and that he is all brawn, bone, and muscle, the reader will be able to appreciate that in tackling him I was up against a pretty tough proposition. In fact, as I have already intimated, Mr. de Frece made his offer originally more by way of a joke than anything else, and he was considerably surprised when I took it on, merely stipulating that the club purse should, no matter which of us won, be given to the Music-hall Artists' Benevolent Fund, the cup of course going to the victor. To this, Apollo, like the good sportsman he is, at once agreed.

The weights were announced by Mr. Bettinson as follows: "Apollo, the Ideal Athlete, 15 st. 10 lb.; Carlton, the Human Hairpin, 11 st. 10 lb." My opponent had for his seconds Charlie Mitchell, ex-heavy-weight champion of England, and Jake Hyams. In my corner were Jim Driscoll, the feather-weight champion of the world, Dai Dollings, and the club's second.

The battle looked like being over before it had properly begun. I had thought that my opponent would have sparred for an opening. Instead, however, directly the gong sounded for the start he rushed across the ring like a mad bull, and landed me a terrific punch under the heart.

Down I went, and I knew no more until I heard "nine" counted, and realised that I had to struggle to my feet before the fatal "ten." I did it, but that was about all; and how I managed to last out the round I don't know to this day. I dragged myself to my corner at the end of it feeling more dead than alive, and the sixty seconds that elapsed before the gong sounded for us to begin again seemed the shortest minute I ever spent in my life.

Curiously enough, though, once I was on my feet for the second round I felt much better. I watched carefully that Apollo did not again get in a blow under my heart, and about half-way through the round I managed to split his lip with a lovely straight left. This made him wild, and he forced the pace, using all his weight, but did me very little further damage, although I felt pretty tired by the end of the round.

Driscoll bucked me up during the interval, telling me that I was winning easily on points, which was the truth.

He also made me promise that in the next round I would give Apollo an opening, and wait until he led a straight left. Then I was to take a half step back, and counter with my right.

This was all right in theory, but in practice, in my case at all events, it didn't work "worth a cent," as our American cousins would say. I did my best from the moment when I stood up for the third round to do as I had promised, but Apollo seemed to know all about it, for I got a terrible pasting waiting for the straight left that never came. Being so tall and thin, I caught the majority of his punches on my shoulders and arms, and mighty glad I was when the round ended.

Well, they massaged me in my corner, and Driscoll kept on saying, "He's bound to lead a straight left directly, then down he'll come, and, don't forget, the bigger they are the heavier they fall." I smiled rather sickly, for I was not so sure.

Towards the end of the fourth round Apollo made another of his mad, tearing rushes at me, and this time he got me over the ropes. I am 6 ft. 2½ in. tall, and the new, thin, wire-like rope cut me right across the small of the back. His whole weight was on top of me. I slid and slithered along the rope, scraping all the skin off the hollow of my back. It was like being flayed alive; far worse than all the punching.

This was practically the end of the fight. Almost directly afterwards Apollo shot out with his right, catching me full on the nose, a terrific punch, and down I went, covered in blood.

My head hit the floor—whack. I saw stars. I also heard "stars"—the "pro.'s" applauding. But I was by no means "out." I heard the timekeeper counting. "One—two—three—four"—and so on!

CARLTON AND HIS TRAINER, DAI DOLLINGS, THE FAMOUS WELSH ATHLETE, STRIPPED READY FOR HIS FIGHT WITH APOLLO

All the while I was thinking what a mug's game it was; so far, that is to say, as I was concerned. My hands were paining me terribly; and they, I reflected, were my capital—my livelihood. I came to the conclusion then that I had done quite enough for one night for sweet charity's sake, and that the cup might go hang for all I cared. I had no money interest in the contest personally, be it remembered. So I stayed down for the fatal ten seconds; when, of course, Apollo won.

Then the cheering burst forth, and lots of people crowded round me, slapped me on the back, tried to shake me by the hand, and told me I had put up a regular game, plucky fight against a far heavier and stronger opponent. Amongst those foremost in congratulating me was Charlie Mitchell, Apollo's second. "By God, Carlton!" he cried; "but I'm glad it's all over. Why, he might have killed you."

When I went up to my dressing-room my seconds rubbed me down with embrocation, and after ten minutes' rest or so I felt all right; but my left arm and shoulder were black and blue, and my nose didn't properly stop bleeding for three days afterwards. This, as I pointed out to my wife at intervals after

I returned home, seemed a rather unusually long time. "Yes," replied she soothingly, "but then yours is an unusually long nose." Which was true, but not flattering.

Women, however, I have long since discovered, are not sympathetic, except in the story books. When I reached home that same evening, for instance, not wishing to disappoint my wife I told her a fib.

"Marie," I said, "I've won the fight."

"You look it," she said, eyeing me stonily. Then added: "Where's the cup?"

I had forgotten for the moment all about this item in the programme, and so had to tell another fib in order to cover up the first.

"Somebody's pinched it," I said. "Tell you all about it in the morning. Just now I want to go to bed."

I went.

Next morning the pillow was red instead of white.

But all the same I performed as usual that evening.

I was once asked by Mr. "Peggy" Bettinson, the manager of the National Sporting Club, to box Jimmy Wilde, fly-weight champion of the world, on the occasion of a benefit performance in aid of the Music-hall Benevolent Fund. These sort of performances are not easy for the amateur, for most professional boxers hit hard even when they are not "out for blood," and on this occasion I had to let Wilde show his ability, while also letting the audience see that I too knew something, at all events, about boxing.

Roars of laughter greeted our appearance in the ring, the contrast between me, standing 6 ft. 2½ in., and the diminutive Wilde, who only stood 5 ft. 4 in. and weighed 7 st. 2 lb., being a striking one. And when we started off boxing, and I allowed Wilde, on his making to hit me, to run between my wide-opened legs, as under an arch, the merriment of the onlookers knew no bounds.

CARLETON AND JIMMY WILDE AT THE NATIONAL SPORTING CLUB

One of my spoofs, however, very nearly miscarried, and had it quite done so Wilde would have known it, for I can hit hard on occasion. It was during the third round. I had got him in a corner, and made up my mind to raise a good laugh. So, watching my opportunity, I put out my left arm in front of him, and upper cut with my right, my intention being that the blow should be delivered at least a yard wide, and that then I would look up into the air, as though pretending to wonder where he had gone to.

This, I say, was my intention. But such was Wilde's marvellous, cat-like agility, that he, knowing nothing of what was in my mind, slipped from under my left, and bounded a full yard on one side, with the result that my blow, delivered with all my strength, actually grazed his ear.

After it was all over "Peggy" Bettinson said to me, "Carlton, old man, you nearly caught him with that upper cut in the third round." "Yes," I said, "I nearly did." But I never told "Peggy," or indeed anybody else, that I had really intended missing him by a yard.

Another time I was asked to box with Jim Driscoll, the retired feather-weight champion of the world, for the Hero Boxers' Fund. The affair came off at the Middlesex Music-hall, and in order to raise a laugh I had arranged with my second to hand me a bottle of Bass to drink in the interval after the first round, to bring me a cigar to smoke in the second, and to squirt a syphon of soda water over me at the conclusion of the third round.

These tactics certainly made the audience laugh. But the actual boxing was no laughing matter—for me. Driscoll hit hard and often, and at the finish I was pretty well done up. Seeing this, I suppose, somebody in the gallery called out for the referee's decision, whereupon Mr. Eugene Corri, who was acting in that capacity, stepped forward and gravely announced "Carlton is the winner."

In this way I obtained a decision, given publicly, over the feather-weight champion of the world, by the most famous referee in the world.

This, again, caused a fresh outburst of laughter. But I was lying flat on my back in my dressing-room—gasping like a fish out of water. I lay like that for a full half-hour before I felt the slightest inclination to rise. While I was thus prone, a friend entered to condole with me. "Why didn't you stop his blows?" he asked. "I did," I gasped. "Anyway, I didn't see any go by."

By the way, talking of Jimmy Wilde, the following true story concerning him occurs to me. Down in Wales, where he lives, they call him the "Tylorstown Terror," the "Mighty Atom," the "Giant Killer," and other similar awe-inspiring names indicative of his pugnacity and fearlessness. Nevertheless, it is an open secret in the district that there is one individual whom Jimmy stands in mortal dread of. This is his wife.

His friends say that when he has been out late with the boys, on his return home he invariably throws his cap into the passage of his house before venturing within. If the cap comes flying out again, Jimmy doesn't go in that night. If it remains in the passage for an appreciable length of time, Jimmy follows it indoors.

While on the subject of boxing I may mention that I have frequently been taken for Bombardier Wells, even in the National Sporting Club itself, where he is, of course, well known. This is due, I suppose, to us both being about the same build and height, with similar light-coloured curly hair. I once took advantage of this circumstance in order to extricate myself from a somewhat tight corner.

When I was in Cumberland salmon fishing I was invited by the captain of the Maryport patrol boat to accompany him on a cruise to the fishing grounds. These boats carry trawls in order to try for the best fishing grounds, and those on board are allowed to fish on the understanding that none of the catch is offered for sale, the surplus, after the crew have taken their pick, being distributed amongst the poor of Maryport.

Well, we had quite good sport, and after landing I was proceeding towards my hotel with a string of fine fish—a present from the captain—which I intended dispatching that evening to my home in Surrey, where I knew they would be a welcome surprise to my wife and children. Very soon, however, I was surrounded by a hostile crowd, who demanded to know where I got the fish, and what I intended doing with them.

I explained that I had been out with the patrol boat—of which fact the crowd was perfectly well aware—and that I intended the fish as a present for my wife and family. "Oh, no, you don't," exclaimed two or three voices. "These fish are for poor people; not for stranger 'toffs' like you."

In vain I tried to reason with the crowd. They became more and more aggressive, jostling me, and making one or two attempts to snatch the fish from my hand. Suddenly a happy thought struck me. Drawing myself up to my full height, I exclaimed: "Gentlemen, you don't know who I am." "No," they roared, "and we don't care. But we mean to have those fish."

"Well, gentlemen," I continued, "it's hard lines on me if you are not going to allow me to carry home fish. You all know me—by reputation at all events. I'm Bombardier Wells."

The effect of my announcement was magical. From open hostility the attitude of the crowd changed in a moment to almost embarrassing friendliness. They pressed round me closer than ever, patting me on the back and shaking me by the hand, and not another word was said about depriving me of my fish.

CHAPTER IX
SOME AMERICAN EXPERIENCES

To New York on the *Mauretania*—Gambling on ocean liners—A "dear" old gentleman—Phenomenal luck—My suspicions are aroused—I play the part of a private detective—A puzzling proposition—The light that shone by night—My suspicions are confirmed—An artful dodge—A new use for smoke-coloured glasses—Doctored cards—The most beautiful American city—Los Angeles—Tuna-fishing at Santa Catalina—Monsters of 400-lb. weight—The Tuna Club—A record catch—Fishing with kites—Wild goat stalking—Outwitting a gambler—Diamond cut diamond—A ride on an ostrich—American police methods—An unpleasant experience.

TRAVELLING to America on the *Mauretania* some years back, I had a rather unusual experience. As most people are perfectly well aware, these crack trans-Atlantic liners are frequently infested by card-sharpers, who prey upon the unwary amongst the passengers, and often reap large harvests in ready cash as the result of their misdirected enterprise.

I always, when travelling, make it a point to study these gentry, and as a rule it is no very difficult matter for me to detect their particular methods of swindling; when, of course, I make it my business to quietly warn such others of the saloon passengers as may be in the habit of playing cards in the smoke-room.

On this occasion, however, there was amongst the card-players one whose methods frankly puzzled me. He was a most benevolent-looking old chap, white-haired and bespectacled, very pleasant and affable, and hail-fellow-well-met with everybody. Nevertheless there was something about him that convinced me that he was a crook.

His luck was simply marvellous. For three nights I watched him win with uncanny regularity; yet, though I studied him closely all the while, following his every movement with my eyes, I could detect nothing wrong with his play. All the same, however, I became more and more convinced that I was not mistaken in my estimate of him. The man was a sharper, beyond the shadow of a doubt. I could tell by watching his play that he knew what cards the other players held.

On the fourth evening, after play, during which he won as usual, the cards happened to be left behind on the smoke-room table. I quietly pocketed them, and took them down to my cabin, where I spent over an hour examining them one by one by the aid of a microscope. My labour was in vain. I could detect absolutely nothing wrong with the cards, which were those ordinarily sold on board ship at eightpence a pack.

On the following night I again watched him closely, and was more than ever convinced that I was not mistaken. On this occasion poker was being played, and his winnings amounted to over £200. During the game one of the other players, either because his suspicions were aroused, or perhaps simply with the idea of changing his luck, ordered another pack of cards, and these were duly supplied by one of the stewards in the usual sealed package, which was opened by the man who ordered and paid for them.

This, of course, seemed to do away entirely with any chance of his having been able to mark the cards beforehand. Yet still he went on winning, and still I continued to watch him, like a cat watching a mouse. The sole result was that I was more puzzled than ever. The thing began to get on my nerves. Here was I a professional card-manipulator, a man who knew, or at all events thought he knew, every trick on the board; and here was a man whom I knew in my mind to be a card-sharper, and yet I could not detect his method of swindling. It made me wild.

The day before we got into New York he had another good night, by far the best he had had during the voyage. His luck was the talk of the ship. "Luck!" said I to myself, and ground my teeth in rage to think how he had outwitted us all. He had not had any of my money, it was true. I had seen to that. But nevertheless I was furious to think I could not find out how the trick was worked.

Again I secured possession of the cards he had been playing with, and again I examined them under the microscope in the quiet seclusion of my own cabin. I spread them out on my dressing-table, and sat there for a couple of hours or more, studying them, peering at them, fingering them back and front. The net result of it all was the same as on the previous occasion. I could detect nothing whatever wrong with them, and in the end I gave it up as a bad job, switched off the light, and tumbled into bed, leaving the pack of cards backs uppermost on the dressing-table.

About four o'clock in the morning, and when it was still quite dark, I awoke, and had occasion to get out of my bunk. While on my feet, groping round for the electric light switch, I saw something sparkle on the dressing-table, and thinking it might be my diamond ring, I reached out my hand in order to pick it up. To my surprise it was not there. I switched on the light and the sparkle disappeared. Investigation showed me that my diamond ring was safe in a little covered box I used to keep my jewellery in. There was the usual litter of things on the dressing-table, but nothing, so far as I could see, that was at all likely to sparkle in the dark.

Somewhat mystified, I switched the light off again, and at once the tiny twinkling point of fire flashed into being again. Then I knew. It emanated from the pack of cards; from the topmost card, that was exposed back uppermost.

Once more I switched the light on, and laid the cards out face downwards on the table. Then I switched it off again; and the mystery stood revealed. Every single card was marked on the top right-hand corner on the back with a luminous substance, which I found out later was a patent preparation of phosphorous oil.

The marks were only tiny dots the size of a pin-point, and each card was marked with two dots, no more and no less. The position of one dot indicated the suit, the position of the other the value of the card. The dots were arranged in positions corresponding with the figures on a watch-face. For instance, one dot placed where the big hand would be at half-past the hour, meant that the card was a six, another dot indicating the suit. Similarly if the dot was where the big hand would be at a quarter-past the hour, it meant that the card was a three, and so on. The knave and queen were eleven and twelve o'clock. The king, the thirteenth card, was shown by a dot placed in the centre where the hands meet. Looked at in the light, the tiny marks were quite invisible. They could only be seen in the dark—or by a person looking at them through dark-coloured glasses. The old gentleman, I suddenly recollected, always wore, when playing, spectacles of a peculiar smoky hue.

One thing, however, still puzzled me; and that was how the old rogue had obtained possession of the cards in order to mark them. I jumped to the conclusion in the beginning that he was probably in league with one of the under-stewards, who had access to the place where the packs for sale to the passengers were kept in stock. But this, I discovered later, was not so. What had happened was this:

On the second day out the dear, affable, old gentleman had organised a whist drive for the ladies, himself providing the prizes, and had ordered in advance from the chief steward a dozen and a half packs of cards. Only eight of these were used, as he had easily foreseen, there being only eight tables. The ten unopened packs he had returned to the chief steward the next morning, with the remark that he had overestimated the number of players taking part in the drive.

This much was clear. The rest I had to guess. But there was no difficulty, in my mind at all events, in supplying the missing links in the chain of evidence. He had had the twelve packs in his possession one whole night. What was easier than for him to steam them carefully open in the seclusion of his cabin, mark them with the phosphorous oil, and then re-seal them? The chief steward would hardly be likely to examine the packs very critically when they were returned to him, and even if he had done so, he would not in all probability have been able to detect that they had been tampered with.

Well, I felt pleased as Punch at having solved the riddle. The only question that agitated me now was whether I ought to expose the old rascal. I thought the matter over very carefully, and in the end I decided not to do so. For one thing, any action of that kind would quite possibly have led to his being arrested on his arrival at New York, and myself being detained there as a witness; an eventuality which would not at all have suited my plans. For another thing, I reflected, the mischief was already done; he could win no more money that voyage, seeing that this was our last day at sea. So I let him go, and I noticed that he was one of the first over the gangway when we arrived at New York.

Later on I instituted a few discreet inquiries about the old gent from a New York detective whose acquaintance I made, but I could not get him to admit that he knew him, or even that he haled from New York at all. "He's probably a Chicago crook," he remarked. "There's a lot of snide gamblers make Chicago their headquarters."

That's the Americans all over. They are awfully proud of their own particular city, and can never be got to admit that there is anything wrong with it. Almost the first question a stranger is invariably asked on his arrival in, say, New York, or Boston, or Philadelphia, is whether he doesn't consider New York, or Boston, or Philadelphia, as the case may be, the finest and most beautiful city he was ever in.

For my part I always used to answer the questions in the affirmative, no matter where I might be, but my own private opinion is that Los Angeles is far and away the most beautiful of American cities. It was while I was performing there, by the way, that I had my first and only experience of tuna-fishing. This was at Santa Catalina Island, which lies off the coast of California in the Pacific Ocean.

The tuna is a gigantic mackerel, weighing anything from 80 lb. up to 400 lb., and even more, and is the strongest and gamest fish that swims. "When you go tuna-fishing," I was told, "you must be prepared to hook something like a thirty-knot torpedo-boat."

The favourite haunt of the tuna is the warm shallow water round Santa Catalina. He comes there after the flying-fish, which form his favourite food, and angling enthusiasts flock there in the season from all parts of the world in order to enjoy the sport of killing him.

There are two species of tuna found at Santa Catalina, the blue-finned and the yellow-finned. The first-named is by far the bigger. I had to be content with the latter, as the blue-finned kind was not in evidence during my stay on the island. I regretted this greatly, for I was assured on all sides that to kill a genuine blue-finned leaping tuna with rod and line was something to be proud of—a feat to be remembered and talked about for the rest of one's life.

This I can quite believe, judging by the stories I heard. I was told, for instance, of a new-comer on the island, a perfect novice at the game, who at his first attempt played a gigantic blue-finned tuna for five hours without assistance, and finally killed it. The youthful angler—he was little more than a boy—was taken ashore fainting, a fingernail gone, a thumb dislocated, the palms of both hands skinned, blistered, and bleeding, and his strained arms rendered useless for days. But he was radiantly happy; for he had qualified on his very first day for the Tuna Club—the blue riband of ocean angling.

To become a member of this exclusive association the fisherman must catch and kill with unbroken rod a fish weighing not less than 100 lb. It need not, however, necessarily be a tuna. A barracouta will do, or an albicore, or a black bass. Some of these latter fish run up to 500 lb. (nearly a quarter of a ton) and are as fierce and game as tigers. I was told of one of 327 lb. weight that was played for seven and a half hours. At the end of that period it broke its captor's wrist by a sudden sidelong jump. A second angler then came to the rescue, and played it for another five and a half hours before killing it.

As regards tuna, the record weight for one of these fish brought to boat by rod and line is, I was informed, 251 lb. But monsters of this size are comparatively rare, and still rarer is it for them to be captured after this fashion. To do so demands of the angler a combination of skill, strength, nerve, judgment, and several other qualities, plus any amount of dogged determination and abnormal staying power. As illustrating my meaning I may mention that a former president of the Tuna Club, Mr. Charles F. Holder, had his boat towed ten miles by quite a moderate-sized fish (183 lb.) which fought gamely for hours on end, never sulking a minute. Another angler was dragged more than fourteen miles under similar circumstances, and had his arm broken into the bargain.

None of these exciting experiences, I need scarcely say, came my way; for, as I have already intimated, the big blue-finned tuna had not then arrived off the island, and I had to be content with trying my luck and skill on the smaller yellow-finned variety. With these, however, I was, so I was assured, quite unusually successful. My partner and I between us killed altogether thirty-three fine fish in eight hours. Of these twenty-six were tuna, two rock bass, and five skipjack.

This, I was told, constituted a record for novices, such as we were, and we had our catch photographed. I have a copy of the picture in my possession, with underneath it the following inscription: "Record catch of yellow-finned tuna by 'Carlton,' the English Magician, and Dr. Lartigau of San Francisco, aggregate weight 350 lb., caught on 9-9 tackle in eight hours. Catalina Island, April 10th, 1911. (Signed) P. V. Rogers, Official Photographer to the Tuna Club."

The day before this record catch I went out alone with a boatman, in order to get my hand in, so to speak. It was well I did so, for I discovered that tuna-fishing, like most other things in this world, wants some learning. I hooked my first fish all right, but after playing him for an hour or so I had to give up. My arms ached as though they were being wrenched from their sockets, and my hands were all blistered. Next day I wore gloves, and my boatman taught me that afternoon how to play a fish with my whole body, throwing it backwards and forwards as in rowing.

The motor-boats that are used for tuna-fishing are, I should explain, fitted with sliding seats, like our racing craft here at home, and with leather holdfasts for the feet, and this makes it much easier to play a really big fish, once one has learnt the knack of it. I had also explained to me how to use the patent reel, with which the rods used in tuna-fishing are fitted, and which only runs out at a certain pressure; not freely, as in the case of an ordinary reel.

I forgot to mention that the bait used for the yellow-finned tuna is a sardine, that for his big blue-finned cousin being invariably a flying-fish. Both these tuna are the same species of fish, be it understood, but bearing about the same relation to one another in point of size as the trout does to a salmon.

In angling for the big tuna a kite is sometimes used. This is flown over the sea, and attached to it is a line with a flying-fish (the bait) dangling at the end of it on or near the surface of the water. The motion of the kite, driven by the wind, causes the bait to bob up and down very much as does the live flying-fish, and the tuna leaps out of the sea after it just as a trout does after a fly. When the big fish swallows the baited hook he of course drags the kite down with him.

Another curious feature in connection with Santa Catalina Island is that boats built with glass bottoms are in use there. This is done to give the visitor an opportunity of studying and admiring at his leisure the wonderful sea flora that everywhere carpets the comparatively shallow ocean floor in the immediate neighbourhood of the island.

The beauty and variety of this latter must be seen to be believed. It seems almost a profanation to apply the hackneyed term of "seaweed" to these lovely forms of subaqueous tropical vegetation, although this, I suppose, is practically what they really are. Many of the species, however, are as big as small trees, and all colours are represented, from brightest tints of green to vivid crimson, that in an instant pales to lavender, quivers to gold, or slips into molten ruby or sapphire as the angle of view alters.

OFFICIAL PHOTOGRAPH OF A RECORD CATCH OF YELLOW FIN TUNA CAUGHT BY CARLTON AND ANOTHER FISHERMAN JOINTLY AT SANTA CATALINA

These wonderful undersea glades spring from a groundwork of coral no less beautifully tinted, and spread about the interstices, and strewn thick on the patches of golden sand, are the most beautiful shells imaginable. On one of my trips out I took with me a professional diver, a half-breed Mexican Indian, and he went down several times, and brought me up a very fine collection of shells, corals, and so forth. I have most of them still, and they have been greatly admired. Hiding deep down amongst the coral and seaweed, too, one catches glimpses of many weird fishes that no angler has ever succeeded in catching.

Altogether I was very pleased indeed with my experiences at lovely Santa Catalina, the tuna-fishing more particularly appealing to me greatly. As regards another form of sport that is peculiar to the island, however, I was somewhat disappointed. This was wild goat stalking, of which I had heard big things. The animals are supposed to have descended from some left there long ago by the old Spanish voyageurs, and were pictured to me as being very wild, shy, and difficult to approach.

Naturally I concluded I would like to have a shot at one or more of them, especially as I was assured that it was quite the correct thing to do; so a day was fixed, and I set off very early in the morning in quite high spirits. I was looking forward to something between a chamois hunt in the Swiss Alps and a day's deer-stalking amongst the Highlands of Scotland. Alas, how different was the reality from the expectation! After riding on the backs of ponies along interminable mountain tracks, ascending higher and higher until we reached a region of utter sterility and barrenness, we at length came upon the goats—an entire herd of them. But they were not the least bit wild. On the contrary, they were quite disgustingly tame. They did not even attempt to run when I approached them, but stood stock-still and "baa-a-d." I thought of Tennyson's line about "catching the wild goat by the beard." It would have been a quite easy feat as regards these goats.

To shoot them was, of course, quite out of the question. There was nothing for it but to retrace my footsteps to the lowlands whence I had come, which I accordingly did. My guide could not understand it. "So easy a shot!" I heard him muttering to himself. "Such beautiful horns! How splendid a trophy! What a chance thrown away!"

Los Angeles is one of the most up-to-date places imaginable, with its blaze of electric lights, its scurrying tramcars and innumerable swift automobiles. So, too, of course is San Francisco, and most of the other big Californian cities and towns; but some of the smaller mining camps up in the mountains are pretty rough. I once visited one of these which was known far and wide throughout the State as a "hard town," being in fact a regular Mecca for gamblers and others of the light-fingered gentry.

While strolling round my attention was attracted by a leather-lunged individual who was appealing to a group of miners to the effect that he would bet he could cut the ace of spades, or any other card designated, in a pack which had been thoroughly shuffled by anyone.

The interest was at fever heat, and the miners wagered freely on the outcome. Over 100 dollars were in fact lying on the table when I addressed the gambler saying:

"I'll take ten dollars of that if you will let me shuffle the pasteboards."

"Why, certainly, stranger," he replied. "It's all the same to me."

I placed the bet and shuffled the cards.

"Now, gentlemen," said the gambler, laying the deck upon the table, "I win if I cut the ace of spades."

So saying, he whipped out a huge knife, and with a mighty swing he cut the cards clean through.

"Gentlemen," he yelled as he quickly scooped up the money, "the cash is mine as I cut the ace of spades."

"Oh, no, you haven't," I cried. "I have the ace of spades."

I had palmed it while shuffling the deck.

"Say, stranger!" was the gambler's only comment. "I reckon that the feller as said that no man cud beat another at his own game was a gol-durned fool."

While in Los Angeles I had my first, last, and only ride upon an ostrich. This was at the Pasedena Ostrich Farm, one of the sights of the place. It was not a success, at all events, so far as I was concerned. The ostrich was hooded when I got on his back, and quite quiet. But directly the hood was removed, the huge ungainly bird ran like mad under the railings, nearly breaking my leg, and glad was I to get off him.

It was here, too, that I had my only experience of the autocratic methods of the much-talked-of American policeman. I was strolling leisurely back to my hotel late one evening from a cigar store, where I had been smoking, chatting, and throwing dice for "rounds" of cigars and cigarettes, a favourite pastime, by the way, with the Yanks, when a burly Irish policeman suddenly pounced upon me. He carried a big club and a big revolver, so I thought it best not to attempt to get away. In fact I imagined at first that he was having a game with me.

I was soon undeceived, however. "Come along!" he shouted roughly, seizing me by the collar, "I want you."

"What for?" I asked.

"You'll soon see," he answered, and marched me to a telephone-box, which he unlocked with a key he carried, and asked over the wire for a patrol waggon to be sent along immediately.

Into it, as soon as it arrived, I was unceremoniously bundled, and driven to the police-station. Here I was charged with being drunk and disorderly. I tried to explain, but had hardly opened my mouth before I was roughly ordered to be silent by the Inspector on duty, and the next moment I was seized from behind and hustled into a cell.

There I remained until after daybreak the following morning. The time seemed endless, and all the while I was wondering what my wife would say, left alone in a strange hotel in a strange city. At length there was a stir outside, a rattle of keys, and an officer appeared, and what is called out there, I learnt afterwards, the "daylight court" was convened.

I stated my case volubly, and with considerable heat. The officer interrupted me.

"You're English?" he asked.

"Yes I am," I replied, "and I'm going to have satisfaction for this outrage. I'll go to the British consul. I'll——"

"Get out!" he interrupted.

"But I say I wasn't——"

"Get out!"

"I've been insulted and——"

"Get out!"

What could I do? I got out. When I reached my hotel I found my wife in hysterics. I comforted her as well as I could. Then I rushed off to the Los Angeles Record office and saw the editor. He only laughed.

Afterwards I saw the manager of the music-hall where I was performing. He laughed too. Then he winked slowly.

"Why didn't you tip the cop a dollar?" he asked.

Then I understood. But, alas! the understanding came too late to be of use.

CHAPTER X
MORE AMERICAN EXPERIENCES

Through the Great American Desert—A land of desolation—An adventure at Santa Fé—"Hands up!"—Railway strike methods in the wild and woolly West—At Kansas City—The Magicians' Club—"Welcome to our city"—A disappointing show—In the land of the Mormons—Salt Lake City—Brigham Young's seraglio—The Mormon Temple and Tabernacle—Something like an angel—Brigham Young's statue—My worst Press notice—A journalistic tragedy—In New York—I am served a scurvy trick—Hammerstein's—A row with the management—Sharp Yankee practice—I perform in the New York Synagogue in the presence of the Chief Rabbi—A unique honour—Rubber-neck cars—The almighty dollar—The Statue of Liberty—A suggestive pose—New York hotels—A tip as to boots.

LEAVING Los Angeles for the East, we travelled by the Southern Pacific Railway, and plunged almost at a bound, so to speak, from one of the most lovely regions in the world into one of the most dreary and inhospitable.

This is the rightly named Great American Desert. For a thousand miles or so, practically all the way to Santa Fé in New Mexico, the railway runs through a wild and barren country—flat, dreary, and wholly uninteresting. Here and there patches of thorny "mesquite" bush alternate with vast stretches of grey and red sand and dazzling expanses of snow-white alkali. Other vegetation there is none, except that occasionally some gigantic cereus—emblem of barrenness—rears its contorted form into the thin clear air, and at night casts weird shadows athwart the moonlit level.

The first portion of the line, as far as Fort Yuma on the Arizona border, is the worst. For nearly two hundred miles the track runs over what was once in prehistoric times the bed of the Pacific Ocean, and which is now a wilderness of billowy shifting sand, devoid of either animal or vegetable life, and of course totally without permanent inhabitants. The greater portion of this horrible desert is below sea level. It is, as might be expected, entirely destitute of fresh water, and in the old pre-railroad days its ever-changing sand-dunes formed the only graves of many hundreds of poor wretches vainly seeking to reach California by what was then known as the "Southern Trail."

At Santa Fé, where we arrived at ten o'clock at night after one of the dreariest journeys imaginable, there was a wait of two hours, and I got out of the train to stretch my legs a bit, and strolled down the line, taking with me for company my contortionist, Harry Cardoe. By the side of the track there was a kind of covered-in stall, kept by a Mexican, where liquor of a sort was dispensed, and we turned in for a chat and a drink.

From the proprietor of the shanty we heard that a big railroad strike was in progress, and it was said that the strikers had blown up the line in several places, and were threatening to dynamite the trains. This was lively news, and I thought I might as well return to my car, where were my wife and kiddies; which I did, leaving Cardoe still in conversation with the Mexican.

An hour or more passed, and I was half asleep, when I was aroused by our train being put in motion, and a minute or so later there was a big commotion, and Cardoe, livid, dishevelled, and in a half-fainting condition, came stumbling into the car, and sank, gasping and panting, into the first seat he came to. So exhausted was he that it was full five minutes before we could get anything out of him. Then, when at length recovered his speech, he unfolded the following remarkable story.

It appeared that he had stayed some time after I left, chatting with the Mexican keeper of the grog shop, when he was startled at hearing the warning clangour of a bell, and at the same time he saw a train drawing out of the station, or "depôt," as the Americans prefer to call it. Imagining it to be our train, he made a bolt for it, and just managed to jump on the rear platform of the last coach, which he presently entered, after a brief pause to recover his breath.

"Hullo!" quoth the conductor, eyeing him suspiciously. "Where in h—ll did you spring from? Where's your ticket?"

"Mr. Carlton's got it," answered Cardoe, with easy assurance. "He keeps the tickets for the whole crowd of us."

"Don't know no Mr. Carlton," cried the conductor brusquely. "Where you goin' to?"

"Kansas City," said Harry.

"Huh!" exclaimed the conductor. "This train don't go to Kansas City. Off you get!" And, suiting the action to the words, he suddenly pounced upon my poor contortionist, and flung him bodily out of the car.

By this time he had, of course, travelled some distance away from Santa Fé, and after picking himself up, and carefully feeling himself all over to make sure that no bones were broken, he started to walk back along the railway track. But he was not yet at the end of his troubles. He had not gone far, when two big men sprang up from the darkness alongside the track, thrust in his face two big revolvers, and curtly cried, "Hands up!"

Now any American under such circumstances would have known what to do, and would at once have raised his hands above his head to avoid being shot. But poor Harry was unused to the summary methods of the wild and woolly West, and instead of doing as he was ordered he simply stood stock-still, and gazed at his captors in hopeless bewilderment. The next instant, however, he was on the ground, another member of the patrol—which had been sent out by the railway authorities to guard the track—having sprung upon him from behind and downed him.

Then, having pinioned his arms, they started to cross-examine him. Of course, directly he began to speak in answer to their questions they knew that he was no striker, and presently they let him go. They told him, however, that he had narrowly escaped being shot dead in his tracks, and warned him on no account to attempt to walk back to Santa Fé along the line, lest he should meet some other patrol the members of which might very likely shoot first and challenge afterwards. As a result, the poor chap had to make a wide detour into the desert, and only just managed to reach the "depôt" and scramble into the train as it was on the point of starting.

At Kansas City I had a somewhat disconcerting experience; which, however, was not without its humorous side. I arrived there, after travelling all night, in the early morning after breakfast, and as I was billed to give my first show at a matinée the same day, I was in a bit of a hurry. I was hustling round seeing to the baggage, when an old gent with a long white beard came up to me, accompanied by quite a number of other people, and, beaming at me through his spectacles, inquired:

"Are you Mr. Carlton?"

"Yes," I said.

"Well," he went on, "I am Dr. Wilson."

"Oh!" I replied, somewhat mystified.

"Dr. Wilson!" he repeated. "You've heard of me, of course? I'm the President of the local Magicians' Club, and these gentlemen"—indicating his companions by a wave of his hand—"are members of the deputation organised in order to bid you"—here he made a long and impressive pause, and beamed upon all and sundry—"to bid you," he repeated, "welcome to our city."

"Much flattered and obliged, I'm sure," I replied, as each member of the deputation was introduced to me in turn. And each member of the deputation—there were about thirty of them in all—remarked effusively:

"Welcome to our city."

Next, the old gentleman who headed the deputation made a speech. He said that he and his friends had heard of my fame, which was indeed world-wide, and that he and they wished me most cordially:

"Welcome to our city."

By this time the baggage was loaded, and I was on thorns to be off. But another old gent, who introduced himself as the editor of the *Kansas Magicians' Magazine*, butted in with yet another speech. He told me that the magicians of the place had booked the front row of the stalls for the coming matinée, and had arranged to entertain me to dinner after the performance, in order to show their appreciation, and to bid me—I knew what was coming by this time:

"Welcome to our city."

Now mine is of course, in its essence, a spoof show. I rely on my patter for effect, and on my sleight-of-hand to draw the applause of my audiences. These people, I gathered later on, expected me to perform some wonderful illusions with the aid of a lot of complicated apparatus.

When I first went on the stage there was a lot of applause and hand-clapping from the front row where the magicians were, mingled with shouts of:

"Welcome to our city."

But as I proceeded with my show, I could see that their opinion of me was rapidly undergoing a radical change. "The fellow's not a magician," they exclaimed to one another; "he's an impostor. Why, we could do better tricks ourselves."

They mostly quitted the theatre before the show was over, and I heard no more of the proposed dinner. But I pleased my audience all right, which was of course the main thing, and the unstinted applause which came from all parts of the house, both then and thereafter, proved to me that they, at all events, wished me:

"Welcome to our city."

I had heard a lot about the Mormons—who has not?—and I was quite looking forward to visiting Salt Lake City, where I was billed to appear at the Orpheum Music-hall. As a matter of fact, however, I was rather disappointed with the place, which has little to recommend it to the casual visitor.

Of course we "did the rounds," and saw all the sights worth seeing, notably the Temple and the Tabernacle. The former is a very fine building, but we only saw it from the outside, no others than Mormons being permitted to enter its sacred precincts. It is said to have cost £600,000, and to have occupied forty years in building. On the topmost pinnacle, dominating the whole city, is a statue of the angel Moroni, over twelve feet high, of beaten copper, covered with purest gold. Moroni is the angel who, according to Mormon mythology, is supposed to have revealed to Joseph Smith, the founder of Mormonism, the existence and location of the golden plates on which were inscribed in mystic characters the writings afterwards translated and published as the "Book of Mormon."

Salt Lake also boasts of a very fine statue of Brigham Young. He stands with his back to the Temple, and his right hand stretched out to the Deseret National Bank opposite. Scoffing Gentiles, of whom there are many in the city, say that the pose is characteristic of the man. We were also shown the Bee House and the Lion House, as they are called, buildings joined together by covered passages, where in the old days Brigham kept his numerous wives. Originally it was surrounded, after the fashion of an Eastern seraglio, by a high wall, so that no prying eyes could penetrate its interior; but this was pulled down after Young's death.

It was in Salt Lake City, by the way, that I was treated to absolutely the worst newspaper slating that my poor little show has ever called forth. "Carlton the long magician"—so ran the notice—"has the most disgusting and joy-killing ten minutes the Orpheum stage has offered in recent times. For cheap, slap, stick stuff, he gets the blue ribbon. The Orpheum has no business inflicting such a pest on its patrons. It is easy to believe the statements made by the eastern vaudeville booking agents that good acts are hard to get these days."

This gem of journalism appeared in the *Salt Lake Evening Telegram*. I made inquiries and found that it was written by a lady who was consumed by a furious hatred of everything and everybody English, and that she invariably "slated," to the best, or worst, of her ability, any "pro.'s," whether male or female, hailing from our country. The affair did not bother me in the least, more especially as I got excellent notices in the other Salt Lake papers; but some of the English people there resented it, and went up to the office of the *Evening Telegram* and had a row with the editor about it. Soon afterwards, and before I quitted the city, the lady journalist who had penned the notice went off and drowned herself in the Great Salt Lake. A verdict of "suicide while insane" was brought in; and it is therefore, I take it, a fair assumption that she was mad when she wrote it. In any case I am proud of it and I have had it framed and hung up in my house. An artiste, even a poor artiste, can always get plenty of flattering Press notices. He can even buy them. But he cannot buy one like the above.

In New York I was served what I considered to be rather a dirty trick. I had been on what is known over there as the Orpheum Circuit, a twenty-two weeks' tour through the principal Western American cities, finishing at Milwaukee, when I received a wire from a New York agent to say that he had booked me for four halls in that city, the Alhambra and Palace; the Orpheum, Brooklyn; and one other. In between, a week intervened, and I also received an offer from another New York agent to put in this period at Hammerstein's Music-hall, provided terms could be arranged.

Now I was naturally rather anxious to achieve a reputation for myself in New York, because a name made there counts. What I mean is that just as in England a London success means far more to an artiste than a provincial one does, so it is as regards New York and the rest of the United States of America. So in consideration of their "featuring me," as we say in the "profession," I agreed to a big reduction of my usual salary at Hammerstein's. I also got an assurance from the agent that my name was to "top the bill"—what they call out there a "head liner"—and that I was to come on not earlier than the seventh turn. My reason for making this latter stipulation was that Hammerstein's is something like what the old Westminster Aquarium used to be in this one respect, it is practically an all-day show, and there is, in the ordinary way, hardly anybody there at the commencement. Consequently any "dud" turn does to lead off with.

I badly wanted to see Niagara Falls on the way from Milwaukee to New York, but found that the train arrangements did not fit in, so I had to forgo the experience. Meanwhile a rather curious thing happened. My contortionist overslept himself on the morning he should have started, and as there was no other train, and as I could not afford to miss the one I had arranged to travel by, I left his ticket at the booking office and came on without him, heartily cursing him in my own mind for his dilatoriness.

I, of course, imagined that I should have to open in New York without him, and was very much upset and worried in consequence. As a matter of fact, however, he turned up there at about the same time as I did; he having had the luck to catch a special train which ran on that one day only. And not only that, but his train came via Niagara Falls, and stopped over there for a couple of hours, so that he was able to "do" them thoroughly, a pleasure denied to me and my wife, and to the rest of my company who had been punctual. The moral, in this case at all events, would seem to be: "Take things easy, and they'll come all right in the end."

On arriving in New York I naturally looked for my name on the top of the bill at Hammerstein's as arranged. To my surprise it was not there, and I had to search diligently through a couple of yards or so of print before discovering it in very small type, and right at the bottom, sharing a line with the moving pictures. Naturally I was very much annoyed, and I told the agent who had engaged me so in language that left nothing to be desired in point of plainness.

He was apologetic. Said it was due to a printer's error, and that anyway it would be all right as regards my turn. But it wasn't all right. On the contrary, it was all wrong. When I arrived at Hammerstein's on my opening day, I was shown into a long bare dressing-room, where were about twenty other performers, all strangers to me. I set about getting ready in leisurely fashion, and was only half made up when I was astounded at hearing the call-boy cry out: "Your turn next, sir!"

Thinking that I had miscalculated the time I made a rush for it, but when I got on the stage I was surprised to see that there was hardly anybody in the building. Looking round I saw "No. 2" up, and it was then that I realised for the first time that I had been done once again by the slick Yanks.

They had played me a scurvy trick twice over. Not only had they not put me at the top of the bill, but they had given me the worst turn, and—I was to get only about half my usual salary.

Well, there was no help for it then, of course, but I made up my mind that I was going to get a bit of my own back. And I did. When I went on the stage there was practically nobody in the house, and I led off by congratulating the management at having brought me all the way from Europe at a big salary, and then putting me on when there was nobody there to listen to me.

This patter raised quite a big laugh from the small audience that was there. They, in fact, thoroughly appreciated the joke. Not so the management. Mr. Kessler, the manager, was furious.

"Cut that out," he cried in a stage whisper. "Don't pull that gol-durned stuff here."

What I said in reply wouldn't look well in print. In fact it nearly ended in my breaking my contract, and chucking the engagement there and then. And indeed I think I should have done so but for my wife, who strongly advised me not to do anything of the kind.

"After all," she said, "what does it matter? You've got two years' bookings in England to go back to. Don't throw good money away."

This, after all, was sound common sense, and I took her advice. But all the same I have no very pleasant recollections of Hammerstein's, more especially as because I declined to give a touting advertisement canvasser an order for a page "ad." in his paper—price one hundred dollars—his editor slated me badly, saying that I was a bad copy of half the variety artistes in the United States—performers whom for the most part I had never seen.

At the other halls in New York where I appeared, nevertheless, things went very well indeed. I was given a good "turn," and made a big hit; so much so that Mr. Martin Beck, the proprietor, asked me to give my show in the New York Synagogue before Chief Rabbi Wise. This is an honour that up till then had never been accorded to any music-hall artiste, and I was, moreover, heartily congratulated by Mr. Wise at the conclusion of my show.

So I quitted New York with pleasant recollections after all, but before going, as a sly dig at Hammerstein's, I inserted the following "ad." in *Variety*, a trade paper answering over there to our *Performer*.

"Sorry cannot come to terms with American managers. Boat sails Wednesday next. CARLTON."

A great feature in New York, and in fact in most of the big American cities, is what is known as "rubber-neck cars." These are really observation motor-cars, holding twenty or more people, in which visitors are taken round to see the sights. A man with a megaphone sits in front with the driver, and roars out information at express speed regarding the various buildings, etc., as the conveyance is driven by them, and the term "rubber-neck" is used because you have to twist and turn and bend that portion of your anatomy at all sorts of different and uncomfortable angles, in order to properly view the skyscrapers, etc., he points out to you.

Most of these conductors call out their information in terms of dollars. "Over there," he will say, "is the brown stone palace of old Jacob Astor—cost five million dollars. That white marble mansion to your right was built by one of the Vanderbilts—cost six million dollars. City hall—cost eight million dollars. Post Office—cost seven million dollars. This is the residence of Silas K. Jenkins, the dry-goods king, came to this country without a cent in his pocket—cost four million dollars"; and so on, and so on. All the while I was entering the amounts in my pocket-book, and when I came to add them up afterwards the total came to about 4,000,000,000,000,000 dollars—more or less.

The people of New York are never tired of expatiating on the beauties of their city, and especially are they proud of the gigantic Statue of Liberty, overlooking the harbour. It is noteworthy, however, that they have erected it with its face to England and its back to America.

One word in conclusion regarding the New York hotels. They are fine institutions in their way, but there is one thing they won't do for you. They won't clean your boots. I only put my boots outside my bedroom once to be cleaned. In the morning they were not there. Nor did I ever see them again, and the only answer I got in response to repeated queries was: "In American hotels, sah, folks only put outside their doahs things they don't want."

CHAPTER XI
PANTOMIME SPOOFS AND JOKES

Harry Tate and I—Together we found the order of "The Beautiful Swells"—The Birmingham spoof supper—A mouth-watering menu—The "Beautiful Swells'" anthem—Cockroach soup—Property viands—A mysterious waiter—Ernie Lotinga's little joke—The spoofers spoofed—A pigeon pie that flew—A surplus of farthings—Rehearsing for pantomime—My first rehearsal—I am "fired" out of the theatre—Pantomime in Hoxton—The gallery boy's irony—A cutting retort—I get married—Courting under difficulties—The married chorus-girl and the lovesick manager—Supper for two in a private room—Hoaxing the police—A sham tragedy and its sequel—The fat policeman and the big lobster—Sold again.

DURING the pantomime season of 1910–11 I was principal comedian at the Prince of Wales' Theatre, Birmingham, and Harry Tate filled a similar rôle at the Theatre Royal in the same town. Together we founded there the order of "The Beautiful Swells"—a spoof secret society, with signs, grips, passwords, etc., after the approved pattern.

Out of this spoof society there sprang the famous spoof supper, organised by me, and the full and complete story of which is now given to the world for the first time. It was held at midnight, and "pro.'s" were there from all parts. Nobody would have recognised us for what we were, however; in fact, we could not recognise each other. For I had caused the fiat to go forth that everybody was to make up as somebody else, and the somebody else must be as unbeautiful as possible.

The result was that there were assembled together at the appointed hour as strange and heterogeneous a collection of human oddities as it is possible to imagine. Charlie Peace, the burglar, was not the least beautiful of the guests. Two of them, with cutting irony, had elected to make up as myself; and there were no fewer than four White-Eyed Kaffirs. Three Lloyd Georges vied one with another in ugliness. There was a Scarlet Pimpernel, with a nose the size and colour of a beet. Everybody, in short, was anybody but their real selves, and nobody knew which was which, or who was who.

The price of the supper tickets had been fixed at half-a-crown payable in advance, and part of the arrangement was that this was to be returned after the meal to all who put in an appearance, and fulfilled the stipulated conditions as to make-up, etc.

I had arranged an elaborate menu. The mouths of the guests watered as they read it, and a confused murmur of pleasurable anticipation pervaded the supper-room. "By Jove, Carlton, old man, you've done the thing in style." exclaimed one well-known comedian to me. "It must have cost a pretty penny."

So it had, but not quite in the way he supposed. Here, however, is the menu. Let the reader judge for himself.

Hors d'œuvres.
Royal Natives.
Plovers' Eggs.   Melon Cantaloup.

Soups.
Real Turtle.   Consommé Marie Stuart.

Fish.
Loch Tay Salmon.   Filets de Sole Carlton.

Entrée.
Ortolans aux Raisins.

Joints.
Haunch of Venison.   Saddle of Mutton.

Sweets.
Soufflé au curaçoa.   Ice pudding.
Wines.   Liqueurs.   Coffee.

The proceedings were opened by Harry Tate, the chairman, who announced that all were to sing standing the "Beautiful Swells' Anthem," written by himself. It ran, as nearly as I can recollect, as follows:

Good evening, my beautiful swells,My rollicking pippins as well;My golden russet, my sweet-scented friend:Is this the beginning or is it the end?We're just beginning to like you,So lots of money we'll spend.Then join in this ditty,And have a sweet nippy,My piscatorial friend.

Chorus:

For we're all getting older and older,
Older ev'ry day.
We're all getting older and older,
Soon we'll all be grey.
So if you want some wrinkles,
To keep you young and frisky,
Keep late hours and drink plenty of whisky.
Casey Jones got another papa,
Casey Jones, the Cunard Line.
Casey Jones got another papa,
Got another papa on the Cunard Line.
Pom-tiddly-om-pom! Pom—pom! pom!

This latter part of the ditty was emphasised by the banging of fists, knives, bottles, glasses, in fact, anything to make a noise; and the resultant din, as may be imagined, was terrific. So was the cheering at the end, and the general hilarity; but the latter was checked somewhat, so far at all events as regards the major part of the assembled guests, on seats being resumed, for these found that while they had been upstanding the waiters had deftly removed their beautifully printed menu cards, and had substituted in their place others not nearly so ornate and which read as follows:

Hors d'œuvres.
Very likely.

Soups.
If lucky.

Fish.
Very sorry it's off.

Entrées.
Hard lines.

Joints.
You never can tell.

Sweets.
Perhaps.

Choice Wines.
I don't think.

THE "BEAUTIFUL SWELLS" SPOOF SUPPER—A PAGE OF CARICATURES BY TOM WEBSTER

Some of the guests now began to suspect that the whole affair was a spoof, but many did not; and the altercations between these innocent ones and the waiters, the latter of whom were all in the know, were frequent and highly diverting. A man, for instance, would order salmon, or venison, or saddle of mutton, and would have pig's trotters and potatoes, the latter boiled in their jackets, almost literally thrown at him. No matter what anybody called for, the result was nearly always the same—pig's trotters and potatoes.

The soup was of the cabbage-water variety, in which floated "property," cockroaches; these the waiters would remove with their fingers, purposely grimy for the occasion. To add to the confusion some few of our guests, here and there, were actually served—by my instructions—with the venison, salmon, or whatever else they ordered.

Those sitting to the right and left of these lucky ones regarded them with envious eyes, and tried to force back on the waiters their own unsavoury trotters and potatoes. As a result, of course, confusion soon became worse confounded. Nor was it allayed in any degree by the tactics of Harry Tate, who was continually jumping up from his chair in order to make some such announcement as follows, delivered in tones of becoming gravity: "Gentlemen: I am sorry, but the plovers' eggs have not arrived; gentlemen, I regret to say that the salmon is off; gentlemen, it is very annoying, but I'm afraid we shall have to dispense with the ortolans—there are none to be had in the market."

In despair some of the guests tried to eat their bread, but found that the seemingly crisp and inviting-looking little rolls were filled, as regards their interiors, with nothing more edible than cotton wool. Everything on the table, or served up at the table, in fact (bar the trotters and potatoes), was of the "property" variety, got specially from Paris at considerable trouble and expense. The eggs and bacon looked real, and they were, in fact, served with real gravy; but the eggs were china imitations, and cemented to the plates at that, and the bacon was of similar material. The luscious-looking peaches and grapes on the central fruit-stands were waxen imitations. Those who tried the cheese spat it out again hurriedly; finding it to be soap—mottled for the gorgonzola, yellow for the Cheddar. The coffee and the liqueurs, the soda and the whisky, were anything and everything but what they were supposed to be. Even the cigars and the cigarettes went bang directly one started to smoke them.

The waiters acted their parts to perfection, especially the head waiter; who indeed, as time went on, began to rather over-act his. At least so I commenced to think. So, too, did Harry Tate, when the fellow shot a load of hot potatoes and trotters on to the seat of his chair when he (Harry) was in the act of standing up to speak—and left them there. Harry sat down in them; with what result may be imagined.

The climax came when this particular waiter upset a huge dish of gravy all over me. "Here," I said, "don't you come it too far.

I told you beforehand that you were not to play any games on me or Harry."

"Oh, you go to h——ll," replied the fellow. "Who do you think you are? Damn you and your spoof suppers. I'm a waiter, I am; not a bloomin' knockabout comedian. Pay me my money, and let me go."

I jumped to my feet at this, really angry, and was proceeding to give him a piece of my mind, when in a changed voice, that I knew well, he cried: "All right, Carlton, old man; keep your hair on."

I gasped in amazement. So did all the others standing round. It was Ernie Lotinga. He had made himself up as a waiter after sending us a spoof telegram from London regretting his inability to be present, had bribed the real waiter I had engaged to allow him (Lotinga) to take his place for the occasion, and had spoofed us, the spoofers, and every other person in the room during the entire evening.

It was the most wonderful piece of play-acting, and the most perfect piece of disguising, that has ever come to my knowledge. Every man in the room knew Lotinga perfectly well. Yet not one of us had suspected him for a single instant. He had altered his voice, as completely as he had altered his facial appearance.

After the roar of laughter created by this unexpected discovery had subsided, Harry Tate rose to make a few remarks. We had had our little joke, he said, and he hoped nobody had taken it amiss.

Several voices: "No! No! Harry! But"—plaintively—"we're deuced hungry."

"Quite so," replied Tate. "I'd thought of that, and there's one thing good to eat that we have provided, and that I can pledge my word is what it purports to be, and that's a pigeon pie."

With that a burly waiter bore into the room an immense pie, and placed it before Harry to carve. He inserted the carving-knife and fork solemnly and deftly, while the mouths of our famished guests once more watered in pleasurable anticipation. Then he removed a generous portion of the crust—and out flew a number of live pigeons.

This was the last of the spoofs of the supper proper; the remainder of the time being occupied in consuming sandwiches, bottled beer, whisky and soda, and in smoking the supply of very excellent cigars and cigarettes we had provided. It took some time, however, to persuade our guests to settle down to the consumption of these; for, after the evening's experience, they feared being hoaxed over again.

When all were at length comfortable, an impromptu entertainment was held, each guest being required to give an imitation of the character he represented. It was great fun. Lastly came the refunding of the money paid for the supper tickets, as previously announced. The guests entered an ante-room one at a time, having first been blindfolded, and after being subjected to sundry mock tests and ceremonies of the order that would not look well in print, each had his half-crown returned to him, or rather its value—in farthings.

There were more than fifty guests present, so that over six thousand farthings were paid out. I had previously arranged for these through one of the local banks, and for days afterwards certain of the Brummagem "pubs" habitually frequented by "pro.'s" were deluged with farthings, greatly to the disgust of the landlords, some of whom resented being tendered sixty-four farthings in exchange for a couple of whiskies and sodas.

This particular supper was arranged to celebrate the close of the pantomime season. It sounds perhaps rather odd to the uninitiated outsider to talk about "celebrating" the close of a season that means a steady and settled income, so long as it lasts, for every performer engaged in the run of the piece. But as a matter of fact pantomimes are not popular institutions with music-hall artistes. The money they receive for performing in them is. But that, as Kipling would say, is another story.

Rehearsals are particularly galling. I recollect that at the very first pantomime I ever rehearsed I got into hot water almost directly. This was at the Chester Theatre Royal, where Mr. Milton Bode was producing "The Babes in the Wood." I was cast for the part of Bumble, the village beadle, and of course I was perfectly ready and willing to rehearse the special "business" pertaining to the part, but Mr. Bode insisted on my rehearsing my own specialities as well.

This struck me as being supremely idiotic, and a waste of time into the bargain, and I said as much. Bode, who was by way of being a bit of an autocrat, flew into a violent temper, and threw his hat at me. One word led to another, and in the end he ordered me out of the theatre.

I went—as far as the "pub" opposite. "That's done it," I said to myself. "You silly ass! Here have you been wishing for a panto engagement ever since you've been in the profession, and the very first chance you get, you take and chuck it away. You ought to go and kick yourself to death."

Presently, enters Milton Bode. "Hullo, Carlton! Have a bottle?"

I ventured to remind him of what had happened less than an hour previously.

"Oh, that's nothing," he replied genially. "You don't know what the responsibility of producing a pantomime is like. Why, I've just thrown my hat at one of the chorus-girls, and told her to go away somewhere and drown herself. She won't take any notice, and neither must you. It's all in a day's work. Don't forget—rehearsal to-morrow morning again at ten sharp." And he bustled out, all smiles and geniality.

Another pantomime reminiscence! At the Variety, Hoxton, one Boxing Night, "The Forty Thieves" was produced. The panto was not precisely up to Drury Lane standards, either as regards the scenery, or the number of performers engaged. Instead of there being forty thieves, there were only ten, and these marched from the wings into the cave, then out at the back, and round to the front again, said operation being repeated four times, so as to make it appear as if the orthodox number was present.

The gallery boys were not deceived, however, as was evident from a chorus of voices demanding, "Hi, guv'nor, where's the other thirty thieves?"

Quick as a flash came the retort from the chairman: "They're up in the gallery."

There was a roar of approving laughter. The Hoxton gallery boys realised that the chairman knew what he was talking about. Some amongst them possibly had had the "honour"— and a very great honour it was considered there and then—of sitting at his little table with him, and incidentally standing him a drink.

It was while performing in pantomime at Leeds that I met and married my wife, who was also on the stage there at the time. We had never met one another before, and I had to do most of my courting behind the scenes in between the acts, with stage carpenters bustling round, and chorus-girls pushing backwards and forwards between us without so much as "by your leave."

However, we fixed it up all right, and got married while the piece was still running. The wedding was celebrated at the Oxford Chapel, in the City Square, which was packed with people, the happy event having been well boomed beforehand. A cinematograph operator was there ready to film us, but the press was so great that he and his machine were both overturned, and we were not "featured" after all.

As soon as the ceremony was over we were whisked back in a motor-car to the theatre for a matinée performance, and the same evening the "book" of the pantomime was considerably altered, though unofficially, owing to practically every performer with a speaking part introducing a "gag" having some reference or other to the "happy event."

The orchestra, too, took it upon themselves to strike up the "Wedding March," on my first appearance on the stage; and news of the marriage having got bruited about, the theatre was packed from floor to gallery, amongst the audience being the Lord Mayor of Leeds.

Shortly before the termination of my pantomime engagement I asked the manager of the —— Theatre if he would give me a week's engagement to follow on, seeing I had done so well there; but I was told, none too politely, that my terms of £40 a week that I was then asking were ridiculous.

I rather got my back up at this, and so as not to be done I took the Coliseum, Leeds, a huge place, capable of seating between four and five thousand people. It was in fact so big that nobody had ventured to open it as a music-hall before, it having been used mostly for musical festivals, and things of that sort.

I paid £80 for the use of the hall for a week, and about as much again for advertising my forthcoming show. All this, of course, as a preliminary! Managers and artists alike said that I would never make it pay; that I was mad.

Maybe! But anyway there was method in my madness. I reflected that, as usually happens at the termination of a provincial pantomime engagement, practically all the artistes at the two pantomimes running in Leeds would be "resting," which means, of course, being temporarily out of a job, and that they would probably be willing to engage with me at a very reasonable salary. And this, as a matter of fact, the majority of them were only too glad to do.

Then I hired a coach and four, and drove myself round, made up as on the stage, to all the schools. There are about forty schools in Leeds, and my method of procedure was the same in each one of them.

"Good morning, sir," I would remark, addressing the head master. "May I have permission to entertain your little scholars gratis for a few minutes?"

In every case permission was readily given, whereupon I would give a short conjuring show, bringing in the usual "bunny rabbit" trick, always a prime favourite with children, and a few others.

Naturally they were highly delighted, and as soon as the applause died away I made a short speech something after this fashion: "Boys and girls, I am glad you appreciated my little performance. Now, as some of you may have heard, I got married the other day, and to celebrate the event I have taken the Coliseum for a week. All the principal artistes now performing at the two pantomimes will be there, and I would like you all to come and see them and me. These tickets"—here I handed round one to each child—"will admit you at half-price, *if you come accompanied by your parents.*"

The result of this little plan of mine was that I had the hall packed every evening, and had to give extra matinées, and I cleared £287 for myself after paying salaries and all other expenses.

I rather think that that manager was sorry he didn't engage me and pay me the £40 I asked.

A few months afterwards I was running a show of my own at a well-known music-hall in the West End of London, and my wife took a part in the performance. After the first performance, enter the manager of the theatre into my dressing-room:

"Nice lot of girls you've got in your show, Carlton!"

"Fairish," I replied.

"Humph! There's one of 'em I've rather taken a fancy to. Will you introduce me? She might be willing to come and take supper with me after the show."

"Very likely!" I said. "Which one is it?"

"The little dark girl in the corner," he replied.

"All right!" I said, smiling inwardly to myself. "Come round to-morrow night after the show, and I'll introduce you."

The next night he was there to time, extra spruce and well groomed, and with a big white camelia in his button-hole. I pretended not to notice him, however, and bundled the girls off directly they had finished their performance. Afterwards I made pretence to be awfully sorry, saying that I had forgotten all about the matter.

"But," he exclaimed ruefully, "I've ordered supper, a bird and a bottle for two, in a private room at the X——," mentioning one of the swellest and most expensive restaurants in Town.

"Never mind," I said, "it won't be wasted. You and I will eat it between us. Then you can order another one for to-morrow night, and I'll speak to the girl in the meantime, and fix things up for you with her."

"All right," he agreed. "But don't forget a second time."

Well, we ate the supper, and the next night he was behind the scenes while my show was on, hopping about here, there, and everywhere like a cat on hot bricks. Directly it was over he advanced, smirking and smiling; and the introduction he craved was performed—as follows:

"Mr. So-and-So, this is Mrs. Carlton—my wife: Marie, my dear, this is Mr. So-and-So, the manager, who is desirous of making your acquaintance."

I never saw a man so utterly taken aback in my life. He didn't know what to say or do, but simply stood stock-still, and stared, and gasped. Afterwards we had a hearty laugh together over the incident.

"You had me properly," he said; "but you might have told me."

"Well," I replied, "let it be a lesson to you not to go running after the girls in a show without first making sure that they're single."

At a certain northern town where I once performed in pantomime the police were inclined to be somewhat uppish and disagreeable, and the male artistes who were there at the time formed themselves into a committee of the whole house, and resolved to be even with them. So one night the neighbourhood near the central police-station was aroused by a tremendous disturbance coming from the inside of a third-story room of a house situated almost opposite. The police turned out in force. A crowd collected, gazing excitedly upward.

A tragedy was being enacted before their eyes. There was a light burning inside the room, and on the drawn blind were silhouetted the figures of two men furiously struggling. Presently the blind was torn aside, and one of the combatants, a big, strong fellow, threw the other bodily out of the window. A shriek of horror burst from the crowd, and the policemen on duty below rushed forward to try and break his expected fall.

However, the man who had been thrown out did not drop immediately, but grasped the window-sill with his hands. His assailant, bent apparently on killing him outright, started to beat him about the head and shoulders with what looked like a heavy iron bar. The next instant four or five policemen rushed into the room, having darted upstairs and burst the door open.

Then they discovered that the man who was hanging out of the window was in no danger of falling, being secured by a strong thin line. The "iron" bar, with which he was being belaboured, was a "property" one of soft rubber.

"Why, what's the meaning of all this?" asked the puzzled inspector.

"Oh," replied the man inside the room, as he assisted his chum to clamber back through the window, "we're just rehearsing a scene for next year's pantomime; the one in the harlequinade, you know, where the Bobby comes in."

One of the constables who climbed the three flights of stairs to the room on this occasion was fat and somewhat wheezy, and he naturally felt hurt. A few nights later he tried his best to get a bit of his own back. A friend and myself were bidding one another good-bye outside the theatre after the performance, when he thrust himself roughly between us and told us to "move on there."

Knowing that expostulation on our part would only lead to our being locked up on a charge of loitering and obstructing the police, we said nothing, but promptly did as we were bid. The next morning, however, we shadowed our tormentor from a distance, and discovered that he was stationed on point duty of an afternoon not far from a big fishmonger's shop in one of the main streets.

On the day following, in the middle of the afternoon, my friend sidled furtively up to the shop. A fine lobster was prominently displayed in the centre of the marble slab. The fat policeman was there.

Suddenly my friend put out his hand, seized the lobster, and took to his heels. The policeman took after him. There was an exciting chase of a mile or more, but eventually my friend allowed himself to be caught, and haled back in triumph to the shop.

"What's the matter?" cried the fishmonger, coming out on to the pavement.

"This fellow has stolen your lobster?" panted the policeman.

"Have I?" inquired my friend innocently, addressing the fishmonger.

"Of course not," he replied. "You bought and paid for it an hour ago."

"Sold again!" cried my friend, turning to the policeman; and the crowd, to whom the joke now became apparent, roared with laughter; while the officer walked away in high dudgeon, muttering under his breath things that cannot be set down in print.

As a matter of fact my friend had purchased the lobster, at the same time telling the fishmonger that he need not wrap it up for him. "Leave it on the slab where it is," he remarked as he handed over the purchase money, "and I'll call for it presently, and take it away just as it is."

Which he did.

CHAPTER XII
AFRICA AND THE ORIENT

Bound for Cape Town—A pleasant voyage—Ships' games—A contrast in voyages—"Cock-fighting" at sea—"Chalking the Pig's Eye"—"Swinging the Monkey"—Marine cricket—A new kind of golf—Cycling at sea—Sweepstakes on the vessel's run—Races on the ocean wave—Mock breach-of-promise trials—By bullock waggon to Kimberley—I perform before Cecil Rhodes—Get shot in a street row—Contrast on my second visit—The great strike riots in Johannesburg—Fire and dynamite—A night of horror—A gay but expensive city—Dear drinks—Performing in the back veldt—Eggs for throwing—At Pretoria—Kruger's house—Where Winston Churchill swam the river—A disappointing stream—My prize giant—A Jo'burg sensation—Buying a forty-shilling suit to measure—A disgusted tailor—Special railway travelling—My giant proves his agility—In Colombo—Indian fakirs—Their conjuring skill overrated—The boy and rope trick—Two versions of a similar story—The whole thing a fake—The evidence of H.H. the Maharajah of Jodhpur—I offer £100 to any native who can do it—No takers—The mango seed trick—Outwitting a fakir—"Let me plant the seed"—The camera in action—The Tree of Life—Cobra and mongoose fight.

THE voyage out to South Africa is an exceedingly pleasant one. The passengers invariably settle down soon after leaving Madeira into a sort of happy family party, and all kinds of games and sports peculiar to ship-board are entered into with zest.

To a certain degree, of course, this is true of all ocean voyages. Going out to America on the *Mauretania*, for instance, we played all the usual ships' games, and I recollect that I won everything, with the exception of the pillow fight. Indeed, as regards the blindfold games, such as, for example, "Chalking the Pig's Eye," I was bound to win; for a reason I shall explain later. But then, of course, I never claimed the prize for these, but always let it go to the second best, or put it up for competition over again.

But the Atlantic passage is too short, and often, alas! too stormy to lend itself readily to a set programme of games. The

P. & O. and the Orient liners make, it is true, longer voyages in quieter seas. But the trip is broken into chapters, as it were, by a succession of stopping-places—Gibraltar, Malta, Port Said, and so forth—at which passengers arrive and depart, destroying the continuity of the excursion and usually rendering futile any attempt at organised recreation.

The moment, however, a Union or a Castle liner lifts anchor at Madeira, her passengers know that there lies before them a clear fourteen days' run, and—they make the most of it. Spasmodic attempts may, indeed, have been made by some few athletic enthusiasts to get up a scratch match at cricket or golf ere the ship was well clear of the English Channel, but these are more often than not foredoomed to failure. It is the fashion of old South African voyagers to protest that the pleasures of a Cape trip do not really commence until Madeira is left behind, and there is a certain amount of truth in this. The crossing of the Bay is usually provocative of more or less seasickness, and, as a natural consequence, both saloons and decks are practically deserted. Besides, the passengers do not usually begin to really know one another in the three days and a half which are occupied in the run to this island.

All this is changed with the disappearance, on the northern horizon, of the white roofs of Funchal. It is felt by all that the real business of the voyage has begun, and the "sports season" is promptly inaugurated by, we will say, a "cock-fight." A ring twelve feet or thereabouts in diameter is chalked out upon the deck, and the "birds" fight with their bare feet, their arms having been previously "trussed" with stout broomsticks, the relinquishing of which entails instant and final disqualification.

After several rounds have been brought to a conclusion, either "Swinging the Monkey" or "Chalking the Pig's Eye" is likely enough to be started. In the first-named game, a man is slung, by a rope attached to his feet, to a boom overhead, with his hands resting on the deck and partly supporting his body. In his right hand is a piece of chalk, and his object is to make with it a line on deck which shall reach further than that drawn by any of his competitors. Considerable skill and judgment are called into play, as, should he prove too venturesome at the wrong time, the rolling of the ship is apt to cause him to lose his balance, and come swinging ignominiously against the bulwarks. "Chalking the Pig's Eye" can be played by both ladies and gentlemen. A pig, minus an eye, is chalked out upon the deck, and the competitors, after being blindfolded and turned round three times, try to fit in the missing optic. The result is usually ludicrous enough.

Marine cricket is played on a cocoanut-matting pitch with a ball of twisted rope-yarn. Nets are stretched along the side of the ship nearest the ocean, and the stumps fit into a specially made block of wood weighted with lead. Owing to the lurching of the vessel, both bowling and batting are apt to be extremely erratic; indeed, nowhere save on shipboard is the proverbial "glorious uncertainty" of the game so clearly apparent. Three matches are usually brought off during a trip—Passengers *v.* Officers, Married *v.* Single, and Ladies *v.* Gentlemen. Golf is a comparatively modern addition to the list of sea games, but is rapidly growing in favour. The "balls" are flat discs of wood, four or five inches in diameter, and a fairly heavy walking-stick takes the place of a club. The "holes" are in some ships represented by spots of chalk, which have to be covered by the discs; and in others by circles about half as large again as the disc, into which they have to be played. Hitting is entirely superseded by pushing, whether for a long drive or a short one. The great thing is not to allow the wind to get underneath your "ball," as it will then almost assuredly rise on its edge and roll away, either into the sea or among the unexplored tangle of ropes "for'ard." Board-ship golf, it may be remarked, naturally produces its own distinctive and peculiar terminology. A "ball," for instance, is said to be "scuppered," "coal bunkered," and so on.

A fancy-dress ball caused a lot of fun, but this was changed to something very like consternation when, right in the middle of it, one of the stokers, nude to the waist, a swab over his arm, and grimed all over with oil and coal-dust, came blundering up on to the upper deck right into the midst of the dancers.

The general opinion was that the intruder was drunk, and there was a wild stampede to get out of his way, the many delicately attired ladies especially fairly racing for safety.

A couple of the ship's officers came hurrying up, and roughly ordered him below, and as he showed no disposition to go, they made as if to compel him; whereupon he cried out exultingly:

"Here, hold hard! I'm Harry Cardoe, Mr. Carlton's contortionist. This is a fancy-dress ball, isn't it? Well, this is my fancy dress."

At this there were shrieks of laughter, and he was the recipient of many congratulations—at a safe distance—from the other passengers. Of course he and I had engineered the joke between us.

It took poor Harry about an hour, however, to get the oil and dirt off his skin, and he grumbled a lot during the operation. But next morning, when he found, greatly to his surprise, that he had been awarded the prize for the most realistic make-up, he was completely mollified.

I have already mentioned golf as being in the nature of a novelty. Bicycle races, six laps to the mile, constitute another innovation, but the machines and riders are almost too apt to come to grief. Obstacle races are, perhaps, among the most generally popular of "open events," the entries being usually out of all proportion to the number of prizes. Nearly every obstacle usually encountered on land has to be negotiated, together with a number of others peculiar to ship-board. Among these latter may be mentioned sets of lifebelts, each swinging loosely and tantalisingly at the end of a solitary rope; funnel-shaped sails, the insides liberally daubed with greasy soot and sprinkled with flour; and rope entanglements of fearful and wonderful construction.

Sack races, flat races, and wheelbarrow races are also organised, the two latter being not infrequently participated in by the ladies on board. The favourite contest with the fair sex, however, is the egg-and-spoon race, varied occasionally by a needle-threading competition. In the former the competitors have to run a certain distance, each carrying at arm's length a very large egg in an exceedingly small spoon. The various dodges adopted by the runners are well worth studying.

At 11.30 the daily sweepstakes on the vessel's run is drawn, the numbers being afterwards put up for auction. This always causes a deal of excitement, and it is an understood thing that a certain percentage of the winnings is handed over to some charity. It is also usual to hold, during each voyage, at least one mock breach-of-promise trial. The "counsel" on either side are arrayed in sailcloth gowns and wigs made of cotton-waste, and the proceedings are carried out strictly in accordance with legal etiquette. The cross-examination of the fair plaintiff—who is, more often than not, some pretty little soubrette bound for South Africa's "City of Gold"—is generally the cause of roars of laughter.

I have made two professional trips to South Africa. The first time I trekked in a bullock waggon from Cape Town to Kimberley, and had the satisfaction of giving a performance before Cecil Rhodes at the Sanatorium there. Those were rough times. Street fights were of frequent occurrence, and on one occasion two miners started firing at each other in close proximity to where I was standing.

I promptly took cover, as did the rest of the bystanders, and was unaware of anything wrong until, feeling my foot wet and heavy, I stooped down, and with my finger and thumb pulled a bullet out of my leg from just under the skin near the ankle-joint. It had been nearly spent when it struck me; fortunately for me.

This was before the war. On my second visit, in 1913, I had the ill luck to arrive in Johannesburg while the great strikes were in progress. Luckily they were soon over, but it was a very terrible business indeed while it lasted.

The affair began over a small matter, that might, one would have imagined, have been easily settled. Five white mechanics working underground at the New Kleinfontein mine were asked to assent to an alteration of hours that would involve their working for the future on Saturday afternoons. They refused, and were dismissed. Whereupon all the white men working at that particular mine went on strike.

The trouble spread. Mine after mine was thrown idle. The mine-owners replied by importing strike-breakers, or blacklegs as the miners called them. This infuriated the workers, and for two or three days over the week-end Johannesburg was given up to something very like civil war. To venture into the streets was to gamble with death. The theatres and music-halls were closed; the newspapers suspended publication. The railway station and the offices of the *Star* newspaper were set on fire by the rioters, and burned to the ground, and many other buildings were either partially or wholly destroyed. Eventually the soldiers got the upper hand, but not before about a score of rioters had been killed, and some two hundred wounded.

Jo'burg, as the inhabitants affectionately term it, is a gay place, but expensive. When I opened at the Empire Music-hall there, I asked half a dozen or so men down to the bar for drinks round. I put down a sovereign to pay for them.

Barman: "Another twelve shillings, please."

I should have taken no notice in these days, for they would now cost almost as much at home.

I gave my show at a great many small towns, and back-veldt settlements where one would hardly have imagined that an audience could be scraped together; but the returns were invariably satisfactory, the reason being that prices rule high out there. The cheapest seat at most of the halls and theatres cost four shillings; a stall is a guinea.

One little mining town we were warned against quite solemnly.

"Don't go there," I was told. "They're a rough crowd. They'll throw eggs at you."

"I don't care," I replied. "It won't be the first time I've had eggs thrown at me."

"Ah! But these are ostrich eggs."

At Pretoria we were shown Kruger's tomb; and we were also conducted over his house. It is quite an unpretentious building, and plainly furnished. Everything in it is supposed to have been left exactly as it was during his life, and the visitor is invited by the caretaker to sit in the late president's favourite chair. The tomb was decorated with many faded wreaths, some of them from English Socialist and Trade Union leaders.

We were also shown the spot where Winston Churchill was supposed to have swum the river when he escaped from Pretoria during the Boer War. I expected to see a broad stream, or at least a raging torrent; something representing some sort of a difficulty at all events. Instead, I was confronted with what was in effect little more than a placidly flowing brook, deep perhaps, but so narrow that I could easily have jumped across it had I been so minded; and which, as a matter of fact, I did do later on.

It reminded me of another disappointment in connection with a river, that befell me while I was travelling in the United States of America. I was shown a muddy, sluggish, malodorous little stream, meandering through a swamp in Florida.

"See that river?" asked my guide.

"I see a dirty little ditch," I replied; "and I can smell it too."

"That *river*, sir," corrected my guide, "is famous. Its name is known wherever the English language is spoken."

"Oh!" I said. "What's it called?"

"The Swanee River!" answered the guide.

And to-day, and ever since, whenever an orchestra anywhere strikes up the well-known air of "Way down upon the Swanee River," like a flash memory calls up unbidden the image of that slimy, alligator-infested creek in the Florida Everglades.

I took a prize giant out to South Africa with me; "Scotty," the King's biggest and heaviest subject. He measured seven feet in height, and weighed considerably over thirty stone.

On the liner, going out, his huge bulk was accommodated in a double cabin; two ordinary cabins knocked into one. Of course it was all done for advertisement; a rather costly advertisement, by the way; but as the company I was travelling with paid all fares this didn't trouble me.

At Cape Town we arranged to have an observation-car attached to the train for his special convenience as far as Johannesburg, and thence to Pretoria. This too, of course, was in the nature of an advertisement; to make people talk, and attract attention, it being pretended that his immense size precluded his passing through the door of an ordinary car, or along the corridor.

ARRIVAL IN JOHANNESBURG OF CARLTON, HIS GIANT, AND HIS DWARF

From Pretoria we went to Durban, and the stationmaster at the former place informed us that no observation-car was available for this part of the journey. By this time "Scotty" had begun to believe that he really couldn't get into an ordinary car, or squeeze himself along an ordinary corridor, and he was quite upset and angry at being denied his usual roomy and luxurious special car.

"I can't possibly do it," he wailed, when the station officials urged him to at least try to enter the train in the usual way.

"Well," exclaimed the stationmaster at last, "you will have to get in here then."

The "here" was an open "Kaffir truck," used only by the natives, and half full at the time with about as malodorous a collection of niggers as anyone would wish to see.

"Come on," said the stationmaster, "the train is just going to start. In you go."

But "Scotty" wasn't having any. One look, one sniff, sufficed. He ran like a deer along the platform, and jumped into the ordinary compartment where we were with remarkable agility, and without the least difficulty.

We had another good joke with "Scotty" in Johannesburg. An enterprising Jew tailor advertised forty-shilling suits for sale, and a day or two after we arrived I called at his shop and selected the cloth for a "made-to-measure" suit "for a friend." "He's a big chap, you know," I said. "No difference at all, sir," answered the tailor, "big men, or small men, the price is just the same—forty shillings."

You should have seen that Israelite's face, however, when "Scotty" came round to be measured next day; and when he found that a five-foot long tape wouldn't meet round his new customer's waistcoat he nearly had a fit. However, he made the suit (but not for forty shillings) and exhibited it in his window afterwards: a good advertisement for him—and for us.

I was greatly struck by the number of Indians in South Africa. They seem to be everywhere, and amongst them were some fairly clever conjurors; but nothing very much out of the common. Indeed, I am personally of opinion that the cleverness of the Indian conjurors has been very much overrated.

In saying this I do not speak without knowledge, for when I was in Colombo, Ceylon, where some of the cleverest conjuring fakirs are supposed to be, I made it my business to investigate the claims of quite a number of them.

Some of the more marvellous tricks attributed to them I have no hesitation in saying are mere inventions, or hoaxes, bred of the credulity of too-easily-impressed Europeans. To this latter class belongs the famous boy and rope trick, of which everybody has heard, but which nobody, in my opinion, has ever seen.

There are two versions of this alleged conjuring trick. One story makes the fakir throw a rope into the air, where it remains suspended; if one may use the term, when there is presumably nothing up aloft for it to remain suspended from. The fakir then orders a small boy to climb the rope, which he does, afterwards drawing it up after him and vanishing with it into space, to presently reappear from somewhere behind the audience at the bidding of his master.

Such a trick, performed after this fashion, would be quite wonderful enough, in fact seemingly unexplainable. But there is another, and in a sense even more wonderful version of the same trick, which has been frequently described in print by people who say they have seen it done.

According to this story the fakir uses, not a rope, which presumably might be climbed supposing the upper free end were attached to anything strong enough to hold it, but a ball of thin twine, such as grocers use. This the conjuror throws up into the air, retaining the free end of the twine between his thumb and forefinger. The ball mounts higher and higher, growing gradually smaller and smaller as it mounts upwards and unravels, until it becomes a mere speck in the upper air, and ultimately vanishes altogether. Lastly the fakir releases the lower free end, and the string remains vertically suspended in the air as far as the eye can follow it.

The fakir next begins to tug violently at the string as if to try and recover the vanished ball, but it refuses to yield an inch, and in affected rage he speaks a few words to a boy he has with him. The little fellow approaches in feigned reluctance, his eyes dilated with terror; but, being urged on by curses and blows, he presently seizes the twine with both hands, and begins to climb up it.

Up and up he ascends, growing gradually smaller until he is a scarcely discernible speck, apparently hundreds of feet from the ground. Then he too vanishes as completely as the ball has done. The fakir waits a few minutes, as if expecting the boy to return. Then he begins calling to him to come down. There is no answer, and the fakir flies into a pretended rage, takes a knife between his teeth, and himself climbs the string, vanishing in his turn as the boy had previously done.

While the spectators are waiting in dumb amazement, wondering what is going to happen next, a distant shriek of pain and horror is wafted down from above. The next moment something round and red comes hurtling downward from the sky. It is the head of the boy severed from the body, with quivering muscles and flowing blood, to prove that it is no figment of the fancy.

Next one severed bleeding arm falls from the sky, and then another; and these are followed by two legs, as neatly dismembered as if cut off by the knife of a skilful surgeon. Lastly, the fakir himself reappears climbing down the string and holding the dripping knife between his teeth.

Calmly collecting the head and limbs he places them in his bag, throws it over his shoulder, and begins to walk away; but before he has gone many paces the spectators notice a movement in the bag. The fakir thereupon places it on the ground, salaams, makes a few mystic passes with his hands and utters a few cabalistic words, and the boy emerges from it, smiling and as sound in body as ever.

I have been at the trouble to recount these two versions of one and the same trick, because they are a source of perennial discussion amongst conjurors, professionals as well as amateurs. Personally, as I have already intimated, I utterly discredit the whole story. Yet I have, I am bound to say, met many people who hold the opposite view. I have even come across four or five people who profess to have seen the trick performed. While in India, and the East generally, the number of Europeans who know other Europeans who have seen the trick is legion.

The best answer to these credulous ones is that the thing is impossible. Consequently no such trick has ever been performed. This, I may add, was the opinion of H.H. the Maharajah of Jodhpur, with whom I had a long conversation relative to the subject. And he ought to know, for His Highness is an authority on Indian conjurors, and Oriental magic generally, having, as he himself assured me, seen practically every native conjuror of note at one time or another. His opinion is that it is just a traveller's yarn, invented by Europeans for European consumption in the dim, far-off days when India was more or less a land of mystery, and handed down ever since as a sort of tradition from generation to generation. "I have yet to meet the educated native who believes the story," were his concluding words.

I myself have asked scores of native fakirs to perform the trick for me, but they all professed themselves unable to do so, although they assured me that it could and had been done. Acting on this information I once caused it to be proclaimed in Colombo that I would pay £100—a fortune for a native—

to anybody who would show me the trick. But the money was not claimed. The only even remotely plausible explanation I have ever heard of the mystery is that hypnotism is the agent. In other words, the spectator is mesmerised by the fakir into believing that he sees things which actually he does not see. But this, to my mind at all events, is the veriest nonsense imaginable.

Another Indian conjuring trick round which a good deal of mystery has been made to centre is that in which a mango plant is produced by the fakir in the course of a few minutes from an ordinary dried mango seed. There is really, however, nothing mysterious about this illusion; to the professional conjuror, at all events. It is a sleight-of-hand trick pure and simple, and one which any of us could easily imitate, if we were so minded.

The way it is worked is as follows. The fakir, with whom usually are two or three assistants, takes an ordinary mango seed inclosed in the dried husk, and hands it round for inspection. It is quite a fair-sized object, measuring some three inches in length by one and a half inches across. This he places in the ground in full view of the spectators, covering it with a little heaped-up pile of dry earth, which he scrapes together with his hands.

Then he waves his loin cloth over it for a minute or so, to the accompaniment of weird incantations by himself and the beating of tom-toms by his assistants, and when he takes it away a couple of inches of green growing plant is seen to have burst its way out of the earth. Again the performance is repeated, and when the cloth is removed the green shoot is seen to have increased in height to fully six inches. A third time, and it is now nine inches. Whereupon the fakir calls a temporary halt, pulls the plant out of the ground and passes it round for inspection, showing the tendrils of the root, and the seed bursted in growing. Afterwards he replaces the mango plant into the ground, and continues his incantations and cloth waving until—assuming a sufficiency of annas and pice are forthcoming—it attains to the dimensions of a small tree, four feet or more in height.

Now I came to the conclusion, after having seen this performance repeated once or twice, that it was just an ordinary conjuring trick, dependent for success on ordinary sleight-of-hand, and quick, clever palming, and I determined to prove it to my own satisfaction. So one day in Colombo, while I and some friends were idling away the time outside our hotel, and a fakir came along and offered to perform the trick for us, I put into execution a plan I had formed.

The fakir asked two rupees as his fee for the performance.

"I'll give you five rupees," I said, "if you will let me plant the seed."

The man at once agreed, and handed me the seed, which I pretended to plant in the ordinary way and cover with earth. Then I told him to go ahead with his show, and took up my position immediately behind him.

Prior to this I had arranged with one of my friends who possessed a camera to take a snapshot of me directly I raised my hand, and this I presently did, choosing a moment when the mango plant had "grown" to about a foot high. In my open hand was the mango seed the fakir had given me, and which I had palmed, unbeknown to him, while pretending to plant it.

Consequently he had by his incantations persuaded his mango tree to grow up from a seed which was not there. This, I think, effectually disposes of the arguments of those who hold that these fakirs do actually cause the seed to sprout and grow by the use of some secret chemical, or other fructifying agent, known only to themselves.

The real truth is that they have concealed about their persons, or their belongings—sacks, etc.—several mango trees in different stages of growth, the leaves folded up very small and tied together with cotton. The rest, of course, is merely a matter of clever palming, and of diverting the attention of their audiences at the critical moment; at both of which arts, I am bound to say, they are exceedingly clever.

I may add that I kept the mango seed I palmed, and I have it now. The fakir never missed it when he came to gather up the earth and stuff and put it back in his bag. Or at all events if he did he judged it best to say nothing of his loss.

Before quitting Colombo I may say that one of the things that most interested and impressed me there was the curious Tree of Life, so called, exhibited in the arboricultural museum attached to the Mount Lavinia Gardens, and the leaves of which seem to be endowed with the faculty of locomotion, in that they crawl about like insects. I was also struck with my first view of a cobra and mongoose fight, arranged for our delectation by one of the many showmen fakirs who abound there. I never saw anything like the rapidity of the movements of the combatants. Greased lightning, as our American friends would say, was not in it. Of course the fangs of the snake had been previously extracted, and presumably the teeth of the mongoose had been similarly dealt with. Anyway neither seemed any the worse for the encounter, which indeed they seemed rather to enjoy, just as a couple of trained boxers might enjoy a friendly bout with each other.

CHAPTER XIII
WHEEZES AND GAGS

The social side of music-hall life—The Vaudeville Club—A telephone wheeze—The swanking "pro." and his mythical salary—About "tops" and "bottoms"—Ring up "625 Chiswick"—"Big Fred" and Fred Lindrum—A queer billiard match—An unexpected *dénouement*—Roberts and the Australian billiard marker—I make of myself a human telescope—Growing to order—Willard the original "man who grew"—Puzzling a Scotland Yard "'tec"—My most wonderful fall—I make a "hit" in a double sense—A Wigan wheeze—The performer who got too much "bird"—A blood-thirsty barber—My worst insult.

THE social side of the music-hall artiste's life centres largely round the Vaudeville Club in the Charing Cross Road, and which is owned and run by the Water Rats, of which I am proud to be a member.

I recall a very funny little incident that happened here not long since. A lot of us were in the place, some playing billiards, some chatting together, etc., when there entered a certain well-known "pro." who was notorious for swanking about the big salaries he commanded.

Going into the telephone-box, and carefully leaving the door ajar, so that we could hear what he was saying, he rang up a number, and the following one-sided dialogue took place.

"Hello!—Hello, I say!—Is that you, Mr. So-and-So?"

(We pricked up our ears at this, for the name he mentioned was that of one of the biggest men in the music-hall world.)

"Oh, it is?—Good!—About Monday next. I—eh? I say about Monday next. I got your letter this morning. Thanks! But two hundred pounds a week is no good to me."

(We gasped, and looked at one another.)

"Eh!—What's that?—You'll make it two hundred and fifty pounds? Not good enough, old chap. Ha! Ha! My terms are three hundred pounds a week, or nothing doing."

(Everybody craned forward their necks, listening intently.)

"What? I can't hear you very plainly. That's better. Oh! You'll make it three hundred pounds? Very well. Have the contract ready to-morrow for me to sign."

Ring off.

Exit Mr. Swanker from the telephone-box. He strolls nonchalantly to the bar.

"Have a drink, boys?"

We assent.

Enter the then manager of the club, Mr. Case. "Excuse me, sir, but that telephone has been out of order since yesterday; we're expecting a man in to see to it directly."

Sudden and complete exit from the club of Mr. Swanker, followed by a roar of laughter from all the other members.

I may add that a "pro.'s" salary, his *real* salary that is to say, is always a jealously guarded secret. Ask, and you generally get told a lie. The public hardly ever knows, in fact I might almost say it never knows. Newspaper "pars" are no criterion. Neither is the position of an artiste's name on the bill. "Tops" and "bottoms" are supposed to be the "star turn" positions. But I myself have topped the bill at £5 a week in my early days, with artistes getting £50 a week in very much smaller type below me. In fact the very first bill I ever topped I got £5 only, and it cost me about £3 in tips to stage hands and others to live up to my that week's (supposed) reputation.

Another little Vaudeville Club telephone wheeze! We were sitting in the smoke-room one day, when a member was smitten with a sudden brilliant idea. Going to the box he rang up about a score of well-known "pro.'s," and told each one who answered his call to ring up "625 Chiswick."

"You're wanted there badly," he explained.

When he had finished we made a dive for the telephone directory, and turned up "625 Chiswick."

Then we did a grin. It was the number of Wormwood Scrubs Prison!

After an interval our club telephone-bell started a perfect crescendo of violent rings many times repeated, and I'm told that the language that came on the wire from the victims of the joke ought to have shattered the receiver.

What the Governor of Wormwood Scrubs thought (or said) about the affair I have no means of knowing. But I can guess.

Yet another amusing happening at the Vaudeville Club occurs to me. There chanced to saunter in there one afternoon a member known as "Big Fred," a Leeds man, who rather fancies himself at billiards. There was also in the club at the same time Fred Lindrum, the Australian champion.

The latter was known to everybody there—excepting Big Fred. The conversation was purposely switched on to billiards, and presently a match, for drinks round, was got up between the two Freddies, the champion having previously let it be known to the rest of us that he would not attempt to show his real form until his opponent and he had each made about seventy, when he would wade in and run out.

"Seventy all!" called the marker.

We rubbed our hands, and smiled. "Cod" bets flew round as thickly as bees in a clover-bed in summer. Big Fred, suspecting nothing, was quite proud of the sensation the match was creating. Lindrum winked at us solemnly behind his opponent's back. It was his turn to play.

"Now the fun begins," we whispered to each other.

The champion played several perfect shots in succession, scoring twenty or so. Then he tried an exhibition stroke, and missed by a hair's breadth.

Big Fred took up the running, scoring eighteen, an unusually big break for him, and leaving the balls in a well-nigh impossible position. Lindrum did his best, but failed. Then Big Fred ran out.

We looked at one another in blank amazement. The impossible had happened. The Australian champion had been beaten, and by a third-rate amateur.

"Have another game?" said Big Fred.

"I don't mind," answered Lindrum.

Big Fred was beaming all over, immensely pleased with himself. "I'll give you ten start this time," he said.

There was a perfect roar of laughter at this. We simply couldn't help it. Big Fred was a good deal puzzled. Also he was somewhat nettled. He couldn't understand what we were laughing at.

"I'll bet any of you chaps a quid I win this game also," he cried.

"Done!" exclaimed half a dozen voices simultaneously, mine amongst them.

Of course the bets were "cod" bets in a sense. That is to say, we should not in any event have taken Big Fred's money. But he, on the other hand, had a perfect right to demand ours—if he won. But we did not stop to consider that side of the question. We were so perfectly cocksure that he would lose—this time.

But he didn't. By one of those million-to-one chances that do occasionally come off, he beat Lindrum a second time. Whereupon the champion broke his cue across his knee in a sudden gust of temper.

Big Fred regarded him in amazement. "Why, whatever's the matter?" he inquired. Then we told him who his opponent really was.

"Well, I'm d——d!" was all he could say.

The next day Lindrum made over eight hundred in one break in an exhibition match against a brother professional at Thurston's, and Big Fred, who was present, called out rapturously at the conclusion of the play: "That's the chap I gave ten start to and beat."

Chorus of sceptics, who knew nothing of the previous day's incident:

"Liar!"

Here is another billiard story, which so far as I know has never before appeared in print, but which was being retailed in all the bars in Melbourne at the time I was there, and which I was assured relates an actual fact.

Roberts was going to Melbourne to play Inman, and found himself stranded at Perth (Australia) with two days to wait for a boat. Accordingly, with an eye to business, he went into the billiard-room of the principal hotel there to see whether there was any chance of arranging an exhibition match.

Boy Marker (a smart, well-set-up lad): "Have a game, sir?"

Roberts: "No, thanks!"

B.M.: "Oh, come, now. Be a sport. I'll give you fifty in a hundred."

R. (with dignity): "I'm Roberts."

B.M. (genially): "Doesn't matter, sir, who you are. I give fifty in a hundred to all the folks round here."

R. (with increased dignity): "I'm Roberts, I tell you. The champion."

B.M. (after a pause for consideration): "Oh, well, sir, if that's so I can only give you thirty in a hundred."

Speaking of billiards, I was once playing principal comedian at the Prince of Wales' Theatre, Birmingham, when Inman and Stevenson—the latter of whom was then world's champion—were there, and we got very pally together.

At this period George Gray had just come over from Australia, and was creating a big sensation in billiard circles by his wonderful breaks off the red.

I noticed that whenever I introduced either Stevenson or Inman to anybody, the first words they uttered almost invariably were, "What do you think of George Gray?"

Now it happened that on the termination of my engagement in Birmingham the three of us, Stevenson, Inman, and myself, travelled up to London together. It was a corridor train, and quite a number of "pro.'s" I knew were aboard it, though not in our compartment.

"Now look here, you two," I said, "I'll bet you five shillings a time that anybody I happen to present to you will ask you what you think of George Gray."

"Agreed!" they said, and a minute or two later a man I knew happened along the corridor. I called him into our compartment, introduced him, and sure enough he promptly rapped out the usual question.

So did the second man, and third. I had won fifteen shillings. Thereupon Stevenson suggested that the next bet should be one for a sovereign.

Of course I raised no objection, and soon another professional friend of mine was roped into the compartment and introduced. He was an enthusiast on billiards, and he talked at great length about the game, recalling many big breaks made by the two players in days gone by. Not a word about George Gray, though! I began to get uneasy. By the terms of our bet I was not allowed to mention the young Australian player by name, but I did my best to lead the conversation in his direction by making such remarks as, "You made a break off the red yesterday, Stevenson, didn't you?"

All to no purpose, however; and my two travelling companions both laughed heartily when my friend eventually left without having asked the required question.

But when we reached London, Stevenson proposed that we should pool the £1 15s. and buy a couple of bottles of wine, explaining that he had previously squared the last friend to whom I had introduced him—and who also happened to be a friend of his—telling him on no account to ask him "What do you think of George Gray?"

This story, by the way, reminds me of another concerning Reece, who was equally good at swimming and billiards. He, too, got very tired of hearing the same query addressed to him; but the climax was reached one day when he was training for his attempt to swim the Channel. He was swimming about twelve miles out when a stranger swam up to him and, treading water vigorously, called out, "Hullo! You're Reece, aren't you? What d'ye think of George Gray?"

Somewhere in the Bible is the following text:

"Can a man, by taking thought, add one cubit unto his stature?"

The Hebrew chronicler who propounded this query evidently thought that there could be but one answer to it. In fact he did not really regard it, I suppose, in the nature of a query at all. He meant to say that the thing was utterly impossible a feat that could not be accomplished under any conceivable circumstances.

Herein he was right. For the Hebrew cubit, according to the best authorities, was probably not less than about eighteen inches long; and one may say at once that it is still impossible, as it was then, for a man—either by taking thought or in any other way—to add a foot and a half to his stature.

On the other hand, it is quite possible to temporarily increase one's height between seven and eight inches. I know, because I have done it; and, moreover, the increase in height, though it cannot be sustained for any great length of time, is perfectly real while it lasts.

It is accomplished mainly by stretching the muscles of the knees, hips, chest, throat, and other parts of the body, and maintaining them rigidly in that position by what is more or less an exercise of will-power. Of this feat I do not pretend to be the originator. A man named Willard, an American, did the same thing in the States. I learnt the trick from him, or rather I should say that I got the idea of it from seeing him do it; and so far as I am aware I am the only man, other than Willard himself, who has succeeded in accomplishing it.

For it must not be imagined that it is an easy thing to do. On the contrary, it is exceedingly difficult. It is also apt to be dangerous. Willard, not long since, overstrained himself while practising it one day; and I myself have found the ill effects so pronounced that I never produced the feat—as was my original intention—in public, and I now only perform it very occasionally in private for the benefit of my friends.

How I first came to know about it was this way. Inman, the billiard champion, was visiting my house, and he brought Willard with him. After lunch we strolled out on the lawn, and I suddenly noticed that my American guest had apparently grown taller; as indeed, of course, he had. Naturally, however, I put it down to my fancy. But a minute or so later, on looking up suddenly from a flower I had been examining, I saw that he was taller than ever, and I suppose I looked the amazement I felt. Anyway, Inman and he burst out laughing, and the former then introduced Willard as "The Man Who Grows."

Afterwards Mr. Willard was good enough to explain his method to me, and that night, after my guests had gone, I started practising on my own account. While I was at it, and still more after I had finished, I felt something of the sensation experienced in the olden days by criminals on the rack. Every bone, muscle, and sinew in my body ached; every nerve seemed on the quiver. But I persevered; and in time I succeeded.

I found, however, that the difficulty of the feat, and incidentally its attendant pain and discomfort, increased enormously with each additional inch. The first one was not so bad. But putting its difficulties, etc., at, say, ten, then those inseparable from the next inch of increase were fully one hundred; the third inch was represented by one thousand, and so on. In short, it resolved itself into a case of what mathematicians call, I believe, geometrical progression.

For these reasons I should not recommend the ordinary man to attempt the feat. He may easily do himself a serious inquiry. The strain told hardly on me, as I have already said.

I may mention that I have succeeded in mystifying a good many people by this growing feat, including at least one famous Scotland Yard detective. I was playing billiards with him, and an argument arose as to our relative heights. He was a tall man, measuring over six feet in his stockings, which is also my normal height. His impression was that he was taller than I, and to settle the point we adjourned to a police station and were measured by a machine that they kept there for recording the heights of criminals.

He, of course, measured his ordinary six feet odd. I stretched myself ever so slightly, and of course without any apparent effort, and beat him by two inches. "Well," he exclaimed, "I should never have thought it!" "Oh," I retorted, "I believe it's the fault of that old machine of yours. It doesn't record accurately. I'm taller than that."

NORMAL HEIGHT

THREE INCHES TALLER

SIX INCHES TALLER

CARLTON AS A "HUMAN TELESCOPE"

"Oh, that's nonsense!" he replied hotly. "Thousands of criminals have been measured by it, some of them several times over and on different occasions, but the measurements never vary by more than the minutest fraction of an inch. I'll bet you anything you like you're wrong."

Of course, I wasn't going to bet on a certainty, so I simply said that I thought he was mistaken, and, placing myself on the platform of the machine, I invited him to readjust the measuring-arm. This time it stood at six feet four inches.

"Well, I'll be hanged!" he ejaculated, in blank amazement. "This beats everything. I can't understand it." "Nor can I," I replied gravely, "because by rights I should measure six feet six inches. Will you please try again?"

Too astonished to reply, he proceeded to do as I had asked. The measuring-arm registered six feet six and a half inches. "Half an inch too much," I said. "Your machine's no good."

By this time my detective friend hardly knew whether he was standing on his head or his heels. He was dumbfounded—flabbergasted. So, taking pity on him, I explained to him how it was done.

"Well," he remarked thoughtfully, after he had recovered somewhat from his astonishment, "I hope the knowledge of how to accomplish the feat won't spread among the criminal fraternity, for if it does the Anthropometrical Department at Scotland Yard may as well close down."

As I have previously intimated, I don't perform the above feat in public for fear of straining myself. There are plenty of ordinary ways in which a man can hurt himself in my business, without looking about for extraordinary ways. For instance, I once came an awful cropper on the stage through no fault of my own.

It was at the Victoria Palace, London, where I was performing for the first time with a giant. I had also with me my contortionist, and I thought it would be a good gag for me, on my being suddenly confronted with the big man, to throw up my hands above my head, utter an exclamation of surprise, and fall over backwards.

This I did, having previously instructed my contortionist to be behind me, so as to catch me as I fell. But he didn't do it. He forgot all about it, and walked away to the wings. The consequence was that I turned a half summersault, and alighted on the back of my head with a resounding thwack that was heard plainly all over the theatre.

There were shrieks of laughter from everywhere—pit, stalls, and gallery. I didn't laugh though. Neither did my contortionist later on, when I got him by himself. Meanwhile I was suffering from slight concussion, and reeled to and fro about the stage like a drunken man. This caused more laughter. I had hardly ever made such a hit before; a "hit," I may say, in a double sense.

I went through the rest of my show with a lump on the back of my head that was really the bigness of a hen's egg, and which seemed to me to be about the size of an ostrich egg, and "still growing." When I had finished, George Barclay, who was then my agent, and who chanced to be in front, came round on purpose to congratulate me.

"It was great," he said. "I never saw a funnier or more natural fall in my life."

"Oh, that's nothing," I replied airily. "Didn't you ever see me do that before?"

"No," he said, "I never did."

"No," I thought to myself, "and you'll never see me do it again."

After that I cut that part of my show, nor did I ever again rely on being caught behind my back by a man I couldn't see, and who might or might not be there.

Of course it is easy enough for a trained athlete to fall, if he knows he is going to fall. I myself can fall twenty or thirty feet without hurting myself. Only on this occasion I didn't know. A man can give himself a nasty jar, or even injure himself pretty severely, by merely stepping off a kerb, if he doesn't know the kerb is there.

There are other directions in which an artiste's life is not exactly all beer and skittles. A young friend of mine found this out on his first visit to Wigan. His was not a bad turn of its kind, but Wigan is notoriously a "hard" town to work for artistes hailing from the south of England, and the people there didn't at all appreciate his particular business. Monday night was a dead frost. He didn't get a hand.

He couldn't make it out, and he went round to the front entrance as the people were streaming out in order to try and overhear what the audience really thought about his show. Of course, they didn't recognise him without his make-up. Not that it would have mattered much, probably, if they had.

The poor chap heard enough. Those who weren't slating his performance, were asking each other what Wigan had done to have such a "dud" as was dumped down there. Next night he got the bird. On Wednesday he got more bird. On Thursday he got most bird. On Friday morning he decided to take a long walk into the country, and try and forget it all.

He walked, and walked. Presently he came to a village. A barber's pole sticking out caught his eye, and he turned into the shop to get a shave.

Barber: "'Ast bin t'Empire at Wigan this week, laad?"

Pro. (shortly): "No, I haven't."

Barber: "Well, aw did. And aw saw a turn there, worst aw iver saw. If he comes in here aw'll cut his bloomin' throat!"

Personally I think the worst insult I ever suffered was rubbed into me while I was performing at Glasgow, very early in my career. I was working at the old Tivoli and Queen's, a very rough house. I had to give two shows a night for £5 a week, and the return fare from London cost me £3 6s.

Friday was amateur night there. That is to say that on that evening the first performance commenced an hour or so earlier than usual, and all sorts of budding "pro.'s," or people who imagined themselves "pro.'s" were encouraged to come on the boards and make exhibitions of themselves.

Well, the people there didn't approve of my show. My prize jokes were received in dead silence. My best gags evoked no responsive laugh. Finally a voice from the gallery rang out clear and shrill:

"Gang awa, hame, mon, and come agen on Friday nicht."

Another time I was touring the provinces with a cinematograph show depicting the destruction of Pompeii. In between I would give exhibitions of conjuring, card-manipulation, and so on.

These latter, however, were more in the nature of fill-ups. The moving pictures was supposed to be the real attraction. It had cost a lot of money to film, and in those days it was thought to be a wonderful production.

It is the custom of showmen running these sort of mixed entertainments in small provincial towns to stand at the entrance to the hall at the conclusion of the show and be introduced by the manager to the people he knows as they are leaving the building.

One evening I was introduced after this fashion to a typical old Yorkshire farmer.

"Good evening, sir," I said, using the accepted formula for such occasions, "I hope you enjoyed the show."

"Well," he replied dubiously, "I don't know about that. The conjuring was all reet. But that there moving picture wur a fraud."

I explained to him that it represented the very last word in cinematography, and had cost a small fortune to produce, as indeed it had.

"Garn!" retorted the old chap, "tha can't kid me. They never 'ad cinematographs in them days."

In 1912 I was appearing at the Palace Theatre, Lincoln. I was running the show with my own company on sharing terms, so that it was to my interest to draw as full houses as possible.

At this time the "hidden treasure" craze was at its height, and the idea struck me that I might as well utilise it for my show.

So I used to announce, prior to opening, that instead of paying £50 for "turns" on my bill, I proposed to give away this sum amongst my audiences during the ensuing week.

To this end I had a number of vouchers printed announcing that "the finder will receive £1 on presenting this paper to Carlton at the Palace Theatre during the evening performance." These I would take out secretly at dead of night, and hide in various likely and unlikely spots, my usual method being to fold them up into quite a small compass, and run a drawing-pin through them. By these means I was able to pin them underneath a seat where I happened to be sitting, say in a park, for instance, or any other public place, without attracting attention. At other times I would pretend to hide the vouchers in various places where I knew people were watching me and then watch them vainly searching for the thing that was not there. It was great fun.

Of course I did not invariably pin them under seats. I hid them here, there, and everywhere, all over the place. People used to follow me about in the day-time, in order to try and spot where I put them. But, needless to say, they were never successful. I saw to that. Still, it was all good advertisement, and it was fun for me to watch them digging and searching for my vouchers miles away from where I had hidden them.

I used to give out clues from the stage at each performance, giving very easy ones the first night or two, and making them more obscure and difficult as the week wore on. Whenever a voucher was found, I used to have the finder up on the stage, and get him to sign it with his name and address, and these were afterwards pinned up outside the theatre, so that the public could see that my offer was a genuine one.

Well, it so happened that at Lincoln, while I was working this stunt, the late B. C. Hucks, the famous *Daily Mail* flying man, who, it will be remembered, was the first Englishman to loop the loop, was holding an aviation meeting there. I invited him to the theatre, and suggested that I should have him up on the stage and introduce him to the audience. "It will be a good 'advert.' for you," I told him.

Hucks willingly agreed. But he did not know what was in my mind. Otherwise, perhaps, he might not have fallen in with the suggestion so readily. For when I got him on the stage, and after introducing him to the people in front, where needless to say he received an enormous ovation, I went on to say that "Mr. Hucks had very kindly consented to take me up in his aeroplane on the day following, and that I would throw down ten £1 vouchers for the crowd to scramble for."

"That's so, isn't it, Mr. Hucks?" I said at the conclusion of my speech, turning to him and shaking him by the hand; and poor Hucks, taken off his guard, could do no more than nod a smiling assent. But all the while, under his breath, he was addressing remarks the reverse of complimentary to me.

Next day I was at the aerodrome to time. Hucks was there. I half hoped that he wouldn't have been. I had had time to reflect overnight, and I didn't at all relish the experience I was up against. For flying in those days, the reader must remember, was not by any means the safe and easy thing it has since become. Nor were the aeroplanes then what they are now. In fact the early types were just big, power-driven box-kites.

However, I was in for it, and up we went. I was in a blue funk, and when Hucks, after circling round two or three times, asked me if I had dropped the vouchers, I replied that I had forgotten all about them. Which was the fact.

So round we went once more, and I threw them out. "There goes ten pounds," I said to myself, and groaned in spirit. But I need not have worried. We were several thousand feet up, and the wind caught the flimsy pieces of paper and blew them heaven knows where. Not one of them was ever presented.

A story occurs to me as I write, which I will call "The Biter Bit." It concerns the brothers Egbert, better known as the "Happy Dustmen." These two are probably about the most confirmed practical jokers on the music-hall stage. They are for ever playing tricks on somebody. Everybody in the profession knows this, and consequently tries to avoid sharing a dressing-room with them.

Well, these two found out somewhere how to make a substance which, smeared on anything, will explode on being touched, even ever so lightly. They tried it first on Bransby Williams at the Sheffield Hippodrome, smearing a quantity on a seat. When he sat down, it exploded with a report like a bomb, and poor Bransby leapt about six feet, imagining that there was an air raid on.

But this was only a trial spin, so to speak. The following week the two practical jokers were at the Hippodrome, Portsmouth, where they shared a dressing-room with Harry Claff, known as the "White Knight." Harry had not, as it happened, heard of the Sheffield incident, but the reputation of the Brothers Egbert in the matter of practical joking was, of course, well known to him, so that he was on his guard.

The brothers tried hard to get him away from their dressing-room after rehearsing together on the Monday, so that they could put some of the explosive stuff on his seat, his grease paints, his make-up box—anywhere, in short, where he would be sure to handle it or come in contact with it. But try as they would, they could not succeed. Harry stuck to them too tightly.

At length the three of them left the theatre to go to their respective diggings. The brothers saw Harry to his. Then Seth Egbert slipped hurriedly back to the dressing-room, and started smearing the stuff all over Claff's various belongings. Now every theatrical dressing-room is provided with a mirror, and just as Seth had finished baiting his trap he happened to glance up into this mirror, and there, clearly reflected, was the face of Harry Claff, an amused grin on his face. Suspecting that the brothers were up to something, he had followed Seth back to the theatre, and caught him in the act.

I had the curiosity to inquire of the brothers how they made the stuff. Here is their formula; but if any of my readers contemplate making any of it, with a view to playing tricks on anybody, I warn them to be very, very careful, as the compound is exceedingly dangerous, being one of the most powerful explosives known, and used extensively in the late war.

You take sixpennyworth of flaked iodine and one pennyworth of 88 ammonia, together with a sheet of filter paper. Put a small piece of iodine on the filter paper held over a tin can, and pour over it enough ammonia to dissolve it into a paste. This, smeared while wet on any hard substance, such as the handle of a door, for instance, will explode—when dry—with quite a violent report directly anyone touches it. But no more than the tiniest piece, about the size of a pin's head, must be used.

Which reminds me, by the way, that a small piece of metallic sodium thrown into a bath of water, or into a river where anyone is fishing, will zigzag about all over the place in the most erratic fashion. Only, don't use too much sodium; a piece about the size of a threepenny-piece will work wonders, causing great astonishment and roars of laughter amongst the uninitiated.

CHAPTER XIV
THE BIGGEST NEWSPAPER SPOOF ON RECORD

How the great spoof first came into my mind—Hoaxing the newspaper Press of two continents—Telepathy and thought-transference—The incredulous reporter—I propose a drastic test—A representative of the *Bristol Times and Mirror* hides a stylograph pen in an unknown quarter of the city—I am blindfolded and find it—Amazement and enthusiasm of the people—A column report in the newspaper—An insoluble problem—Various theories as to how it was done—An indoors test imposed by the Editor of the *Bath Chronicle*—Blindfolded through the streets of Bath—Vast crowds—I am again successful—Press and public alike bewildered—Hoaxing the Yankees—The Oakland, California, *Tribune's* test—Two hundred and fifty dollars in gold hidden—The Secretary of the Oakland Chamber of Commerce is chosen to secrete the treasure—Again I am successful—My best free Press "ad."—Congratulations all round.

THE idea of the "great spoof," the most colossal thing of its kind, I venture to assert, ever perpetrated on the Press and public of two continents, first suggested itself to my mind in February, 1907, when I was playing in pantomime at the Prince's Theatre, Bristol.

I was being interviewed by a representative of the *Bristol Times and Mirror*, and the conversation turned on the alleged telepathic feats of the Zancigs, then at the height of their popularity. The newspaper man opined that there must be "something in" the theory of occultism in connection with their exhibition; that they were possessed of a sixth sense, for example.

I hotly traversed this view of the matter, but eventually, after some further argument, I pretended to agree that possibly telepathy, or thought-transference, might afford a clue to the solution of the so-called mystery. This I did for an ulterior motive of my own, and in pursuance of a plan that was beginning to shape itself in my mind; for I do not really believe in telepathy, thought-transference, mind-reading—call it what you will. Presently, in the course of the conversation, came the cue question I had been waiting for, and which I had gradually led up to, though without appearing to do so.

"Can *you* read a man's thoughts?" asked the reporter.

"Yes," I replied boldly; "given certain conditions, I can."

The reporter sniffed incredulously. I pretended to get huffed.

"Look here!" I burst forth, as though struck by a sudden inspiration. "In order to prove to you that I can read yours, I am willing to submit to a test; the most drastic, almost, that it is possible to conceive. You shall take some small article and hide it in any part of the city you like, and I will go to where you have hidden it, and find it. Moreover, I will allow you to blindfold me in such a manner that it is impossible for me to see to find my way to the spot where you have hidden the object, even if I knew where the locality was or in which direction it lay. All I ask is that you shall walk behind me and mentally direct me which way to go. You must fix your whole attention on the quest, that is to say, and exert all your will-power to guide me aright. This is all I ask. The rest is my business. There will be no word spoken between us, no questions asked or answered, and, of course, no personal contact. In fact, I should prefer that you remain always at some distance behind me; say, for instance, five or six paces."

* * * * *

The sequel to the above conversation came a week later, when on February 5th, 1907, I found a stylograph pen which had been previously hidden by the reporter in the axle of one of the old Russian guns on Brandon Hill. Of course the affair was well boomed beforehand—I saw to that—and fully three thousand people (according to the report in the *Evening Times* of the above date) were on the hill when I made the discovery, while a crowd of at least two thousand watched my start from the Prince's Theatre, after my eyes had been tightly bandaged with a dark blue silk handkerchief folded in ten thicknesses, and stitched together to prevent any slipping. The width of this bandage was about four inches, completely covering my eyes, and, in order to make assurance doubly sure, I had each eye covered under the bandage with a separate pad of cotton-wool, pressed well down into the sockets.

Thus blindfolded I groped and blundered my way along several streets. Once I ran into a tramcar. Four times I fell down.

But—I found the pen. And so delighted were the crowd at my success, that they seized me and carried me shoulder high to the Prince's Theatre. The full report of the affair, as published in the newspaper, occupied over a column; and the reporter professed himself completely puzzled as to how I accomplished the feat, as indeed doubtless he was.

Yet the whole business was a spoof from start to finish, so far, that is to say, as regards there being any question of telepathy or thought-transference. But it was a spoof engineered entirely by myself, and off my own bat, so to speak. In other words, there was no collusion, direct or indirect, between me and anybody else connected with the affair. Nor, as a matter of fact had I the remotest idea, when I set out on my quest, whereabouts the pen was hidden, nor indeed in what quarter of the city. In the circumstances, therefore, I think the reader will admit that the feat was, on the face of it, a sufficiently marvellous one.

I was blindfolded. I was in a strange city, where the streets and turnings I had to traverse and take were necessarily totally unfamiliar to me. Let the reader turn the problem about in his own mind, and try if he can reach any plausible solution of the mystery. I make bold to say that he will fail, as the good people of Bristol failed, and as many thousands of other people failed before whom I was presently to give other similar exhibitions in various parts of the world.

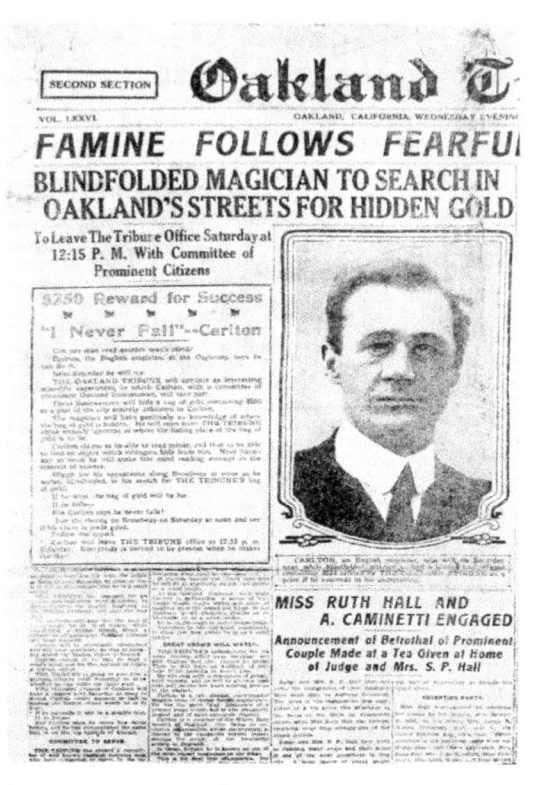

PORTION OF FRONT PAGE OF THE "OAKLAND TRIBUNE" WITH REPORT OF CARLTON'S TREASURE HUNT IN THAT CITY

Telepathy was the explanation most generally tendered, both then and afterwards, and I have in my possession letters from members of the Psychical Research Society warning me against repeating the experiment on account of the strain on my "psychic personality," which might, so they averred, have unlooked-for and dangerous results. That the ordeal I voluntarily underwent was a trying, not to say nerve-racking, one was perfectly true. I felt it mentally and physically for weeks afterwards. Nevertheless, as I have already intimated, telepathy did not enter into the matter at all. Exactly how the trick was worked I shall take occasion to explain later on. Suffice it to say here that I afterwards spoofed the Press and public on the same lines over and over again, and never once did I fail in my quest, nor was the secret of how it was done ever elucidated by anybody.

I have performed the feat in Italian cities, and puzzled university professors, and before committees of professional magicians in India, Egypt, and other Oriental and Near-Eastern countries, and these were deceived as completely as were the shrewd, hard-headed Yankees.

Some of my hardest tests, however, have been undergone in England, in connection with certain of the big English newspapers. In several instances editors whom I have approached have been frankly incredulous in the beginning; so much so, indeed, that they have at first refused to sanction a public test under their auspices. This was the case in connection with the *Bath Chronicle*, whereupon I offered to give a preliminary exhibition there and then in the office before the members of the staff.

The offer was accepted. I was blindfolded with a thick, heavy muffler, folded in four, which was then tied tightly round my head, my eyes, moreover, being first covered with pads of cotton-wool. This done, one of the staff, at my suggestion, took up a piece of chalk and started to draw a line from near where I was standing to whatever part of the building he chose. He could, I agreed, carry the line where he pleased, up and down stairs, into the basement, offices, machine-rooms—anywhere he liked, in fact. This done, he was to hide some small article at some spot near the end of the line, and I would undertake to find it. More than this, I told him that, provided he walked behind me, concentrated all his thoughts on the matter in hand, and willed me so to do, I would follow exactly the chalk-line he had marked out, pacing along all its twists and turnings, until I had groped my way to the end and found the hidden article.

This feat I successfully accomplished, wending my way in and out among machinery—purposely brought to a standstill for the occasion—upstairs and downstairs, under tables and over chairs. As a result everybody was greatly impressed, nobody had any reasonable explanation to offer, and the editor promptly agreed to a public trial, minus, of course, the chalk line.

Accordingly he deputed a member of his staff to hide, "in some public place within two miles of the *Chronicle* office, some article or other." Strict injunctions were given that he was to let no one see him do it, and that he was not to tell a single person what he had hidden, or where he had hidden it.

So impressed was the reporter with the importance of his mission, I found out afterwards, that he waited until after dark to fulfil it, and sallied forth from the office so stealthily, and followed so circuitous and lonely a route, as to convince him that no one could possibly have dogged his footsteps, or had him under observation in any shape or form.

The day following I underwent the test, and successfully located the article he had hidden. The report of the affair in the *Bath Chronicle* takes up about a column and a half, but as the main instances are similar to those narrated above I forbear to quote it in its entirety. I will, however, reproduce the concluding paragraphs, and I would like to direct the reader's particular attention to the words I have italicised, as I shall have something important to say about this particular incident when I come to elucidate the mystery.

After relating various happenings in connection with the earlier stage of the journey, the crowd that lined the route, etc., the report proceeds as follows:

Reaching the turning leading to the Midland Bridge, "Carlton" crossed the road for a few yards, and then went ahead towards the bridge. He marched on, only halting once or twice, as his outstretched hands fumbled the side of the bridge. Crossing and recrossing the road he went on, and the crowd was evincing the liveliest interest in the proceedings. Arriving at the end of the Midland Bridge Road, he turned sharply to the left, and after some manœuvring turned down James Street.

Here he walked into the wall on the left-hand side, his forehead coming into contact with the stonework. This accident loosened the bandage over "Carlton's" eyes, which was at once readjusted. This done, "Carlton" made for the direction of Green Park. He took the right-hand side of the thoroughfare, and for about twenty yards kept close to the railings fencing the Green Park enclosure. The explorer retraced his steps as far as the Park entrance gate, which seemed to excite his lively interest. His hand alighting on the handle, he opened the gate, entered the enclosure, and closely examined with his hands the stonework on which the gate is hung. He was observed by the crowd to stoop down, feel along the ground, and on rising up was seen to be holding a pale blue envelope. Recognising that the search had been successful, the crowd cheered heartily. On opening the envelope "Carlton," amid renewed cheers, displayed the bunch of keys which I had late last night hidden. He had completed his task in an hour.

As a rule the articles hidden by those who tested me were comparatively valueless, and anyhow I was not supposed to keep possession of them after I had found them. But at Oakland, California, I was given a rather pleasant surprise. So cocksure was the editor of the *Tribune* of that city that I could not do what I said I could do, under the conditions he proposed to impose upon me, that he offered to hide two hundred and fifty dollars, the money to be mine if I succeeded in finding it.

Naturally, I was quite agreeable, and as the *Tribune* took good care to boom its "generous offer" beforehand, the crowds in the streets on the day the test was to be performed surpassed anything I had before experienced. The police estimated that there were between thirty and forty thousand people present. The date was September 9th, 1911, and the dust and the heat were awful.

The individual chosen by the *Tribune* editor to hide the money, and to "guide" me to it afterwards, was no less a personage than the Secretary of the Oakland Chamber of Commerce, one of the city's wealthiest and most prominent citizens, and a man whose integrity and *bona fides* were, of course, quite beyond question. By agreement with the Chief of Police, he had selected as a hiding-place for the bag of gold one of the police telephone call-boxes, such as are an institution in most American cities, and to which the police alone are able to obtain access by means of their private keys.

The particular box he chose was fixed to an electric light standard in a remote quarter of the city, and just before I left the *Tribune* building the editor received a telephone message to the effect that the money was still in the box where it had been hidden overnight, and that the key had now been placed on top of the box, which was being guarded by a couple of officers detailed for the purpose. This information, however, was, I need hardly say, not imparted to me. In fact, I knew nothing whatever about the money, except that it was hidden somewhere in Oakland, and that I had got to find it.

How I succeeded is told in the following report, taken from a special evening edition of the *Tribune*, which was selling on the streets within a few minutes of my having accomplished my task:

In the middle of a hollow square and surrounded by thirty thousand persons, shortly after noon to-day, at the south-east corner of Fourteenth and Broadway, "Arthur Carlton," the famed magician, who is nightly performing at the Orpheum in this city, blindfolded found a bag containing two hundred and fifty dollars in gold which had been hidden in a telephone-box at that intersection for the purpose of determining whether or not he was able to read the thoughts of the man who had there cached the precious metal.

The discovery was greeted with enthusiastic cheers by the thousands who pressed in on every side, and who were prevented from raising the magician upon their shoulders only by a cordon of police.

The money was offered by the *Tribune* for the purpose of determining whether or not "Carlton" possessed the power of reading the minds of persons, which he claimed to be able to do. In the event of his finding the coin in the place selected for its secretion, the two hundred and fifty dollars was to become the property of the finder. There was a stipulation, however, that the money was to be cached by a man of standing in the community who should be selected by the management of the *Tribune*; that the hiding-place was to be kept a secret by the representatives of this paper, who had been chosen for the purpose, and that the treasure-trove should be conducted in the light of day and in the presence of every resident of the city of Oakland who might desire to witness the quest.

"Carlton" agreed to every condition and complied with them in a manner which showed him to be not only capable of mastering the thoughts of others without physical contact with them, but at the same time to be a consistent advocate of the science of telepathy, of which he is to-day the most famous exponent in existence.

The achievement of this young Englishman has never been equalled in this city. This is the view of thousands of citizens who witnessed the accomplishment, and who still retain the heartiest appreciation of the work in the same line of Bishop, Tyndall, and other workers in the same field who made reputations in this country about twenty years ago. It has been created by the fact that "Carlton" has done something which none of those distinguished advocates of thought-transference ever attempted. They were able to read the minds of others, but not without being in physical contact with those whose minds they were reading. The persons whose minds were being interpreted were required to hold the demonstrator by the wrist and concentrate their thoughts upon the subject which was to be illustrated, or they were connected by wires with the operator and expected to centre their thoughts both upon the article hidden and the direction which had been followed in the secretion.

The following morning the paper gave up its entire front page to recording my achievement, and then, and for several days afterwards, scores of letters appeared from people who imagined that they had hit upon the solution of the mystery.

As a matter of fact, as I have before intimated, neither in Oakland, nor anywhere else where I have performed the feat, has anyone succeeded in finding out how it was done.

Now for the explanation!

CHAPTER XV
HOW THE BIG SPOOF WAS WORKED

Muscle training on novel lines—How not to be blindfolded—Artificially developed frontal muscles—The advantage of possessing a prominent proboscis—Following one's nose—I study boots—A Sherlock Holmes of footwear—Acting blind—Not so easy as it sounds—Queer happenings at Halifax—A mishap at Leeds—Police stop the performance—A curious mischance at Bath—Ingenious explanations to account for the feat—Invisible wires—Guided by bugle calls—Following the scent.

THE real root secret of the trick, or rather series of tricks, described in the previous chapter may be summed up in four words—muscular training and development.

Not the ordinary muscular training of the gymnasiums, however, be it noted; but muscular training developed along novel and unsuspected lines.

I have always been fond of experimenting in these directions, with the result that I have, in the course of years, achieved what I think I may fairly describe as some rather startling results. I can, for example, as I have already explained elsewhere, increase or decrease my height at will by expanding or contracting the muscles of my legs, thighs, chest, and abdomen. I have taught myself also to move my ears backwards and forwards, a feat performed constantly and naturally by all the lower animals, but the practice of which, as regards man, has become dormant owing to long disuse.

The particular set of muscles I used in my blindfold experiment were those in front of the forehead, and which ordinarily come into play whenever the eyes are shut or opened. These are quite unusually powerful in their action, as the reader can test for himself if he will take the trouble to close his eyes, cover them tightly with the palm of his left hand, and then suddenly open them wide to their fullest extent. He will find that the whole lower portion of the skin of the forehead is pushed up under his hand by the expansion of the frontal muscles, no matter how tightly he presses against it.

Now it is, of course, well known that as a result of long or repeated use all muscles increase in size, and consequently in strength, through the formation of new fibre. Taking advantage of this fact, I set to work to train and develop my frontal muscles, in much the same way as the professional boxer, say, trains and develops his biceps, or the runner his leg muscles.

I spent an hour or more every day for many months on end practising shutting and opening my eyes, rolling them from side to side, moving the scalp up and down, and so on. The result was that I was able presently to so contract and expand the muscles of my forehead and to move the skin up and down in such a way that, no matter how closely my eyes were bound, I could relax the bandage or change its position up or down in relation to my sight, and this, of course, without touching it in any way with my hands.

Nor was it possible for anyone to detect the change, for not only was it quite slight—although always sufficient for my purpose—but if anyone wanted to examine the bandage while the test was in progress, as indeed frequently happened, I had only to close my eyes, throw back my head, and at the same time relax my frontal muscles, when the bandage would at once fall into its proper position, and even the most critical examiner would be fain to confess that in his opinion the wearer of it—that is to say myself—could not possibly see anything whatever, either through it, over it, or under it.

This much as regards the training preliminary to the trick! The intelligent reader will no doubt be struck by the fact that in its inception it bears a certain sort of analogy to that first practised by the Davenports and their imitators. These people allowed themselves to be tightly bound about the body, arms, and legs with ropes, while their muscles were purposely kept by them in a state of extreme tension, and then when lights were lowered they were able to free themselves from their bonds by muscular contraction. Substitute "bandage" for "ropes," and it will be apparent that I worked my blindfold trick on similar lines.

"But," exclaims the reader, "this does not explain how you found articles previously hidden in places unknown to you, and in localities miles away from your starting-point. Even if you were able to loosen your bandage at will in such a way as to permit of your peeping under it, that would not help you greatly in this respect, seeing that you had to find your way unaided, and according to your theory, unguided, through the maze of streets and thoroughfares of a strange city."

Wait a minute—I am coming to that. But first let me say something about the preliminary test which I usually insisted on undergoing at the office of the particular newspaper I had selected to spoof. This, it will be remembered, consisted in my walking along a chalk line that had been drawn by a member of the staff from the centre of the floor in the editorial sanctum to some distant point on the premises. This line, which was, of course, started and completed after I had been—so the onlookers were convinced—securely blindfolded, was carried at my instigation all over the place in a series of zigzags and curves, in and out and across, up stairs and down, so that it not infrequently resembled very closely the ground pattern of some new and abnormally intricate species of maze.

The man who drew the chalk-line would then, as explained in the previous chapter, hide some small item near the end of the line, and then, following behind me at a distance of three or four paces, he would "will" me to go forward along the line, following all its twisting and turnings, until I had reached the end of it and retrieved the hidden article. My great aim and object in carrying out these tests was to impress upon this individual that it was he who was really doing the finding through me, that I was only the medium, so to speak, and that it was his will-power that set me in motion and directed me which way to go.

In order to encourage this delusion I used to tell him beforehand to draw crosses here and there along the line, explaining that, if he succeeded in exercising sufficient will-power, I would stop at each cross to it. This invariably greatly impressed the beholders, and added considerably to their mystification.

The reader will now be able to form a fairly clear idea of how this particular trick was worked, bearing in mind my previous explanation as regards the bandaging, and the contraction and expansion at will of the artificially developed frontal muscles. I forgot to say that in addition to the bandage, folded in many thicknesses, I used to insist, as an extra precaution, on my eyes being covered with pads of cotton-wool. This, however, made no difference. Nature has fortunately endowed me with a fairly prominent nose, and by expanding the bandage and pads, and shifting their position ever so slightly by muscular effort in the manner already described, I was easily able to see down each side of it.

True, the range of vision so obtained was extremely limited. I could see no more than a few inches immediately in front of me. But the chalk-line was there. I had only to keep along it, stop at the various cross marks, and, when I came to the end of it, grope about for the hidden article until I found it—no very difficult task. In fact, it was no more than a cause of following my nose, literally as well as metaphorically.

Of course, there was a good deal of play-acting about the performance. I had to grope and stumble about, for instance, exactly as a blindfolded man would; and yet I had to be very careful not to overdo the part, for the great thing, of course, was to avoid rousing the slightest suspicion in the minds of the onlookers. As a matter of fact, I am quite convinced that none of them at any time harboured any such suspicions. The elaborately tight bandaging, the plugging of the eyes with pads of cotton-wool pressed well down into the sockets, was sufficient to convince the most sceptical. And, of course, they were quite right in assuming that I could not see at the time when they were examining me. It was afterwards, when the frontal muscular expansion came into play, and I made ready to start on my quest, that the element of sight came into operation.

This preliminary test, with the chalk line to guide me, was, however, a comparatively simple matter. It was far otherwise when it came to working the trick in the open streets, without any line, or in fact guidance of any sort, save that which was supposed to come from the man walking behind me, who, moreover, was forbidden to speak to me, and who, of course, was not in personal contact with me in any shape or form.

During the months in which I was engaged in working the trick out in my own mind, and in experimenting privately as regards the best way of successfully concluding the task I had set myself, I found that the only moving objects that were at all likely to come within the extremely limited range of vision allowed me when "blindfolded" were—boots.

Forthwith I became an enthusiastic and critical student of boots of all kinds. Not new boots as exhibited in the shop windows, be it understood; but worn boots—boots on people's feet. I practised my powers of observation on men I met, training my memory in this one direction until I was able mentally to visualize, so to speak, any pair of boots I had once seen. I could see in my mind's eye every crease, each tiny protuberance. Sherlock Holmes himself would simply not have been in it with me in this particular branch of detective science. I learnt to recognise and know men by their boots, and by their boots alone. It was a most fascinating study, once I had warmed to my subject, and fraught with infinite possibilities. Some day I shall publish a monograph on "The Influence of Character on Footwear."

Exactly how this laboriously acquired knowledge helped me in my quest for hidden treasure the reader shall now learn, and I will take as an illustration the test imposed upon me at Oakland, California, where two hundred and fifty dollars in gold was actually hidden. The reader will please imagine me at the office of the *Tribune* newspaper of that city. Outside in the street is an immense throng of curious people, for the affair has been well boomed beforehand. I am introduced to the person who is to "guide" me, and who alone of all those present knows where the treasure is hidden—in this case, Mr. A. A. Denison, of the Oakland Chamber of Commerce.

Prior to being blindfolded by the committee of prominent citizens appointed for the purpose, I am introduced to this gentleman, and we shake hands. Meanwhile I take stock of his boots, while addressing him in some such terms as these: "You will please understand, Mr. Denison, that my failure or success to-day in the task I have undertaken rests with you, and you alone. You are the active agent; I am merely the passive one. In effect it is you who are going to find this treasure, not I. You must exert all the strength of your will power to guide me aright. If you do this, I cannot possibly fail; if you fail to do it, I cannot succeed. Walk behind me, and will me along the right path. If I am going in the right direction, mentally boost me ahead. If I am going wrong, stop yourself and mentally tell me to stop also. This is all I ask—that you shall not will me along the wrong road."

All this, of course, is the biggest bunkum imaginable. But it impresses my auditors. And especially it impresses Mr. Denison. Meanwhile, I am still studying his boots.

Well, I am bandaged to the satisfaction of the committee, who one and all examine me in turn, while some make suggestions, calculated, so they imagine, to further the completeness of the blindfolding business; a little more cotton-wool here, a tightening of the bandage there, and so on. When all is finished a prominent member of the committee of investigation solemnly and emphatically pronounces his opinion as follows: "Gentlemen, if Carlton can see through that bandage and those pads, he must have the eyes of a catamount."

Precisely what kind of an animal a catamount is, I do not know, but I am quite prepared to believe that it possesses abnormally keen eyesight. Anyway, everybody appears quite satisfied, and I step forth from the building, groping and stumbling as a blind man would. The bugles blare, the crowd gives a mighty cheer, and the quest begins. I circle round like a hound casting for scent, only that my movements, of course, are slower. I know that in the beginning I must either go one way or the other; up the street or down, to the right or to the left.

Groping this way and that, with my hands outstretched, but my eyes carefully directed downwards, I am able presently to bring the boots of my "guide" within my very limited range of vision. Naturally the toes are pointing in the direction he is mentally willing me to go. So off I start in that direction, after a little more groping and circling, done for effect, and not of any set purpose.

Now, I have previously taken care to make myself thoroughly acquainted with the topography of the city generally, and more especially with that of the streets in the immediate vicinity of the newspaper office from which I set out. Also I am aware that the bag of gold is secreted somewhere at a point approximately not less than a mile, and not more than two miles, from the starting-point, for this was the arrangement made in advance. So the reader will see that I had a certain amount of data to go upon.

There is, of course, always the kerb to guide me, and in the main thoroughfares there are tramlines. I could, therefore, walk in a perfectly straight line as far as the first turning. But this, naturally, I do not do. Instead, I zigzag from one side to the other, blunder into pedestrians, finger my way along shop-fronts and area-railings, and so on.

By and by I come to a side street. I may have to turn down it, or I may not. In order to find out, I have to grope and circle in such a way as to be able to bring within my view the boots of the "guide" who is following me. A single glimpse suffices. But often I pretend to be at fault.

"You are not exerting sufficient will power," I tell him. "*Please*, sir, do your utmost to guide me aright. Will me along the way I am to go, *please*. I cannot go right without your help." And so on and so forth! It is all the veriest humbug, of course; but I have yet to come across the man whom it does not impress.

In this manner I progress along the route, and at each turning or doubtful corner the pantomime set forth above is repeated. But never in quite the same way, or some among the onlookers might get suspicious, and this is the one thing I have to avoid at all hazards. Everything has to be done naturally; every movement must be executed exactly as a blind man might be expected to execute it. It is not an easy matter. One has to be a good actor. Supposing, for example, I came upon an open grating, or a hole in the road. It would never do to avoid these too markedly. In the case of the grating I "feel" it with one foot, pretending to try and gauge its depth and extent, before circling round it. As regards the hole, if it is not too deep, I may allow myself the luxury of falling into it. It must, of course, be done carefully, and there is even then a certain element of risk, but it adds immensely to the realism of the performance.

In this way, circling, groping, stumbling, but every minute drawing nearer and nearer to my objective, I progress along my way, and in time I am able to locate the hiding-place of the object I am in search of. Never once have I failed.

There have been some curious mischances, though. One of the queerest of these unrehearsed incidents occurred at Halifax, in connection with a test organised at my instigation by the editor and staff of the *Guardian*. The object I was in search of had been hidden under a bridge, over which the road I had to traverse was carried. On reaching the crown of the bridge, I knew, owing to my boot-reading tactics, that the hiding-place was somewhere beneath it; so I pretended to climb over the parapet, knowing, of course, that I should be prevented from doing so, for this would have meant a sheer drop of twenty feet or so.

On being pulled back, and warned of the danger I was supposed to be unconsciously running, I went round another way, and under the bridge. Here I located in my usual manner the exact spot where the object was supposed to be hidden, but, greatly to my chagrin and disappointment, I could not find it. For fully twenty minutes I fumbled round unavailingly. Then the man who was "guiding" me approached, and after himself fumbling about for awhile, he exclaimed: "Mr. Carlton, I am awfully sorry, but it's gone."

CROWD IN BRADFORD WATCHING CARLTON'S SEARCH FOR THE HIDDEN "TELEGRAPH" BADGE

CROWD AT OAKLAND (CALIFORNIA) WATCHING CARLTON'S SEARCH FOR HIDDEN TREASURE

This proved to be the fact. Somebody had discovered the object, and removed it for safe keeping, and it was returned to the *Guardian* office the next day. On this occasion I may be said in a sense to have failed, in that I did not find the article. But as the reason I did not find it was because it wasn't there, my reputation naturally did not suffer on that account. In fact it was rather enhanced, for everybody recognised that I had correctly located the place where by rights it ought to have been.

Another time, at Leeds, the crowd was so great that the whole tramcar service of the city was threatened with disorganisation, and the police stepped in and stopped the performance. This was one of my most trying experiences, for the crowd was a somewhat rough one, and some of the people were in a rather ugly mood, believing the whole affair to have been a put-up job. However, I made them a speech, and soon got them in good humour.

One of my roughest experiences was at Bradford, where the object of my quest was a silver medallion, or badge, the property of the chairman of the Bradford Cinderella Club. The crowds were immense, and to add to my difficulties the medallion had been "hidden" by being actually buried in the ground on a waste plot of land now occupied by the Alhambra

Theatre there. However, after groping among the loose rubble and debris for a while I found it all right. "Then"—to quote the local report—"a cheer went up from several thousand throats as Carlton stood aloft with the silver badge in his hand. For our part we have to congratulate Carlton upon the feat, which we can testify was performed in a genuine manner and without any possible chance of collusion."

At Bath there happened a curious incident, referred to in the account of the affair published in the *Bath Chronicle*. The bandage became loose, and slipped down in such a manner as made it impossible for me to see under it; nor was I able, try as I would, to get it back in its proper position by working my frontal muscles in the ordinary way. In this dilemma I was compelled to resort to a pretty little piece of play-acting. I pretended to blunder into a wall, bumping my head somewhat severely, and incidentally loosening the bandage—of course, on purpose—so that it slipped completely down. This necessitated my being rebandaged, and this time, you may be sure, I took good care to have it tight enough.

In conclusion I should like to emphasise the fact that no one, so far as I know, had any inkling at any time of the manner in which I succeeded in accomplishing what, on the face of it and until the mystery is explained, strikes the vast majority of people as being a wholly inexplicable feat. Literally thousands of letters have appeared in the Press professing to elucidate the way in which I worked it, but in no single instance were the writers anywhere near the correct solution.

Nevertheless, some of the suggestions put forward were exceedingly ingenious, and such as I should certainly never have thought of on my own account. At Oakland, for instance, where buglers were employed (without consulting me) to advertise the show, quite a number of people advanced the theory that I was guided to the left or right, forward or backward, as the case might be, by the notes they emitted from time to time in the course of my progress through the streets.

Another theory that found favour with quite a number of people in various parts of the world was that I was connected with my "guide" by means of "invisible" wires; although how wires were to be made invisible nobody took the trouble to explain.

After one of my performances in Egypt—where, by the way, I nearly got knifed through pretending to blunder into and embrace an Arab woman in the course of my "blindfold" peregrinations—a grave and dignified old Sheikh explained to the public, with much volubility, that the feat was really a quite childishly simple one. Walking in front of me, he opined, was a confederate strongly scented with a special perfume, and I simply "followed the scent," much as if I were some species of two-legged hound.

CHAPTER XVI
TELEPATHIC AND MESMERIC SPOOFS

Real spiritualism and sham mesmerism—Spoof séances—I ring one off on my landlady—The self-playing piano—The spirit that walked upside-down—Some simple explanations—Manufacturing a telepathist to order—Thought-reading extraordinary—The colour test—Telepathy by wire—A brief dream of wealth—A sleepy wife and a hidden match-box—The head-head who was spoofed—A disconcerting reception—Story of Houdini, the "Handcuff King"—More telepathy—Over the telephone this time—A puzzling link—And the explanation.

ONE of the most famous conjurors who ever lived publicly expressed his disbelief in spiritualism. He held the view that it is all a fake, got up by clever swindlers in order to bamboozle credulous fools.

With all due respect to the late Mr. Maskelyne's undoubtedly sincere views I disagree with them. That there is a lot of spoof spiritualism knocking about nobody can deny. In fact I will go further and assert that in the vast majority of instances the ordinary séance, for which one pays one's guinea or two for the privilege of being present, is neither more nor less than a fake and a swindle of the most pronounced kind.

But, admitting all this, the fact remains that there are phenomena in connection with spiritualism that cannot be explained away by any known rule of logic or reasoning. At least, such is my opinion. Why, I have heard a little Cockney wench of sixteen, who to my certain knowledge has never been any nearer to South Africa than the Battersea Park Road, hold forth in pure Zulu dialect while in a state of trance at a private séance in a house near Clapham Junction. And when she came to, she didn't know a word of what she had been saying. She spoke Zulu with the proper native accent, too, and not as an ordinary Englishman or Englishwoman does when trying to imitate their guttural clicks and clucks. I know. I've been there.

All the same, I would not advise any of my readers to "go in" for spiritualism. That way madness lies. I once tried it myself, but had to give it up. Better stick to the things of this world, and leave those pertaining to the spirit world severely alone.

Telepathy stands on an altogether different footing. I don't believe in it one little bit. As I have already had occasion to remark, so-called thought-reading is merely trickery, clever trickery, no doubt, but none the less trickery. To the ordinary man the feats performed by the Zancigs and others seem absolutely inexplicable. But then so, too, do some of my card tricks.

Reverting to the subject of spiritualism! I once engineered a spoof séance all on my own. Not in order to make money; but just for a lark.

I was performing at Hastings, and as it happened the landlady of the house where I was staying was a firm believer. Of course, I was not long in finding this out; whereupon I pretended that I also was one of the elect, and just before the termination of my engagement there I suggested that she should invite a few friends to a private séance. To this she assented, and at my suggestion it was held in my sitting-room, where was the usual collection of plants in pots, gimcrack pictures, and worthless ornaments, together with an ancient and asthmatic piano such as is to be found in most "pro.'s'" lodging-houses.

That evening after my performance at the theatre, and shortly before the witching hour of midnight, the séance began. The landlady asked us all to attune our minds to receive humbly and without scepticism the spirit manifestations which she hoped and trusted were about to be vouchsafed to us. The lights were turned down, and a young lady with a greenery-yallery complexion and straight black hair sang very soft and low "Lead, kindly Light," with mandoline accompaniment.

When she had finished, the landlady invited us to sit round the table and place our hands upon it. This we did. Pretty soon the table began to wobble about and rotate.

"Wonderful!" ejaculated everybody in a series of hoarse whispers.

"Not at all," I replied. Then, in low solemn tones, I called upon the spirit present to manifest itself in regard to an aspidistra plant that stood in the far corner of the room.

No sooner were the words out of my mouth than the leaves of the plant were violently agitated, the rustling noise being plainly audible to everybody.

"Wonderful!" cried everybody once more. "The spirits are indeed with us to-night."

"They are indeed," I replied, "and we'll make the most of 'em."

Then in lower tones: "Spirit, if it be thy will, let us have a manifestation in regard to that vase on the mantelshelf."

Instantly, and without more ado, the vase jumped up of its own accord and came crashing to the floor.

At this something like consternation reigned. By the dim light of the single turned-down gas-jet I could see that the eyes of my neighbours on the right and left were fixed on me in awe, and I could feel their hands tremble as they sought mine on the table.

"The piano!" I cried in a stage whisper, pretending to get wildly excited, and jumping to my feet. "The piano! I'm going to ask the spirits to take it out at the window, and bring it in at the door."

But this was too much for even my landlady. "Mr. Carlton," she exclaimed, "please don't joke. The spirits are all about us. Never before have I seen such manifestations."

"All right!" I replied, "If you think they'd be offended at my asking them to move the piano, why I won't ask them. But I'll tell you what we will do. We'll ask 'em to give us a tune on it."

"No! No!" objected the landlady. "Impossible! Such a thing is unheard of. The spirits can't do it."

"Well, let's try anyway," I said. "Come along!" And suiting the action to the word I got up and went over to the piano, which I locked, and put the key in my pocket.

Then we all put our hands on the closed cover of the instrument and waited. For a while nothing happened. Then suddenly from one of the lower notes there came a deep resonant "boom," followed by another, and another.

There could be no mistaking whence the sound came. Somebody was playing on the closed and locked piano.

At that moment there was a loud shriek, followed by a heavy thud on the floor. One of the women, completely overwrought, had screamed and fainted. That was the end of the séance. Somebody turned up the lights. The girl who had swooned—she was the same who had played the mandoline—was brought to with water and smelling-salts, and the awe-stricken guests took their departure.

Now for the explanation. Before summoning the landlady and her friends to the séance, I had gone to the trouble of fixing threads leading from where I was sitting to the aspidistra plant and the vase, and I had also affixed similar threads, half a dozen of them, to the hammers of the notes of the piano underneath the keyboard, allowing them to dangle down in such a way that I could easily reach them by stretching out my hand.

Simple, isn't it! Yet it spoofed completely everybody there that night; and to this day, I suppose, they believe that they witnessed some very wonderful and perfectly genuine spirit manifestations.

The following morning early I made up my face delicately with hollow eyes, and wan cheeks, so as to suggest a sleepless night, and when the landlady came in with my morning cup of tea I remarked in awestricken tones that I believed her house was haunted by the spirits. "Why," I said, "they've been walking about in the night upside-down on the ceiling above my head."

Instinctively the good lady turned her eyes up to the ceiling. Then she let out a yell, dropped the tray she was holding with a crash, and fell gasping and shaking into a near-by arm-chair.

And small wonder! For there on the white plaster of the ceiling, plainly visible, were the marks of naked feet, circling the room and leading out at the door.

And now for another simple explanation. The next bedroom was occupied by a friend of mine, an acrobat. After the household had gone to bed on the previous night, he had stolen into my room, slightly blackened the soles of his bare feet with soot from the chimney, and then, balancing himself upside-down with his hands on my shoulders, he had made the prints on the ceiling which so puzzled and alarmed the landlady.

So simple! And yet she never guessed.

I once persuaded a fat chap who used to work for my show that he was a telepathist. The beginning of it was this way. I used to perform feats of the so-called thought-reading variety that were as genuine as such feats ever are. The fat chap used to try to imitate them. There was, for instance, the trick of walking blindfold into a room, and finding an article that had previously been hidden.

One day when there were a lot of us together in my dressing-room at the Hippodrome, Sheffield, I turned the conversation on to my assistant's wonderful telepathic gifts, flattering him to the top of his bent. Previously, I had put the others up to it, and they one and all clamoured for an exhibition of his powers.

Fatty was nothing loth, and at my instigation he was taken from the room and blindfolded. An article was supposed to have been previously hidden somewhere within the room by one of the crowd, and I was deputed to walk behind him and "will" him the way he was to go in order to find it.

"You must," I told him, "stand perfectly upright with your heels and toes close together, and presently you will feel my will power urging you forward in the direction you ought to go. Don't resist the influence. Let yourself go. And you will find that, if my will power is sufficiently strong, it will lead you to where the hidden article is."

Now it is a fact, as the reader can easily prove for himself, that if a man stands upright, blindfolded, or even with his eyes tightly shut, and with his heels and toes close together, his body will automatically sway forward; and this is precisely what happened to Fatty.

"I can feel the influence pushing me on," he exclaimed excitedly, and started groping about the room. In a minute or two one of the men present quietly placed a cigarette-case on the table in front of his outstretched hand, and of course he grabbed it.

"Wonderful!" they shouted. "He's found it."

Fatty pulled the bandage from his eyes, and stood triumphant, his big, round, simple face beaming with pleasure and pride.

"I didn't think I could do it," he cried. "I didn't think it was in me. I'm a marvel."

But I pretended to be in doubt.

"Some of you chaps are having a lark with us," I said.

"No! No, we're not. It's all fair and aboveboard; isn't it, Fatty?" they cried.

And Fatty, of course, assured me on his word of honour as a man and a gentleman that he did not even know what was the article he had to find. Which was quite true. And neither did we in the beginning.

"Well," I replied, as if still unconvinced, "I'll mark a penny myself, and we'll see if you can find that."

Again Fatty was led from the room, blindfolded, and the same rigmarole gone through, the penny being slipped right under his hand as he groped along the mantelpiece.

"My God!" he cried excitedly. "I'm a marvel. I've found it."

I pretended to be surprised, but still somewhat incredulous.

"Look here," I said, picking up a piece of paper and an envelope from my dressing-table, "we will have one more test. I am going to write the name of a colour on this sheet of paper, seal it up in the envelope, and place it inside my coat-pocket. Then you must leave your mind a blank, and I will try and will you to tell me the colour I have written down."

This test also succeeded. He named a colour, and it proved to be the one written on the paper inside the envelope I took from my pocket. As a matter of fact I had a dozen or so envelopes in rotation in my pocket, each with a different colour-name inside, so that was impossible that the test should have failed. But this, of course, Fatty did not know.

I made out to be really and truly surprised now. So did all the others. Nevertheless, I suggested one more final test, a drastic one that would place the matter beyond doubt for evermore; or, at least, so I told him.

I knew that he had a brother who was manager of a well-known London music-hall, so when I asked him suddenly if he knew well anybody in Town whom he could send a wire with the probability of being able to get an immediate reply, I was not at all surprised when he answered:

"Yes. There's my brother, who manages the Holborn Empire."

"Right!" I exclaimed. "He'll do." And taking a pack of cards from my pocket, I spread them out face downward on the table.

"Now," I said, "I want you to select one card at haphazard from this pack, and when you have examined it you are to send a reply-paid telegram to your brother asking him what card you are thinking of. You must concentrate your thoughts on your brother, and try and tell him mentally which is the card you hold in your hand. Meanwhile, in order to avoid any chance of collusion, no one is to leave the dressing-room until the answer comes back."

"I'll try," said Fatty haltingly, as if doubtful of the result. "I'll try my best."

He took up a card. It was the ace of spades. Then he wrote out a telegram as follows: "Dear brother. What card am I thinking of? Please wire immediately."

The telegram was given to a messenger to send off. Then we lit cigars, poured out whiskies-and-sodas, and sat down to wait—and chat. Fatty sat by himself in a corner, his head between his hands, intent on conveying a telepathic message to his brother two hundred miles away in London.

Presently the messenger entered with the reply wire. Fatty seized it, tore it open.

"My God!" he cried, reading it aloud. "It says 'the ace of spades.' *Now*, gentlemen, will you believe in me?"

"We will," we said solemnly. "That settles it."

For the benefit of the reader I may explain that the pack of cards I took from my pocket and spread out face downwards on the table was a trick pack, of the kind used by conjurors. Every one of the fifty-two cards comprising it was an ace of spades.

Also Fatty's brother in London, who was of course well known to me, had previously been instructed by me to reply "ace of spades" in case he received a wire from anybody inquiring, "What card am I thinking of?" In fact I have quite a number of people all over England who have received similar instructions, for I frequently work this particular wheeze, but in a slightly different form, at conjuring entertainments at private houses.

I lost sight of Fatty soon after the occurrence narrated above, but I have been given to understand that he believes to this day that he became for a brief while, and under my influence, a genuine, first-class telepathist. Nor did the fact that all his further experiments in the same direction resulted in complete failure shake his confidence in the least. He attributed it to the fact that the people he selected to influence him did not possess a sufficiency of will power.

Another man who used to work for me, and whom we christened Talking Tommy, holds a similar opinion. We worked the spoof on him, too, and he went home, after having a few drinks at about three o'clock in the morning, and tried the experiment on his wife, who was in bed and asleep.

Waking her up, he said: "Get out of bed, dear; I'm a telepathist. I want you to hide this matchbox downstairs somewhere. Then I'll blindfold myself, and you shall will me to find it."

"But I don't want to will; I want to go to sleep," expostulated the poor lady.

"Just this once, darling," pleaded Tommy. "There's a fortune awaiting us if we succeed. I can see us working it on the Halls together at one hundred pounds a week. It all depends on whether or no you possess sufficient will power. Hide the box, then concentrate your whole attention on guiding me mentally to the place where you have hidden it."

Thus adjured, the sleepy lady arose, and for the next half-hour she was wandering round the house in her bare feet, upstairs and downstairs, trying to will her blindfold husband to where the matchbox was. Of course she failed. Tommy fell over the coal-box, knocked two of his choice vases off the mantelpiece, but found no match-box. Then, in the end, he got wild, and told her it was all her fault, she hadn't got as much will power as a she tabby cat.

Tommy was one of the most simple-minded men I ever came across. He had a lawn at home. It was almost as big as an ordinary billiard table, but Tommy was awfully proud of it. One year, however, the grass grew patchy. Tommy was quite upset about it, and used to bewail his ill luck to all and sundry.

"Oh," said one of the dressers, "if that's all, I can easily put things right for you"; and he went and mixed some permanganate of potash in a bottle, and told Tommy to take it home, dilute it with plenty of water, and sprinkle his lawn with the mixture at night before going to bed. "It's the most wonderful fertiliser ever known," concluded this champion liar, "and in the morning you'll find your lawn a lovely velvety green all over."

Tommy did as he was bid. But the lawn wasn't green in the morning. It was a dull brick-red colour, and looked as if it had been devastated by a first-class prairie fire.

Another time Tommy came to me while I was showing at the Oxford, and asked me to pass two or three of his friends in. At first I was rather taken aback, for, of course, it is entirely against the etiquette of the profession for a performer to ask for free admission for even his most intimate friends or relations. And rightly so! We get paid our salaries, and we have no earthly right to try to sponge on managers for seats.

Tommy, however, I could see, had no idea of all this. To him his request appeared in the light of a quite natural one. And this gave me an idea.

I told him to get some cards printed with his name and address, and underneath the words: "Super and Comedian to 'Carlton!'"

"These cards," I said quite solemnly, "will pass you and your friends into the best seats in any Hall in London. All you will have to do is to ask for the manager and hand him one, stating how many seats you require."

Tommy thought this an excellent idea, and went off there and then and got his cards printed.

"Where shall I go first?" he asked me later on in the day.

"Doesn't matter!" I replied off-handedly. "Why not try the Oxford? Come to-morrow night, and bring half a dozen pals with you."

"Right," replied Tommy, beaming with pleasurable anticipation, "I will."

And he did.

Meanwhile I had seen Mr. Blythe Pratt, the Manager, and told him about the joke; with the result that when Tommy appeared, with six rather nondescript-looking friends, he was received with every courtesy, and given a private box for the evening.

Of course he was delighted. Vistas of unlimited free entertainments loomed before his excited imagination.

"Where shall I go to-morrow night?" he asked.

"Oh," I said. "Why not try the T——," mentioning a Hall where there was, I knew, an unusually grumpy and quick-tempered manager.

He went. What exactly transpired there I never heard. But I can imagine the scene.

Tommy was quite upset about it.

"Oh," there must have been some mistake, I told him. "Try the Palace to-night."

And he actually did try it. But that finished it. The reception he met with there finally cured him of all further desire in the direction of cadging for free seats.

By the way, here is a funny story that occurs to me as I write.

Although it is not generally known to the public, it is, nevertheless, a fact that Houdini, the world-famous "Handcuff King," and Hardeen, his rival in the business, are brothers.

They are, however, on the best of terms with one another personally, being rivals only professionally. Once it happened that Houdini had a week's engagement at Leeds at the same time that Hardeen was appearing at Bradford.

Houdini arrived in the former town very late at night, and desiring to see his brother on an urgent matter of business he went over to Bradford, arriving there about two o'clock in the morning, when, of course, everybody had gone to bed.

However, Houdini made the best of his way to where his brother lodged, and after he had been knocking and hammering at the door for about twenty minutes, "loud enough," as he expressed it, "to wake the dead," the landlord put his head out of the window.

"Who are you? What do you want?" he asked rather irately.

"I'm Houdini, the handcuff king, and I want to see my brother, Mr. Hardeen, on important business," was the reply. "Come down and open the door."

The landlord grunted. Then—"Oh, you're Houdini, are you? That there chap as can open any lock?"

"Yes! Yes! That's me!" cried the Handcuff King impatiently.

"Well then," quoth the landlord, "if that be so, why don't 'ee open t' lock o' front door, an' walk right in? What dost want to knock me up for? I'm going back to bed."

And go back to bed he did, leaving poor Houdini cooling his heels on the doorstep, until such time as he chose to take his departure and return to Leeds.

Here is a little telepathic spoof that anyone can accomplish who has a telephone in their house, or if not they can make use of the telegraph service.

Say you have a friend, or friends, dining with you. You lead the conversation round gradually to the subject of telepathy, mentioning incidentally that you yourself possess certain gifts in that direction.

Probably your statement will be received with polite incredulity; whereupon, pretending to get huffed, you take a pack of cards, spread them out on the table face uppermost, and invite any one of your guests to select any card he pleases.

He picks out, we will say, the three of hearts. Then you say to him: "Now I have a friend living at Hampstead (or wherever the place may be) who is telepathically *en rapport* with me. If you will keep perfectly still for a minute or so, I will try and place myself in communication with him, and let him know by means of telepathy which card you have chosen."

You then bury your head in your arms on the table, pretending to be thinking deeply for a short while; then presently you look up with an air of relief, heave a deep sigh of satisfaction, ejaculate "Sakabona! I've got him!" or some similar phrase, and tell your friend to go to your telephone, and ring up a certain number, which you give him.

You then tell him to ask for "Charlie," which, you explain, is your friend's name, and say to him, "What card have I chosen?"

Wonderingly, and not a little sceptical, your friend does as he is bid. But his scepticism vanishes when the correct answer comes back over the 'phone.

"What card have I chosen?" he asks. And almost instantly the answer comes back: "The three of hearts."

Now for the explanation of this very puzzling trick; puzzling, that is to say, to the uninitiated.

Like most other tricks of the kind, it is very simple, once you know how it is done.

There is, of course, no telepathy about it. The real fact of the matter is that the "spoof" is worked by means of a code previously arranged between yourself and your friend at the other end of the wire. On the wall near his telephone-box is a card made out as follows:—

	HEARTS	DIAMONDS	CLUBS	SPADES
1.	Jim	Ronald	Philip	Ted
2.	Bill	Archie	Claude	Adam
3.	Charlie	Reggie	Ernest	Matthew
4.	Jack	Gus	Fred	Doc
5.	Harry	Victor	Geoffrey	David
6.	Brown	Robin	Jesse	Andrew
7.	Smith	Norman	Jacob	Isaac
8.	Robinson	Gerald	Joe	Sam
9.	Eric	Frank	Bert	Mike
10.	Tom	Arthur	John	Mac
Jack	George	Oliver	Hal	Eli
Queen	Stevens	Harold	Ben	Leonard
King	Bert	Stanley	Dick	Hubert

Glancing at this immediately on receipt of the message, he sees that "Charlie," the name he is addressed by, stands for the three of hearts, and he 'phones back accordingly. Had your friend chosen the ten of spades, you would have instructed him to ask for "Mac," and so on throughout the whole pack of fifty-two cards.

CHAPTER XVII
SHARPS AND FLATS

Spoofing a mesmerist—The spoofer spoofed—Spoof card tricks—Racecourse sharps—The "dud" diamond wheeze—I am beautifully "had"—Three-card trick sharps—A Newcastle adventure—Bunny's spoof—Spoofing a "new chum"—The performing elephant and the dude—Wheezes and gags.

I WAS once supposed to have been mesmerised myself. It happened at Newcastle. I was a guest at an hotel there where a professional mesmerist also chanced to be staying.

One day, in the course of conversation, I expressed incredulity regarding his alleged power. "You can't mesmerise me," I said.

"Well," he retorted, "I don't mind trying. But you must promise not to try and resist me. You must remain passive."

"All right," I said, "I will. Go ahead with the show."

He made several passes, during which I kept smiling at him, and shaking my head, as much as to say it was no good.

Then all of a sudden I threw myself into a state of rigidity, a trick I had learnt and practised years previously, and pretended to go off into a cataleptic trance.

The mesmerist was hugely elated. The others present, most of whom knew me, were considerably surprised. Not one of them but believed that he was witnessing a genuine hypnotic phenomenon.

After a while the mesmerist made several passes designed to bring me to. But herein he failed. Again and again he tried. It was no good. The only movement I made was to bite my lip so that it bled, and roll up my eyes horribly, leaving only the whites visible.

The mesmerist began to get badly frightened, and after one or two more vain attempts he ran out of the house to, as he said, fetch a doctor. Meanwhile the others carried me, still rigid, upstairs to bed.

A friend volunteered to stay and watch me, and after a while I came to of my own accord.

"Thank God!" exclaimed my friend, and called out for the others to come up and have a look at me.

"Fine bit of play-acting, wasn't it?" I said.

But the others would not believe me. They were quite sure in their own minds that I really had been mesmerised, and only when I repeated to them practically the whole of the conversation that had passed between them while I was in my supposed trance, did they realise how completely they had been spoofed.

As for the mesmerist, he never came back to the hotel. Instead of going for a doctor, he had made a bee-line for the railway station, and skipped the town. Evidently he thought it was all up with me.

Here is a spoof bet which may be new to my readers. You select a man of obviously bigger physique than yourself, and offer to wager him, say, a sovereign, that you measure the bigger round the chest. If he takes you on, as he probably will, you hand him a tape measure and say, "So as to be perfectly fair, you measure me, and I'll measure you." When the test is finished he will say that he has won. "Oh, no," you reply, "I've won. You are the bigger man of the two, and it was I who measured you." I spoofed one of the "fliest" men in England with this trick on one occasion.

Another time I was spoofed myself at the Empire, Liverpool, where the Macnaughtons took my carefully prepared pack of cards and stuck them together with glue, so that they formed a more or less solid block. The result, when I started to attempt to perform my tricks with them, can be more easily imagined than described.

By the way, speaking of card tricks, the majority of these, though infinitely puzzling to the observer, are usually susceptible of a quite simple explanation. Take, for example, that known as "The Two Queens," and which is not infrequently worked on racecourses with a view to fleecing the public.

The way it is done is as follows: The performer takes the two Queens of either colour, black or red, and holds them up so that the audience can see them. Cutting the remainder of the pack into two lots he places one of the Queens upon the top half. At this point the performer's hat falls off, or his attention is apparently distracted by some cause, and he turns away from the cards, still holding the other Queen. Someone in the company meanwhile quickly places a few cards from the bottom half of the pack upon the Queen, which had been placed upon the top half. When the performer resumes he announces that he will place the second Queen upon the first, and accordingly places it upon the cards. He now asserts that the two Queens are together, and offers to bet that he will produce them in that order. The audience, thinking otherwise, make various bets, and then the performer dealing the cards from the bottom of the pack produces the two Queens one after the other. This is accomplished by means of a confederate. When the performer has shuffled and cut, he notes the top card when the pack is cut. One of the Queens is placed on this card. When the hat falls off the confederate places the other cards as described, and the Queens are really separated. In dealing from the bottom the performer watches carefully until he arrives at the card which he had previously noted when the cut was made. When this is dealt he knows that the next card will be one of the Queens. So, instead of dealing this he pulls it back underneath the pack with the fingers of the left hand, and continues dealing. He produces the other Queen, and it is then a simple matter to deal the first Queen which he had pulled back. A shrewd spectator would notice that the Queens appear in reverse order to that in which they were placed in the pack, but audiences are so amazed that they don't notice a little thing like that.

It is not by means of card tricks alone, however, that the unwary are cheated on racecourses, and elsewhere. I could fill a good-sized volume if I liked with accounts of the wiles of some of the "fly" gentry frequenting these places. One of them once "had" me beautifully, though, I need hardly say, not at cards. It concerned a diamond ring.

The man, a well-known Birmingham racecourse frequenter, brought it to me while I was playing there, and asked me to buy it, saying that he had won it at cards. This story, I reflected, might or might not be true. Anyway, it was nothing to do with me. I am a good judge of diamonds, and I examined this one very carefully.

I saw at once that it was a splendid blue-white stone, and worth certainly not less than £80. The man asked me £40 for it. I offered him £20, which sum, after some hesitation, he agreed to take. "Hand over the money," he said, "and the ring is yours."

This conversation took place in one of the hotel bars in the centre of the city, and I had not so much money on me. I accordingly told him to bring the ring round that night to the theatre where I was playing, and I would let him have the money; which he did. The stone was to all appearance perfect, blazing with fire, and I put it in my waistcoat pocket, thinking what a nice surprise it would be for my wife.

So it was a surprise, but not in the way I intended. For next morning all the blaze and beauty had gone out of the stone. It looked like a piece of ordinary glass. I rushed round to a jeweller's with it. "You've been had," he explained. "The stone is not a diamond at all, but a jargoon, a gem whose lustre, especially if it is well polished, exactly resembles that of the diamond. Only it is extremely evanescent." I may say that the stone I first examined was a genuine diamond, and worth fully four times what I agreed to pay. It was afterwards that the jargoon was substituted for it, and in the hurry of dressing I did not notice the difference.

Here is a tricky way of tossing for drinks and winning. It cannot be described as cheating, being rather in the nature of forced suggestion. You say to a man, "Come on, I'll toss you for drinks round," at the same time pulling out a coin and placing it flat on the counter, or elsewhere, with the tail uppermost, and, of course, covered so that he cannot see it. "Come on," you say, speaking very rapidly, yet distinctly. "Cry to me. Which is it? Heads or tails."

In nine cases out of ten the man will cry heads, but it must be done quickly, without giving him time to think; and you want to lay a little emphasis, but not too much, on the word "heads." Anybody can try this for themselves, and they will find that what I say is true.

Another coin-tossing trick! Where you are asked to "cry to pieces," a favourite trick with men who are not too particular is to say, with affected carelessness: "Oh, I'll have the same as the top one." In this way, if the first coin is a head, he starts off with one to the good, and the man who puts down the coins is, of course, handicapped to that extent.

Speaking of racecourse sharps, I once was tackled by a gang of three-card men under rather peculiar circumstances. I was working at the Empire, Newcastle, where I topped the bill as the World's Premier Card Manipulator. With me were the

Poluski Brothers, and Sam Poluski, who is well known in the profession as a sportsman, introduced me to a local tout, called Bunny, who used to back horses for him, and incidentally, if he heard of a "good thing," he would tell Sam about it, and Sam would tip him for his trouble if the horse won. If it didn't win, then Bunny got his commission from the bookie with whom he placed the bet, so that he was all right either way.

Bunny was perfectly straight himself, but he, of course, knew all "the boys." Well, on the Friday of the week I was there, there was what they call up there "a flapper meeting"; that is to say, a small race meeting got up under National Hunt rules among the farmers and others. I went there alone, but took Bunny with me as a sort of bodyguard, and to show me the ropes.

The place where the meeting was to be held was about half an hour's run from Newcastle by train, and I arranged for Bunny to meet me at the Central Station. I got there first, and I must say that I had seldom seen a tougher-looking crowd assembled anywhere. By and by Bunny turned up, and I took two first-class tickets, for I didn't like the look of the mob on the platform, and I thought that by this means, and if we waited until the train was just about to start, we might manage to get a compartment to ourselves. If we could do this, I reflected, we were all right, for the train, a special race one, did not stop until we got to the course.

I was at this time a youngish lad, with curly hair, and looked, I suppose, a typical "pie-can," which is the bookies' way of characterising a "mug." The train was a bit late at starting, and while we were waiting I distinctly saw Bunny "give the office" to a gang of "the boys."

"Here, Bunny," I said, taking him to one side. "No larks. What's the game?"

"All right, Carlton, old man," he replied. "Don't get alarmed. I'm only going to have a lark with some of these chaps."

I wasn't at all reassured at this, for the gang didn't look to me at all the kind it was in the least advisable to play larks on. However, there was not time to say anything further, for at that moment the whistle blew, and Bunny jumped into an empty first-class compartment and I after him, so too did five or six of the boys; the same Bunny had given the tip to. Just as the train was starting a detective poked his head in the window, and cried warningly, "Beware of card-sharpers." I quickly slipped my diamond pin out of my tie, and stuck it in the back of my waistcoat. Then I buttoned up my coat over my inside pocket, where the bulk of my money was, and waited.

I hadn't long to wait. Within a minute or two the three cards were produced, and the old familiar performance gone through; the men, all apparently strangers to each other, winning and losing alternately. Bunny also took a hand and won. Was he not, in a sense, "one of the boys"? It was, of course, all stage-managed for my benefit.

But I wasn't having any. Or at least I pretended I wasn't. When I did at length yield to their repeated entreaties, I won a sovereign, and declined to bet any more. Thereupon they began to get nasty; so, thinking the thing had gone far enough, I said: "Look here, boys, you took me for a pie-can. Well, I'm not. But I'm a sport. I don't want your money. Here's your quid back, and here's another to get drinks with."

Then, picking up the cards, I remarked quite casually: "Let me show you how we work the three-card trick down where I come from."

So saying I took out three cards, including the Queen of Spades, and throwing them down on their faces, I invited them to pick out the "lady."

One of them selected a card. It was the wrong one. Then another of the gang chose another. It also was not the "lady." Then I myself turned up the remaining card. And that also was not the "lady." There was no Queen there. I had palmed it, and substituted a plain card for it.

The sharpers gazed at me in blank amazement. Bunny, in his corner, rolled in his seat, and screamed with laughter.

Then, when he had recovered his breath, he said: "Don't you know who it is? Why you were all with me last night at the Empire, and saw him on the stage there. It's Carlton, the world's premier card-manipulator."

And he went off into another fit of laughter.

But "the boys" didn't laugh. They had wasted the journey, to say nothing of their fare money. And the language they used to Bunny was quite unprintable.

Of course none of them had recognised me without my stage make-up.

I don't know why it should be so, but it is a fact that we professionals are exceedingly prone to play larks on one another. A new-comer in the profession is especially likely to find himself made a butt of. It is good-natured chaff, and if he takes it in good part—well. If not, why so much the worse for him.

Once, when I was performing at Liverpool, I recall that there was a "new chum" there who was doing some sort of show business in a sketch. He was rather stuck-up and touchy, and he was put through it rather unmercifully in consequence. One night, for instance, he would find his boots had been securely nailed to his dressing-room floor. Another time the sleeves of his coat would be sewn together, and so on.

Well, one night he was waiting in the wings for his cue to go on, and was holding a tall hat in his hand, which he used in his performance. Suddenly this was snatched from him from behind, and jammed on his head.

"There you are," he cried to the manager, without turning round. "These fellows are always playing larks on me before it is my cue to go on. It puts me off my business. I wonder you allow it."

"That's all right from your point of view," replied the manager. "But the culprit in this case is too big for me to tackle. Better have a go at him yourself."

Whereupon the victimised "pro." swung round on his heel in order to take stock of the offender. He found himself face to face with one of Lockhart's elephants. The beast had been trained by its master to do the trick, and seeing the hat held temptingly had taken advantage of the opportunity.

When the dog-muzzling order was previously in force, Dan Lesson, who was one of the best-known practical jokers in the profession, one day fixed a needle to the front of his dog's muzzle, allowing it to project an eighth of an inch. And—well you know how friendly dogs are. Another "pro." fixed a similar needle arrangement to the "push" of his electric bell.

Yet another wheeze of his was to address about fifty envelopes to as many of his friends and acquaintances. These he posted, but omitted to put stamps on. Inside was a card, with these words neatly inscribed on it: "Bet you a penny you paid twopence."

I think that the following incident is about as perfect an example of the "double cross" as it is possible to conceive.

I was playing in a certain town in the Midlands, and amongst the other performers there was a bright, particular "Knut" who was, as he himself expressed it, "dead nuts" on the girls. The rest of us took advantage of this to, as we thought, play a game on him.

One day he received a letter, written in a disguised feminine hand by one of us, which ran as follows: "Dear Mr. Blank,—I have seen your show from the front and I think it's simply ripping. But not more ripping, I am sure, than you are yourself if one could only get to know you. May I have that pleasure? If so, meet me opposite the fountain in the park to-morrow afternoon at three. I will wear a blue navy costume trimmed white, suède gloves, and a red rose in my bodice. Signed: One of your admirers—Bessie."

All the next morning the recipient of this missive strutted about looking awfully pleased with himself, but, of course, said not a word to anyone. Meanwhile we were busy helping a female impersonator, who chanced to be playing at the same hall, to make up as the supposititious Bessie.

Shortly before three he took his place on a seat near the fountain, blue costume, toque, suède gloves, and rose, all complete. We were hidden in the undergrowth at the back, on tiptoe of expectation, ready to enjoy our carefully planned joke.

Presently along comes Mr. Knut, dressed to kill. The female impersonator put on his most engaging smile, and half rose to greet him, when to his and our astonishment and dismay a real girl dressed in exactly the same fashion stepped forward from another direction, and taking his arm, proudly marched off with him.

He had, of course, tumbled to our little joke, and had double-crossed us. Needless to say we felt rather small.

Here is another "girl story." I had in my employ at one time a big, handsome chap who was also, like the knut mentioned above, exceedingly fond of the fair sex. He was a favourite with them, too, so that he practically had a sweetheart in every town we visited.

He used to boast to me of his many conquests, giving me names and full particulars. Of these I made mental notes.

Finally he became engaged to be married to one of his numerous flames, the wedding being fixed for a certain day at noon. Early that morning I sent off prepaid telegrams to the managers of various halls in towns where we had performed, and where I knew that old sweethearts of his resided, asking them to wire the bridegroom as per the formula I sent them. These telegrams I arranged to arrive at the bride's house, addressed of course to the bridegroom, shortly before the ceremony.

I was not there, but I heard afterwards graphic accounts of what happened. It appears that the first wire arrived a few minutes before the happy couple were due to leave for the church. The bridegroom, quite unsuspicious, seized it and opened it, imagining it to be a telegram of congratulation.

But directly he glanced at it, his face fell, and he tried to put it in his pocket. The bride, however, seeing that something was wrong, snatched it from him, and read it herself. Then she gave a scream and fell in a faint.

The telegram, which was from Halifax, read as follows: "You base deceiver. Shall be there to forbid the marriage. Think of our child. Alice."

In vain the poor chap protested. Nobody would believe him; and to make matters worse, a few minutes later another telegram arrived, from Manchester this time. It read: "Are you going to desert me like this after faithfully promising to marry me? Beware! Jennie."

Other similar wires came to hand at intervals, and the bride insisted, on arriving at the church, on showing the whole batch to the clergyman who was to perform the ceremony. He, good man, insisted on postponing the marriage for an hour in order to see if anybody turned up to forbid it. Naturally, however, and of course, nobody did; but in order I suppose to make assurance doubly sure, when he came to the part where any person desirous of forbidding the ceremony is invited to come forward, he repeated the words slowly three times before finally uniting the couple.

I may say that I never really thought that my little joke would have been taken so seriously by all concerned, or I would most certainly never have perpetrated it.

Another practical joke in which a "dud" telegram played a part rather misfired towards the end. The affair happened at Brighton, where, as it chanced, a famous theatrical star (whom I will call Estelle), a well-known mimic (who shall be Smith), and myself were performing.

Each of us was putting up at a different hotel, Estelle (I think) at the Grand, and Smith at the Metropole, where he had engaged rooms for himself and wife, who was devoted to him, and who was also very, very jealous of him.

Knowing this, I got my assistant, a man named McMillan, to disguise his handwriting, and dispatch to Smith a fake telegram as if from Estelle, couched in imitation French, and asking him (Smith) to come round and see her at her hotel that evening. The wire, I may add, ran something like this: "Voulez vous mi sheri sus soir? respondez tuts weet.—Estelle."

I got McMillan to send the wire off from the Brighton Post Office early in the morning, and it was delivered to Smith, as I had foreseen, while the couple were in bed.

Smith read it, and tried to smuggle it on one side, but his wife snatched it away and read it also. Then, of course, the fat was in the fire. The good lady was out of bed in an instant, and throwing on some clothes, rushed round to Estelle's hotel.

"You try to steal my husband!" she screamed indignantly to the astonished and but half-awake actress. "You wicked woman!"

In vain did poor Estelle protest, and that with almost equal indignation. "I no want your husband. Your husband—pouf! I can have kings! Kings, I tell you!"

"A king!" corrected Mrs. Smith, with emphasis.

"Well, then, a king," agreed Estelle. "And he is very good to me. Everyone knows that. What I want with your husband?"

There was a lot more talk, and in the end Mrs. Smith, still unconvinced, went back to her hotel, packed up her things, and took the first train back to London.

Soon afterwards Smith came to me and told me all about it, asking my advice.

"Somebody's been having a game with you," I said. "Let's go round to the Post Office, and try and get a look at the original of the telegram."

We went, and after some demur the postmaster allowed us to see the telegraph form. Smith scanned it carefully, but McMillan had well carried out my instructions as to disguising his handwriting, and he could make nothing of it.

Then, in an evil moment, it occurred to him to turn the form over, and there at the back, in the space provided for the name and address of the sender, he read, "Carlton, Hippodrome, Brighton." My dresser, instead of putting the name and address of the actress, had, in a moment of temporary forgetfulness, inserted my own.

Smith, I will say, took the matter in good part; but I had a rough time explaining matters to his wife.

A joke I once saw played by one friend on another struck me as being amazingly funny. One was clean-shaven, the other had a long thick beard, into which his friend stuck some half-dozen prawns, without, of course, his being aware of it. It did look funny. Try it yourself. But don't try it on a man who is bigger than you, or possibly awkward results may ensue.

The late Dan Lesson, as I have already remarked, was a rare hand at these sort of practical jokes, and speaking of prawns somehow naturally reminds me of kippers. On one occasion Dan was dissatisfied at the way the orchestra played his music, so he got a none too fresh kipper and tacked it inside the bass viol. In a few days that orchestra was the sickest orchestra in England. The smell was something awful. It was hot weather, and the theatre was a bit close anyhow. They pulled up the boards. They even tore up the drains. But they didn't succeed in locating where the smell came from. For all I know the mummified remains of that kipper, now of course no longer smellable, is in that viol yet.

The trick, I may add, is an old one with music-hall artistes who want to get even with a bad landlady, the kipper in this case being nailed under the leaf of the table near the centre. I knew of one case where the local sanitary inspector was actually called in. He had all the drains up, and then failed to find out whence the overpowering odour emanated from.

Another similar "stunt" is to put a pinch of gunpowder in a bloater, and hand her the doctored fish with strict instructions that it is to be grilled, not fried.

Many funny stories could be told by performers of their experiences with their landladies. Of course, there are good and bad of every kind, good cooks and bad cooks, honest women and dishonest women.

My Christmas dinner in Edinburgh where I was performing in pantomime some years ago I am not likely to forget. My mother sent me a Christmas pudding, and she prided herself on her skill in making them. I bought a fine turkey, and invited all my pals round to my special Christmas dinner. Of course in Scotland they do not recognise Christmas Day, and all the theatres and music-halls are open, New Year's Day being the big holiday there. However, to get back to the Christmas dinner! I had previously told all my pals how nice my mother made Christmas puddings, but imagine my surprise when my landlady served up the turkey—she had stuffed it with the pudding!

On another occasion when I was performing at the Theatre Royal, Dublin, my wife asked me what I would like for supper, and I answered, "sausages, mashed potatoes and onions," telling her at the same time to be sure to ask the landlady if she knew how to cook them. She replied, "Av coorse," adding that she had cooked them hundreds of times before. When I got them, however, they were served up like Irish stew. She had put the beautiful Cambridge sausages, the onions, and potatoes in the pot together, and said, on being remonstrated with: "Sure, that's the way we cook them in Oireland." This incident was capped later on at Cork where I fancied a shoulder of mutton. The landlady fried it in a frying-pan.

I remember once a very dishonest landlady in Leeds, the pick of the bunch. I used to go out and buy my own things in those days and always kept my tea, sugar, etc., in a little cupboard in my combined room. Everything used to vanish, but she always had an excuse on the tip of her tongue, so after half a bottle of whisky had gone one night I put some jalap in another whisky bottle. I had to laugh, for she was running up and down stairs all night long complaining of pains in her stomach, but although half the contents of the whisky bottle containing the jalap had gone, she persisted in declaring that she had never touched it. Later on, when my tea had nearly all vanished from the caddy, and she had the audacity to complain to me as to how much tea I drank, I carefully caught a fly and put it alive in the tea caddy. When I got home, and took down the caddy to put my tea in the pot, the fly had gone, but even then she would not admit her dishonesty. So I made up my mind to catch her properly the next time. I carefully counted six potatoes, not letting her know I had counted them, and asked her to boil them for my dinner; but she had me again, she mashed them!

To "have" the average man on "a little bit of string" is quite easy, and some of the simplest "gags" I have found the most effective. For instance, you ask a man if he is good at mental arithmetic. The probability is he says that he is. You then ask him two or three exceedingly easy questions, such as, for example, what is twice seven, how many times does six go into eighteen, and so on. Then you say, "How many penny buns make a dozen," followed, when he has answered it correctly, by the catch question, "How many half-penny ones?" He is practically certain to answer on the spur of the moment, "Twenty-four."

Here is another equally simple catch. You take a piece of white paper, tell a man to place his forefinger on it, and offer to bet him you can draw a ring round it with a piece of lead pencil that he can't lift his finger out of. You then draw a small ring on the paper round the tip of the finger, and ask him to lift his finger out of it. Of course he does so quite easily. You repeat this once or twice; then you draw your ring round the forefinger itself.

Or you get a man to put an easily fitting ring on his little finger, then join the tip of your little finger to the tip of his, and ask him if he thinks it possible for you to remove the ring from his finger without moving yours. He will almost certainly pronounce the feat an impossible one, when all you have to do is to slip the ring off his little finger and on to yours, and the trick is done. The ring is no longer on his finger. It is on yours. And the connection between the two fingers, yours and his, has not been severed for an instant. Then you say: "And now do you think it is possible for me to take the ring off *both* our fingers without severing the connection." He is sure to say, "No." Whereupon you just lift the ring so that it does not touch either, and the trick is done.

These little "spoofs" sound very simple after they are explained, but all the same I have "had" some of the smartest men for "drinks round" with them. Once, too, in Denver, I recollect a professional gambler rather got on my nerves by bragging about the amount of money he carried about with him.

"Look here," I said suddenly, withdrawing my closed fist from my trousers pocket, "I'll bet you five dollars I've got more money in my hand than you have."

"Done!" he cried, and diving his hand into his pocket he withdrew it stuffed full of gold pieces.

Mine held a matter of a few cents. "I've won," he cried, exhibiting his fistful of wealth.

"Not at all," I retorted, "I said in *my* hand. That money is not in my hand; it's in yours. You've lost. Pay up."

Which he did, with the best grace he could.

A few days later he met me, and told me that he had won over five hundred dollars from fellow gamblers by means of the trick. And these men were supposed to be among the "widest" on the American continent.

Here is a trick game with matches which sounds as if nothing could be fairer, and which yet is, in reality, an arrant swindle. The man who wants to practise it starts off by telling his opponent (and dupe) that it is a Chinese gambling game. This tends to throw him off his guard.

He then takes a number of matches and places them under his hat. Next he tells the other fellow to take any number of matches from the box, place them on the table, and lift the hat. "If," he says, "you have put down an even number of matches, and the sum total of both heaps of matches, yours and mine, is even, then you win. If you have put down an odd number, and the sum total of both heaps of matches, yours and mine, is odd, then also you win. Otherwise you lose."

This seems perfectly fair and aboveboard, yet in reality the game is entirely in the hands of the man who puts the matches under the hat. If he puts an even number of matches (say six) there, and the other man puts down an even number (say four) then the total (ten) is an even number, and the other fellow wins. If the other man puts down three he also wins, he having put down an odd number, and the sum total of the two heaps being odd.

In short, if I, who am supposed to be working the trick, choose to put an even number of matches under the hat in the first instance, then the other man must win. But equally, if I put an odd number, he must lose, for in that case if he puts an odd number down the sum total of the two heaps is bound to be even, and if he puts an even number down the sum total is bound to be odd.

Here is a trick which invariably creates a good deal of fun and amusement. I call it "The Vanishing Hair."

At an evening party, or other similar gathering, you pluck a hair—first asking permission, of course!—from the head of one of the ladies present. This, you say, you will cause to vanish mysteriously, and you get someone to tie a knot in it so as to identify it. This, to create an impression.

You thereupon call for a small flat tea-tray, into which you pour a tumbler of clean water, forming a light film upon the surface, on which you place the hair, where it floats serenely, plain for all folk to see.

"Now," you say, "you all see the hair is there. Watch closely while I count three, and at the word 'three' you will see it suddenly and mysteriously disappear."

At this they all crowd round, bending closer down and peering intently at the hair floating on the thin film of water.

"One—two—three!" you say, and bring your hand down flat with force on the hair, when, of course, the water flies up into their faces and they hurriedly back away wiping their eyes. Meanwhile the hair most certainly does disappear. You see to that.

CHAPTER XVIII
FLOTSAM AND JETSAM

Sharing terms—Some tricks of the trade—Spoof telegrams—A Bradford dispute—I engage to fight "The Terror of the Meat Market"—A packed house—I enter a lion's den—And am glad to get out again—A trick the police foiled—Tricks of trick swimmers—I learn a secret or two—Pigeon shooting extraordinary—Satan's Dream—Royalty at a side-show—My mother hears me over the electrophone—At Wentworth Woodhouse—A kind reception—My embarrassing mistake—An angler's paradise.

I THINK I can truthfully lay claim to have been one of the very earliest pioneers in the Music-hall world of the system now generally known as "sharing terms."

This means that the star turn for the week takes a certain fixed percentage of the gross profits, and also takes over the artistes already engaged by the management, adding at his own discretion, and, of course, at his own expense, whatever other turns he thinks fit.

In this case it is, of course, greatly to his interest to draw as full houses as possible during the period of his engagement, and many and varied are the dodges I have resorted to in order to, in my case, bring about this very desirable result.

One of these, of my own invention, I may call the Fake Telegram Wheeze. In the old days, before the war, duplicate telegrams used to be taken at threepence apiece, provided they were not over twelve words, and that the same words were used for the whole batch of telegrams handed in. Taking advantage of this concession, I would sent off perhaps a couple of hundred wires as follows: "See 'Carlton' Empire to-night. He's marvellous. Love. Annie."

These would be dispatched to different addresses selected at random from the local directory of the town where I was showing, and used inevitably to set people talking: which was what I wanted. I am a great believer in the late Mr. Barnum's motto: "Talk about me! Good or bad! But for God's sake talk about me!"

At the Palace Theatre, Bradford, once I was working on sharing terms, the arrangement being that I was to receive fifty-five per cent. of the gross takings and pay the company. When I arrived at the town on the Monday morning I was somewhat surprised to see bills up all over the place announcing a grand boxing tournament for Friday afternoon, at which the finals for the amateur championship of Yorkshire were to be decided.

The manager of the Palace at that time was named Harrison, and, of course, I asked him about the matinée. "Oh," he said, "that's a special event. I shall have a packed house, I hope; certainly not less than £150 in it."

"Good!" I exclaimed. "That'll mean £70 or £80 for me."

Harrison laughed, then winked. "Don't you wish you may get it?" he said.

"Well, of course," I replied. "But why wouldn't I get it?"

"Why it's nothing at all to do with you," he retorted, beginning to look serious.

"Oh, isn't it?" I said. "You just look at our contract. It says that I am to have fifty-five per cent. of the gross takings for this week. If you're going to wedge in a matinée I'm entitled to my fifty-five per cent."

There was a lot more talk, and in the end he said he washed his hands of the whole business, and I'd better telephone through to Mr. Macnaughton, in London, whose tour it was.

This I did, and after a lot of palaver I issued an ultimatum to him in the following terms. "Look here, Mr. Macnaughton," I said, "I agree that a mistake has been made. But the mistake isn't mine. Now you're a sportsman, so am I, and I'll tell you what I'll do. Instead of fifty-five per cent., to which I am legally entitled according to the strict letter of my contract, I'll take twenty per cent., and I will myself fight anybody Harrison likes to put up, as an extra attraction. Then you *will* have a full house, if you like."

"Agreed!" he said. "That's a bargain. Send Harrison to the 'phone."

In five minutes it was fixed up, and the agreement was signed there and then.

But Harrison was a bit nettled over it, and turning to me, he said: "It serves you right. I've got a chap here who's a terror.

They call him the 'Champion of the Meat Market.' He was unlucky enough to get beaten on points in the semi-finals last week. I'm going to put him up against you, and I hope you get a jolly good hiding."

"All right," I said. "I don't care. Put up whom you like. For forty pounds or so I'll take the hiding, if it comes off, and be thankful."

That afternoon I made inquiries in the town, and everywhere I heard alarming accounts of the hitting powers of my prospective opponent; so I promptly went into training for the intervening three days.

Meanwhile the bills were got out, and the affair at once became the talk of the town. Every seat that could be booked was taken in no time, and when Friday afternoon came round the "house full" boards were up in ten minutes after the doors were open.

I was in my dressing-room getting ready, when in stalks a brawny giant and inquires: "Are you Carlton?"

"That's me," I answered.

"Well," he said, "I'm the Champion of the Meat Market, and I gotter win. Unnerstand that! I don't want to hurt you. But all my pals are in front, an' I just gotter win."

"All right," I said. "We'll see about that when the time comes."

Well, we entered the ring, and the first round had no sooner started than I saw he meant to knock me out if he could, so I let him have a straight left, and repeated the dose at what I considered suitable intervals. In the beginning of the second round we clinched, and the big man whispered in my ear: "Hi, you go easy with that left of yours." "Right!" I whispered back. "But you stop swinging that right of yours."

After this the going was a bit easier, and in the end I won easily on points; greatly to the disgust of the Champion of the Meat Market. My share of the takings came to £34, and I enjoyed myself immensely. My opponent got ten shillings, and I don't think he enjoyed himself at all. Harrison was frankly annoyed.

Another adventure I had, out of which, however, I got no enjoyment whatever, was when I was trapped in a den of lions at the Theatre Royal, Oldham. They were Madame Ella's lions, she being in the bill with me that week. During rehearsal on Monday on the stage I got near the cage where the animals were, and an attendant pushed me away, saying that the lions were dangerous, and that one of them had just clawed the hand of a railway porter.

"Rot!" I replied. "They're as quiet as kittens. Why, I wouldn't mind doing my show in their den."

"What's that you say, Carlton?" interjected Mr. Dottridge, the proprietor of the theatre, who was seated in front watching the rehearsals.

"These lions!" I replied. "They're as quiet as kittens. I wouldn't mind giving my show in the den."

"Really?"

"Certainly," I said, never dreaming that he would take it otherwise than as a joke.

Nothing more was said, and that night I gave my two shows as usual. On Tuesday morning on leaving my lodgings I was thunderstruck at finding the hoardings covered with big, flaming posters announcing that "on Friday night 'Carlton' will enter the lions' den and referee a billiard match between two local publicans on a miniature table—twenty-five up."

Round I went to Mr. Dottridge, but I found him unsympathetic. "Why, man, they're as quiet as kittens," he said.

I saw then that I had got to go through it, but I didn't relish it one little bit, and all the rest of the week I was thinking about the lion clawing the hand of the railway porter.

Madame Ella somewhat reassured me, however, by saying that she did not intend to take the two most ferocious lions into the cage, and that she would have a couple of trained boarhounds in with us. The lions, she added, were afraid of the dogs, and she didn't see how, under the circumstances, anything could happen.

Well, Friday night came. A big cage had been built all round the stage, and after I had drunk a stiff brandy-and-soda I went in, accompanied by Madame Ella and the two publicans. The game began, but after a few strokes had been made one of the players, both of whom were obviously in a state of considerable trepidation, accidentally dropped his cue.

This startled one of the lions, which let out a terrific roar and jumped from its perch. Both the players thereupon darted for the door. So did I, but in my excitement I tried to escape by opening it on the hinged side, and, of course, did not succeed. Meanwhile the lions were darting this way and that, Madame Ella shouting to me to get out quick, and lashing with her whip, while the dogs kept chasing them about the cage.

Frankly, I was frightened out of my life. I thought my last hour had come. One of the lions switched me with his tail as he rushed by. The audience roared with laughter to see me tugging at the wrong side of the door in a vain attempt to open it, but for me it was no laughing matter. How I got out at last I have no clear recollection. All I know is that I got out somehow, or was pulled out by the attendant; I am not sure which. Four weeks after one of these same lions got loose at Gloucester and killed his keeper.

Another extra draw that I worked while on sharing terms at Hull, Huddersfield, and elsewhere, consisted in a variation of my old box trick. I used to have a packing-case made by some local carpenter, out of which I would escape after it had been nailed together, and roped and sealed, all in full view of the audience. The packing-case used to be on view outside of the theatre during the week, and on the Friday night the house was invariably packed as full as it would hold. This was in 1903.

Once, too, I conceived an idea for a variation of this trick, which I am convinced would have created a big sensation, and been heard of all over England, had I been allowed to perform it. My intention was to charter a tug, and allow myself to be dropped over into deep water inside the box. It wouldn't have made any difference to me, for I could have got out of the corded and locked box while it was under water as easily as I could on dry land.

I had made all the preliminary arrangements. The crew of the tug were to drop me over the side, and if I did not release myself and come to the surface in three minutes by the watch, they were to haul the box up again in order to save my life. Meanwhile it was my intention to have dived under the tug's bottom after releasing myself, swim quietly away, and remain somewhere in hiding for a couple of days. I could picture to myself the consternation of the crew when, the stipulated three minutes having elapsed, they should haul up the box and find it empty, and also the excitement that would follow on my "mysterious disappearance." It would have been a splendid "ad." But, alas! I could not persuade the police that there was no danger in it, and at the last moment the scheme had to be abandoned.

At Bradford Palace, on one occasion when I was there, some trick swimmers were performing in a big tank, and Harry Arnold, the manager, knowing that I rather fancied myself as a swimmer, challenged me to try and see which of us could pick up the most coins under water from the bottom of the tank. I readily agreed, and Harry invited a lot of local people there to witness the trial, which it was arranged should take place after the regular evening performance.

Twenty-four pennies were dumped into the tank, then we threw dice for choice of entering the water. I won. They were my dice.

I told him to go first, which he did, and much to my surprise he gathered up all the coins. Then it was my turn. I dived in the water, but found it was practically impossible to keep down. Nor could I easily find the pennies, for they, being the same colour as the copper bottom of the tank, were practically invisible. In the end I did manage, however, to gather together three or four, and came up again thoroughly exhausted. But I got even with them the next night.

Just before the act was going on I threw a pennyworth of permanganate of potash into the water. The moment the swimmers started diving and stirred up the water, it became blood-red. You can imagine the rest.

Afterwards Harry explained to me how the wheeze was worked. In the first place a man cannot possibly keep down in shallow water where there is no room for him to move about. He invariably bobs up to the surface, like a cork does. Trick swimmers who perform in these tanks always wear a leaden belt round their loins under their tights. Harry had borrowed this, and used it. Also, the pennies he had fished up were fastened together with invisible thread in the corner of the tank. After this explanation I did not feel chagrined any more at having been so completely beaten.

This reminds me that there are tricks in all trades. I was once shown by a pal of mine how to win money at pigeon shooting.

I had arranged a match with a man for £5 a side and twelve lunches; 26 yards, 5 traps, best of 11 birds. The arrangement was that each was to supply the other's birds, the match to take place in a week's time.

The odds were supposed to be ten to one on my opponent, as I was not shooting very well at the time. But my pal, who was up to all the dodges, assured me that he knew of a scheme that would ensure my winning.

He was himself a great pigeon fancier, and possessed a fine strong lot of homing birds, which he kept in a barn at his place near Ilkley, in Yorkshire. We used to go over to his barn and catch a dozen or so of these birds in the dark, and shut them in a basket such as pigeon fanciers use.

Then, for five mornings running, we took them out one at a time and put them in a trap. Round about were a lot of boys, some with old tin cans to bang upon, some with handfuls of sand to throw at the pigeon directly the trap was sprung, and so on. We used these birds at the match for my opponent to shoot at, and, naturally when the trap was sprung there each pigeon thought that the same sort of thing was going to happen, and was up and away like a rocket.

As a result my opponent only got two out of eleven birds. I got nine, and scooped in a lot of bets at long odds, for nearly everybody made sure the other chap was going to win. "Where on earth did you get these birds from, Carlton?" asked my opponent over the lunch that followed; "I'd like to buy some."

Billy Grant, the open champion of Scotland, and the proprietor of the King Edward Hotel, Bath Lane, Newcastle, saw me shoot a couple of times, and presumably he rather liked my form. Anyway, he made me join the Hotspur Gun Club, and suggested to me that I should go in training with him. "We can make a tidy bit of money," he said, "and we'll go halves in everything."

I agreed, and I may say at once that between us we never lost. At the big shoot for the Sterling Cup presented by the Club, and open to all the North of England, held on February 4th, 1909, I killed twenty-two birds out of twenty-three. This was accounted a wonderful performance for a novice.

For the benefit of those who are not familiar with pigeon shooting, I may explain that one is faced by five traps, and the man who is shooting does not know out of which trap the bird will be released. The pigeon must be killed within the thirty-five yards' boundary.

As I was only a novice nobody took much notice of me at the start, but after I had shot twelve birds running the "bookies," and others who had bets on, began to look a bit worried, and some of them started making remarks with a view to putting me off my aim. "I'll take three to one you don't kill this bird," one of them would call out, just as I had my gun in readiness to shoot. I would turn half round to take the bet, and then get ready again, when another one would call out, "I'll take three to one you don't kill," and the whole performance would be gone over again.

This sort of thing was, of course, very disconcerting, but I went on killing my birds, and by and by there were only two of us left in. When we had each shot twenty birds, my opponent missed his twenty-first, and I had only to kill mine to win. I shot my bird, but it dropped just outside the boundary.

CARLTON AND BILLY GRANT, THE OPEN CHAMPION PIGEON SHOT OF SCOTLAND

The excitement was now intense. It was my opponent's turn to shoot. He fired, and again he missed his bird. Again I had only to kill mine to win, and the bookies started once more renewing their attempts to put me off my aim. So I lined them all up—there were six or eight of them—and laid them £3 to £1 each that I killed. Then I took up my position on the mark, the string was pulled, and I killed my bird within a yard of the trap.

Now for the explanation of how I accomplished the feat, a wonderful one for a novice, as everybody who understands pigeon shooting will readily agree. During the fortnight or so preceding the match, Billy Grant had taken me out every morning to a quiet place in the country, and there set me shooting at sparrows released from a trap similar to a pigeon trap.

"They're cheaper than pigeons," remarked Billy simply when I asked him why he employed sparrows. Later on, when I came to shoot for the cup, I understood his real reason. The pigeons looked to me like ostriches after the tiny sparrows, and I felt I simply couldn't miss them.

Later on I shot for the championship of England at Hendon, where I thought myself unknown; but I was quickly undeceived. Each competitor was allowed to take up to five chances at £5 a chance, and half-a-crown for each bird. I took three chances.

A man named Dillon was the handicapper, and when I asked him where I stood he indicated the 28 yards mark. I was taken aback at this, for I had reckoned on being placed on the 25 or 26 yards mark, and I had my gun bored accordingly. Any good pigeon shooter will understand the importance of this. A gun in these contests is bored to allow of a certain "spread" at a certain fixed distance, and mine being bored for 25–26 yards, at 28 yards the spread would be too big. I could not expect to get the proper concentration, and even if I hit the bird I could not be sure of bringing it down within the boundary.

"Oh, but, Mr. Dillon," I objected, "I'm only a novice. Surely you're not going to put me back to 28 yards."

But Dillon was adamant. "You can't 'kid' me," he retorted. "I know all about your performance up at Newcastle last February."

After this, of course, there was no more to be said. I took my stand on the 28 yards mark, thereby giving three yards start to a man who had won the *Grand Prix* at Monte Carlo. As regards two of my shares I got knocked out in the fifth round, for though I shot my sixth bird on each occasion I did not succeed in bringing it down inside the boundary, owing to the shot spreading, exactly as I had foreseen.

With my third chance, however, I killed eleven birds running before the same thing happened. The winner was the man who had carried off the Monte Carlo *Grand Prix*, and who shot off the 25 yards mark. His was the "unlucky" number thirteen.

Most "pro.'s" have had the honour of appearing before royalty; or they say they have. It really did happen to me. I was showing at Earl's Court at the time; a little side-show, entitled "Satan's Dream; a Supernatural Illusion." It was an illusion of the kind that was just then all the rage, a girl's head on a pitch-fork, with the prongs sticking through, and straw hanging down. Why "Satan's Dream," I'm sure I don't know. But, anyway, it was a good drawing title, and I was coining money easy all day at sixpence a time for admission. "What's in a name?" they say. My answer is: "Everything—when it comes to the show business."

Well, one day I was standing outside my pitch as usual in the intervals of showing, pattering for an audience, when the late Duke of Cambridge came along, accompanied by Princess Beatrice and her children, and attended, of course, by the Earl's Court directors. Directly I saw them coming I made up my mind that I was going to have them inside my show, so I waited until they were a few yards away, and then I opened wide the gate, took off my hat, and bowed low.

The Duke evidently thought that it was all part of the programme arranged for him, for he walked right in, and Princess Beatrice and her children followed as a matter of course. Naturally the directors could do nothing but follow on also; but they looked at me very sternly, I noticed, as they trooped in. "A fine show," said the old Duke to me quite genially, when he passed out. Five minutes afterwards I had a big board up: "Patronised by Royalty."

The following year, encouraged by my success, I put a really big show on, with ten or twelve tip-top illusions. But, alas! this was a failure. I was in a bad position, right behind the Big Wheel. I wanted to close down, but the directors wouldn't release me, and I had to go on showing to the end, losing money all the while. It was a heart-breaking experience.

Speaking of Earl's Court reminds me that it was while my poor old mother was there on a visit one day that she heard me perform on a regular stage for the first and last time in her life. They had an electrophone there, a novelty at the time, and by arrangement with the man who was running it, I got him to allow my mother to be at the receiver just before I was due to appear at the Palace, in Shaftesbury Avenue.

As everybody knows who has ever listened to a performance over the electrophone, not only is every word uttered on the stage by the performer clearly audible to the listener at the other end of the wire, but one hears the applause of the audience as well, assuming that there is any. As it happened I went very well that night, and the old lady was both surprised and delighted.

In the middle, between two of my gags, I called out: "Are you there, mother? Can you hear me?" Whereupon, so I was told afterwards, the poor old lady broke down and cried like a child. She was very infirm at the time, and a cripple, and she died very soon afterwards. But it pleased me, nevertheless, to think that she had at least heard me perform, although she had never seen me on the stage.

Reverting to my story of how I entertained the Duke of Cambridge and Princess Beatrice and children at my little Earl's Court side-show, I may remark that although this was my first appearance before royalty, it was by no means my last. And this leads up naturally to the subject of private entertainments before more or less eminent personages; a side of an entertainer's life which is pleasant or the reverse, according to the people with whom he has to deal.

Speaking generally, it has been my experience that the bigger the people are socially, the less "side" they put on, and the more courteous and considerate they almost invariably show themselves towards the performer or performers they summon to their houses. It is the newly rich, and the hangers-on to the fringe of society, who relegate, or try to relegate, the artiste to the servants' hall for his refreshments, etc., and otherwise show him by every means in their power how deep is the social gulf they imagine exists between the mere performer for money and themselves.

As an example of the other kind of treatment, meted out to me by people of the highest social standing, the following plain, unvarnished account of a professional visit I paid in the autumn of 1915 to Wentworth Woodhouse will serve. This magnificent mansion, the Yorkshire seat of Earl Fitzwilliam, is one of the most beautiful and stately ancestral homes in England; and to give some idea of its vast size I may state that in the front of the house alone there are more windows than there are days in the year.

The occasion of my visit was a garden-party and entertainment given by Lady Fitzwilliam in aid of one of the war funds. Half-a-guinea was charged for going over the house, and from this source alone over £1,000 accrued to the fund, so the number of guests present may be imagined.

Soon after my arrival I was taken in hand by a pleasant affable lady, who conducted me all over the mansion, and who showed me, amongst other things, the royal suite of rooms, and the bed the King slept in when he visited the house, and wound up by ushering me into the magnificent marble hall on the ground floor where the performance was to take place.

Here champagne cup and other refreshments were served, and my guide, when I had all along taken to be a governess, or something of that sort, moved away from me after shaking hands very cordially. I seized the opportunity of being alone for a moment to ask one of the many footmen standing about which was Lady Fitzwilliam.

"That is her ladyship over there," replied the man, pointing to the individual I had supposed to be a governess.

I confess I was never more taken aback in my life. Naturally I took an early opportunity of apologising, saying, what of course was the truth, that I had no idea as to her identity. Whereupon her ladyship laughed heartily, but quite good-naturedly; and, in order to put me at my ease, asked me if I had seen the grounds.

I replied that I had, and that I was greatly impressed by the size and beauty of the lakes, and I ended up by inquiring if there were any fish in them.

"Yes, lots," replied her ladyship. "Are you fond of fishing?"

I answered that I was, whereupon she gave me an invitation to come over the next day, take a morning's angling, and have luncheon with the family.

Of course, I gratefully accepted the kindly offer, and the next day, when I drove up in my car, I found awaiting me at the lodge gates Lord Fitzwilliam's agent, who went with me to the big lakes and told me the best places to fish.

I angled all the morning, but for some reason or other I had no luck to speak of, and when I went in to lunch, and in answer to inquiries I said as much, Lady Fitzwilliam remarked: "Never mind, you shall fish this afternoon in the private lake where the trout are bred for the table."

I was really almost overwhelmed by so much kindness, and still more did I realise all it meant when I went out and told the head keeper.

"My word!" he exclaimed. "You *have* got a privilege."

"Are there many trout in there, then?" I asked innocently.

The man smiled. "Come along and I'll show you," he said. "We're just going to feed 'em."

We went, and the keepers started throwing handfuls of fish offal into the water. Instantly all was commotion. Never had I seen such a sight. Hundreds of trout, great speckled beauties, rushed together, churning the water to foam, and leaping into the air in their excitement.

Then we took a punt and went out on the lake, and oh the sport I had. I caught ten brace, which I was informed was the limit, and then put back to bank.

Nor was this all. The following Christmas I was performing in pantomime at the Hippodrome, Sheffield, when to my unbounded surprise I received yet another invitation for a day's fishing. On this occasion also I had the honour of lunching with the family, and I was likewise introduced to Earl Fitzwilliam, who had just returned from the Front.

He was affability itself, and before I took my leave, hearing from me that I intended shortly to pay a professional visit to Paris, he gave me a personal letter of introduction to the Hon. Maurice Brett, our Provost-Marshal there.

CHAPTER XIX
IN EGYPT IN WAR-TIME

My trip to the land of the Pharaohs—Giants and dwarfs on a P. & O. liner—We are ordered into Plymouth—Submarines—An exciting experience—Destroyers to the rescue—The dwarfs and the lifebelts—Sports at sea—My contortionist is taken ill—Anxious days—Kindness of the Maharajah of Jodhpur—Arrival at Port Said—Cairo—I engage another contortionist—Pelted with money—Pigs at Port Said—Captured Turkish pontoons at Cairo—Turkish prisoners playing tennis—Interned enemy ships at Alexandria—Wounded soldiers—At the Pyramids—Ammunition from India—On the way home—Across France in war-time—The Channel passage—Elaborate precautions—Submarine nets—Paris in war-time—Madrid in war-time.

TOWARDS the end of May, 1915, as I was feeling a bit "hipped" and run down, I decided to take a short sea voyage to Egypt, a land I had always wished to see.

I had heard that there were numbers of wounded there, as well as a large number of unwounded soldiers, and I decided, therefore, to take my company with me; arguing that if by so doing I was able to clear working expenses so much the better, and that in any case I should be sure of appreciative audiences amongst the convalescents and the less seriously injured.

My company at this time consisted of six persons: myself, three dwarfs, a giant, and a contortionist. Two of the dwarfs, Signor and Madame Gondin, were reputed to be the smallest man and wife in the world, and their appearance in Egypt, and on board ship going out, created no end of interest and excitement.

We embarked at Tilbury on May 29th, 1915, on the P. & O. steamship *Malwa*. We were not a big crowd at first, but some of us—this does not apply, of course, to my humble self—were very distinguished. There was, for instance, Lady Peirse, wife of Admiral Sir R. Peirse, in charge of the Mediterranean Station. Lady Peirse took great interest in a charitable entertainment we got up on board, and later on, when we arrived at Port Said, her ladyship invited me to take tea with her and Sir Richard Peirse at their hotel.

Mr. Justice Bucknill was another notable on board. But the most striking and interesting personality of all was that of the youthful-looking Maharajah of Jodhpur, who came straight to the ship from Buckingham Palace, where he had been dining with the King. He was travelling in great state with a splendid suite, yet he was most affable and unaffected, entering with zest into whatever sport or entertainment was going.

The Maharajah had already raised some thirty-five thousand troops in his dominions, and remarking on this I ventured to say: "Well, your Highness, you have certainly done your bit." His reply was: "Bit be d——d! I'm going back to raise some more." His state, I may mention, is larger than any of the smaller European countries, and somewhat bigger than Saxony and Bavaria combined, while even in peace time the Maharajah maintains a force of eight thousand infantry and cavalry with one hundred and twenty heavy guns.

The original intention, or at least so we were given to understand, was for the *Malwa* to proceed direct to Gibraltar. But there was evidently something more on the board than we passengers knew of, for soon after leaving the Thames we were stopped by a patrol boat and told to alter our direction, and this was repeated every four or five miles, so that we steered an altogether zigzag course.

Eventually we were ordered into Plymouth, where we took on board some 250 bluejackets. These did duty during the voyage in various parts of the ship; and especially aft, where was mounted a big 4.7 naval gun, obviously for use in case of our being chased by submarines.

That this was no idle precaution we had good reason to know, for on resuming our voyage, and when we were about four hours out from Plymouth, a destroyer came racing up at so terrific a speed that she actually collided with us before she could turn, slightly denting her side. Her captain shouted an order to us to put back into port immediately, as there were submarines about; and this, of course, was immediately done. At the same time all passengers were ordered to don lifebelts.

There was considerable excitement, although not so much as one might suppose. The chief aim and object of practically everybody seemed to be to try and get a glimpse of the submarine or submarines, but in this we were unsuccessful, although several passengers declared afterwards that they saw a periscope. I myself saw nothing, although I was ready with my camera, and keeping an eager lookout. I did, however, succeed in getting a good picture of the collision between the destroyer and our ship; but this was afterwards abstracted from my cabin—whether by the authorities, or by some individual who took a fancy to it for his own private collection, I do not know.

Harking back to the lifebelts, I had almost forgotten to say that the members of my company, owing to their diverse size, underwent probably the worst experiences of anybody on board in connection with these always trying and clumsy contrivances. The contortionist contorted as he had never done before. The giant could not find one to fit him, and was rushing about the decks, imploring the stewards, with tears in his eyes, to get him "an extra outside size in lifebelts." The dwarfs, on the other hand, were unable to find any small enough, and were likewise wildly excited in consequence. In the end Signor and Madame Gondin solved the difficulty by sharing one between them. It accommodated them both, although it was rather a tight fit, and I could not help reflecting that if we were destined to go to the bottom the little couple would at all events do so as securely united in death as they are—I hope and trust—in their lives. The giant solved his difficulty by wearing a couple of belts which he lashed together, one of these being the property of one of the dwarfs.

Well, the destroyer escorted us back to Plymouth, where we remained for a while; and when we resumed our voyage we had an escort of two torpedo-boats, one on each side of us, and a destroyer leading the way. These kept with us till darkness set in, when, of course, as we steamed with all lights out, there was little to be feared from submarines.

The rest of the voyage was uneventful, except that when we were nearing "Gib." a lot of talk arose about the submarine peril, and one evening after dinner the engines stopped suddenly without warning, and for several minutes the steamer remained motionless.

The passengers looked at each other in an anxious manner, wondering what was the matter.

Presently one of them, a portly, pompous person, advanced to the captain.

"What seems to be the trouble, captain?" he inquired.

"Too much fog," answered that worthy curtly.

"But," persisted the other, "I can see the stars overhead quite plainly."

"Maybe you can," came the grim reply. "But unless the boilers burst, or a German submarine pops up, we aren't going that way."

At Gibraltar we stayed rather longer than usual, in order to unship the big stern gun, which was wanted for the next homeward-bound steamer. Between Gibraltar and Malta we gave an entertainment, assisted by volunteers from amongst the passengers, the proceeds being divided equally between the mine-sweepers and the Music-hall Benevolent Fund. There were also sports, the blindfold boxing for prizes amongst members of the crew being especially funny. Afterwards the prizes were presented by Lady Peirse, and my two male dwarfs gave an exhibition of trick wrestling, which was greatly appreciated.

This particular dwarf of mine was quite a smart little fellow, and once, during a voyage to South Africa, he got the better of my giant in a rather ingenious fashion. He bet the big man a sovereign that he could reach further than he (the giant) could, each to stand bolt upright with his back to the wall, and to use an arm and hand only, and not to bend or sway any part of the body out of the perpendicular. The stakes having been duly wagered, the dwarf took up his prescribed position, back to the wall, and, reaching down, made a mark with a piece of chalk close to the floor on the wainscoting. This of course the giant could not do without bending, and the dwarf, therefore, won his bet.

The only drawback to a very pleasant trip was that my contortionist developed a bad attack of appendicitis, whether owing to his unwonted exertions in connection with the lifebelt or not I am unable to say. We were all greatly upset, and the captain and the ship's doctor both recommended his being put off at Malta, in order that he might go into hospital there, and be operated upon. But the poor chap, with tears in his eyes, begged us to take him with us: "Mr. Carlton," he said, "I've been with you so long; let me stay on now till the end."

So eventually we yielded to his entreaties, but when we were about three days from Port Said he became very much worse, and the ship's surgeon, after consulting with another doctor who chanced to be on board, advised an immediate operation. As this, however, would have meant that he could not possibly have been taken ashore at Port Said, but would have been obliged to go on to Australia, and as furthermore an operation on board ship in anything but the calmest weather is always an exceedingly risky business, the patient himself negatived this proposition.

When at length we arrived at Port Said the poor fellow was hovering between life and death, but we managed to get him down the side, and eventually to Cairo, where he was at once admitted to hospital. Here he was promptly and skilfully operated on, and in the end, I am thankful to say, he completely recovered. I should like to add that the people on the boat, from the captain downward, were most kind and sympathetic. There happened to be two nurses on board going out to Cairo, and these rendered invaluable help to the sufferer. His Highness the Maharajah of Jodhpur, too, expressed genuine concern for him, and before we quitted the boat at Port Said he slipped a ten-pound note into his hand, to help him during his convalescence.

By rights, on disembarking at Port Said, I ought to have proceeded to Alexandria, where I was to open under a contract previously entered into with Signor Dalbagni, the proprietor of the Jardin Rosette Music-hall there. But I decided that I should not be justified in quitting the sick man until I had seen him safely into the hospital at Cairo, and to that place accordingly I went.

Now Signor Dalbagni, besides owning the Jardin Rosette at Alexandria and another music-hall at Port Said, is also the proprietor of the Kursaal at Cairo, and as luck would have it he happened to be at the latter place when I arrived; so, having left the patient in good hands, and feeling relieved of my responsibility in that direction, I set off for the Kursaal to interview him. I was in somewhat of a quandary, for I had contracted to give a complete show with a full company at all three of his halls, beginning with the one at Alexandria, and now, of course, I was minus my contortionist, and how to get another in Egypt I had not the remotest idea.

Besides, it struck me as just possible that Signor Dalbagni might take advantage of my misfortune to try and dock me of part of my agreed remuneration, as the Germans and Austrians had done under somewhat similar circumstances, and this I had firmly made up my mind I was not going to put up with. It was, therefore, with somewhat mixed feelings that I presented myself before him.

To say that he was surprised to see me is stating the case very mildly. "Good God!" he exclaimed. "Why, what are you doing here in Cairo? Didn't you know that you are to open tomorrow night in Alexandria? The bills are up all over the city."

I told him I knew that, but that I had to come to Cairo, and I explained the circumstances fully to him. "I shall have to do without the services of one of my men," I said in conclusion, "but that need not necessarily affect my show adversely, and I shall expect the same money as if he were present. I came out here principally for a change, and for my health's sake, as you know; and if there is going to be any question of docking me, I would rather pack up my traps and return to England by the next boat."

"No! No, Mr. Carlton. I would not do a thing like that," was his reply. "But," he added, "cannot you find a substitute to take the sick man's place?"

"Why, certainly!" I replied. "Nothing easier! I'll set about engaging one at once, and communicate with you later on in the day."

Now, I may remark right here that in saying this I was far from expressing my real feelings. In fact I was affecting a confidence I was far from experiencing. I had not the remotest idea whereabouts in Cairo I was going to engage a contortionist, nor had I, of course, any knowledge of the city, never having set foot in it before. But I *had* a knowledge of showmanship, and this I relied upon to stand me in good stead in the emergency.

The first thing I did was to go and get a drink—a good stiff brandy-and-soda. Then I put on my considering cap, and lit a cigar. As a result of my cogitations, I started to get into conversation with the barman; a likely-looking, well-set-up young fellow. He told me he was a Roumanian by birth, and that he had formerly travelled with a circus in India.

"You're my man," I exclaimed to myself.

Then, aloud to him: "Do you like the bar business?"

"No, I don't," he replied.

"Then why not chuck it," I said, "and come with me? I'm in the show business. Will you?"

"What shall I have to do?" he asked.

"Oh, nothing much. Just come on the stage and pretend you're mesmerised, fall off a chair, and simple things like that. I'll explain it all in the train later on. What wages are you getting here?"

He mentioned a sum.

"I'll pay you double that," I said.

"All right," he replied, "I'll come."

"Good!" I cried. "We start for Alexandria to-morrow morning at seven o'clock. Be sure and be at the station in time."

"But," he objected, somewhat taken aback at my precipitancy, "I can't do that. I've got to give a week's notice here."

"Pay a week's money in lieu of the notice," I said. "I'll give you five pounds right now if you'll agree."

"Right ho!" he cried, "I'm agreeable." And I drew up the contract there and then in the bar, and he signed it. Then I went back to Signor Dalbagni, and told him that I had met and engaged an old acquaintance of mine, a circus performer just back from India, that he was twice as good a man as the other was, and that I had to pay him twice as big a salary (as a matter of fact it was about half), and so on, and so on.

Dalbagni was quite pleased, and so was I, although I had to lay awake pretty well all night rearranging my show in my own mind, and spend all day rehearsing him in the train on the journey up. However, everything went off all right even in Alexandria, and during the fifteen days we played there I was able to teach my new man a lot, so that he was fairly efficient when we opened at our next hall.

In fact I was greatly pleased with the success of the venture throughout, a success which was largely due to the patronage accorded me by our officers and soldiers. They were always in the jolliest spirits imaginable, and up to all sorts of larks. When performing at Cairo, for example, in the course of my patter I introduced an old gag of mine as follows: "Oh! Isn't he marvellous? Let's throw some money at him."

This I did for three evenings running. On the fourth night, when I again repeated the words, a lot of young officers in the stalls suddenly started showering handfuls of small coins at me. I was rather taken aback, for although I have often used the gag before in all sorts of places, nobody up till then had ever taken me seriously. However, I thought that as they had thrown the money on the stage, I might as well have it; so directly the curtain rang down, I ran on, and gathered up all I could find, to the number of between two and three hundred pieces. I was quite pleased with myself, and grateful to the officers too; until I discovered that the coins were millièmes, the smallest piece of Egyptian money, and worth no more than about one-tenth of a penny apiece. Of course it was meant for a joke, and as such I took it. The coins were handy for distributing to beggars, of which there are a goodly assortment in Cairo.

There is no need for dustbins in Port Said. The pigs do all the scavenging, and very effectually. I remember that on one occasion, very late at night, or rather early in the morning, I was sitting on the verandah of my hotel, enjoying a final "peg" before turning in, when about fifty of these animals came trooping up the street. They rooted into every doorway, scurried up every close and alley, and out again, devouring every scrap of garbage.

This, I was told, was their regular nightly custom. There is nobody to mind them, but hunger makes them do their work thoroughly. The city is divided into districts, each with its own platoon of pigs, and no porker from one district dare trespass on the domain of its neighbours. Personally I am rather partial to pork, but I barred it as an article of diet during the remainder of my stay in Egypt.

Going to Cairo by train we passed the place where the Turks tried to get across the Suez Canal the previous February. The old trenches were still there. Our soldiers captured intact four of their pontoons, and these are now on view in the Zoological Gardens at Cairo. I went to look at them. They are beautifully made, of aluminium, and wonderfully strong and well finished.

In them the Turkish invading army carried their water supply over the Desert of Sinai, and they afterwards used them, or attempted to used them, as boats, in order to bridge the Canal.

We stayed some time at Cairo, going about the different camps, and giving our entertainment. There were an enormous number of wounded here, some very bad cases, but all quite merry and bright. Sometimes we gave our performance in the hospital wards, and sometimes to the convalescents in the grounds, and everywhere our efforts to amuse met with the heartiest applause.

Going to Alexandria I was greatly struck by the wonderful system of irrigation. It is quite modern hereabouts, I was told, but the result is that what was barren sand a few years ago is now covered with cotton fields. The natives draw the water from the river by means of small screw pumps, which they keep incessantly turning by hand. The combined resultant noise is terrific, resembling a series of motor explosions magnified a million-fold.

At Alexandria were some 150 to 200 interned ships, big and little, that once flew the German or Austrian flags. It was a wonderful sight to see them all lying there in long serried lines, and gave one a fine idea of the all-powerfulness of the British Navy. We also saw here, for the first time, a number of Turkish prisoners. They were behind barbed wire playing tennis. I don't exactly know why, but Turks at tennis struck me as being distinctly funny.

Alexandria was then the main base for the Dardanelles, and wounded men were everywhere about. We went the round of the various hospital camps, often performing in tents by candlelight, and walking across the desert in the dark in between whiles, challenged every few yards by armed sentries. It was rather a tiring, nerve-trying experience.

I forgot to say that while we were at Port Said we gave a special matinée to the convalescents in the Theatre Khedival. The house was packed from floor to roof, and most of the audience attended clad in pyjamas. It was amusing to see them walking through the main streets in this airy attire. As I was watching them a Greek came along with an ice-cream barrow, and I told him to dish out his creams to the pyjama-clad Tommies until I told him to stop. He cleared his stock in no time. I never realised till then what an appetite for ice-cream the British soldier can acquire in a hot climate, and when recovering from wounds.

Of course we went to have a look at the Pyramids, and with my usual luck I managed to lose my brand-new hat down a deep excavation there. However, it was retrieved by an Arab boy, who was lowered by a rope from above. A ticklish proceeding, but he didn't seem to mind it a bit.

Arriving back at Port Said we found the *Germanic* there discharging. She was doing duty as an Australian trooper. Another little object-lesson in the silent might of our Navy. Near her was the P. & O. steamship *Khyber*, unloading five million rounds of ammunition for the Dardanelles operations. She had, I was told, another five million rounds on board, destined for Marseilles. All this was made in India by native labour.

We left Port Said on July 22nd, a day late owing to the time occupied in unloading the ammunition. On the way back we organised another charity entertainment, the proceeds this time being divided between the French Red Cross and the M.H.A.B. Fund. "Tipperary" was rendered, first in English, and then in French by two Parisian members of an opera troupe who were on board, and everybody enjoyed themselves hugely.

At Marseilles I left the ship and travelled overland to Boulogne. We were, of course, out of the war area proper, and nothing much out of the common happened, barring sundry delays and side-trackings, due to troop trains proceeding to the front. At Boulogne I had to have my passport *viséd* for the last time; it was nearly filled up and covered now with signatures and seals. Also we had to submit to a very strict search, and any suspects, known as "special cases," were taken aside and examined separately. The main object of these precautions was to prevent gold from being taken out of the country. No more than eight sovereigns, or the equivalent in French gold currency, was allowed to be taken by any one passenger; the balance had to be in paper money.

This, as I have already said, was in 1915. A year later, in the summer of 1916, I was again in France, this time for a stay of three months, during which time I was appearing at the Folies Bergère, Revue, Olympia, and the Alhambra, Paris.

Contrary to what I had been led to expect, I found the city quite gay and the citizens leading practically a normal life; no restrictions as to lighting, treating, or anything of that sort, and all the time I was there I never saw a single searchlight.

This was all the stranger to me, because, of course, the war was very close. Just outside Paris, at St. Cloud, one could hear the guns quite plainly.

There were lots of French soldiers there, and a sprinkling of English ones as well. The "poilus" I found were rather jealous of our "Tommies," chiefly because the latter were better fed and better paid. Seeing an aeroplane flying overhead, they would say: "There goes some more buttered toast and ham and eggs for Tommy's breakfast." From this it must not be inferred, however, that they bore us any ill-will.

From Paris I went to Madrid, where I was engaged to play at the Circo Parish for twenty nights. The return fares for myself and company, five people, amounted to £64, and the journey meant two full days and nights in the train.

On my arrival I found an ominously strong German element in the city, and a large amount of pro-German feeling prevalent. Germans and Spanish pro-Germans walked about everywhere sporting the Hun colours, but I did not see one British flag worn.

This perhaps ought to have warned me as to the reception I might expect to receive, especially as when I was dressing for my show I could hear the German artistes in adjoining dressing-rooms chewing their beloved gutturals. Some inkling of what was in store for me did, I admit, cross my mind just then. But I have ever been an optimist, and I started in at the Sunday matinée hoping for the best.

Hardly had I commenced my performance, however, when I got the "bird" properly. Not just the ordinary "bird," but about three thousand people hissing, howling, shouting, shrieking, and stamping. I had never heard anything like it in my life before. The news had apparently got spread abroad that I was English, and the Germans, reinforced by the Spanish pro-Germans, had turned up in force.

Furthermore, the majority of the Spaniards apparently would not believe that my conjuring show was a burlesque one. Many of them thought I was fooling them. This does not speak highly for the Spanish sense of humour, and perhaps explains why the Spanish music-hall stage contains scarcely a single comedian.

Well, I did not like giving in easily, and I determined to go on again for the evening performance. But things were even worse then. The din was terrific. I could not hear myself speak. Nevertheless I went through my performance in what was practically dumb show, and when I came off I decided that my Spanish engagement was at an end. I accordingly asked the manager to release me, which he did, paying me one day's salary only; and after three days' sightseeing I returned to Paris, where I put in another engagement at the Alhambra, in order to fill in my time before returning to England.

When I was in Paris the celebrated Italian sculptor Sabati presented me with a splendid statuette of myself in my make-up. I had this copied in plaster of Paris and Mr. Reynolds, of the famous waxworks and museum in Liverpool, begged me to give him one for his show. Imagine my surprise when I walked into the waxworks next day to find myself in a glass case with a tablet underneath, "Carlton, the World's Famous Comic Conjuror," on my left being Charles Peace and on my right Crippen!

I did not find Madrid a particularly interesting city. The people there seem to me to be either very rich or very poor. There does not appear to be any middle class.

On the last day of my stay there I was sitting in the smoke-room of the Palace Hotel with a friend of mine who was running a company at the Teatro Princesca, when a messenger came that the King of Spain intended to be present that night. We immediately motored to the theatre, and found about fourscore of detectives there. There were eight or nine behind the scenes, a lot more up on the roof, others behind the royal box, and scattered about among the audience, while outside there was a regiment of soldiers stationed.

They told me that a bomb might be thrown at any moment, so I got on the opposite side of the theatre, as far away as possible from the box, where the King sat with his English wife, our Princess Ena. It was then that I reflected that, spite of all my troubles, I would rather be "Carlton" than the King of Spain.

And now, in conclusion, here are a few odd stories that I could not possibly work in anywhere else—as in all my tricks it will be seen that I take the public into my confidence. Here they are—the stories, I mean.

The majority of performers in this country live in "digs" or apartments. In America it is just the opposite, all travelling performers live in hotels. On the occasion of my last voyage back from the States there were a lot of American "pro.'s" coming over who were very anxious to know the ropes here. They were looking forward to cosy "digs," with a comfortable sitting-room and a nice fire, instead of the artificial steam heat, so they asked me to tell them of some good rooms in London. I told them I knew some tip-top ones. They thanked me, and I wrote down the address in their book, "10, Downing Street." When they arrived at Euston Station they got all their "props" on to a taxi and immediately went to the address I had given them. I have kept out of their way since, so exactly what happened I do not know, but I heard that they duly drove up and asked for apartments. I wonder whether Lloyd George was at home?

I was once in the smoke-room of a very fashionable hotel in the Provinces, where the sporting fraternity meet. The subject of conversation turned to running, and a smart Yank who was present, together with some of his compatriots, offered to bet £50 that he would run a mile in 4 minutes 20 seconds on the road. As the record is 4 minutes 22 seconds, he was promptly accommodated, and the money put up, the event to come off the following morning between two agreed mile posts on a straight road in the country. Everybody turned up with their cars and bicycles, and off he went, and he was some runner, believe me, for to the consternation and surprise of everybody, he did it in 4 minutes 19 seconds, thereby beating the world's record. The money was promptly paid over and we never saw the Yank again, but I found out afterwards that he and his pals had gone out the night before in the dark and shifted one of the milestones about two hundred yards nearer to the other.

Dick Ford, an American comedian, was a great practical joker. He always took particular delight in annoying Irish policemen. I remember once in Kansas City he went up to an officer on point duty and asked him the hour about twenty times a day. The policeman stood it until Friday, and then, when he asked him for about the twenty-first time, "What is the time, officer?"

the policeman hit him on the head with his club, and said, "It has just struck one," adding, "and sure it's a damned good thing it isn't twelve!"

The public does not generally know that the manager of a provincial music-hall on the big tours is not really a manager at all. These "managers" do not even know what their programme is until it is sent through from the head office in London on Wednesday or Thursday in the previous week, neither do they know the salary of the artistes until they receive the salary list, generally on Friday mornings. But on Monday they watch the show, and have to report to the head office in Town what they think of the acts, and what they value them at; so when a certain manager of a music-hall in the Provinces came to me on the Monday morning during rehearsal, and said, "Hullo, Carlton. How are you? Now, let me see, what is your salary this week?" I replied, "I am only getting £150 this week, but of course it is a very old contract." So, being—in his own estimation—a very clever chap, when he made his report out he valued my performance at £150 per week. He wanted to let those in Town know what a good judge he was, but when he paid me less than half on Saturday night, he told me they had written to him from the head office telling him what a rotten judge he was. He wanted to know what I meant by saying my salary was £150 a week. Of course, I said I was only joking. I have worked this many times, and it has not done me any harm.

I remember once the Manchester bookmaker, George Gunnup, coming to London to look after the box office for the late Dick Burge at The Ring, Blackfriars. He always used to rave about London cured fish, and told me one day in great confidence that he had found a shop down the New Cut where a pal of his smoked haddocks in real oak sawdust. They were marvellous, he said, and he promised me a bag of his pal's fish to try. At this time he and his wife were staying with Marie Lloyd on her house-boat at Thames Ditton. One day he 'phoned up to my house at New Malden. I was away working four shows a night at the time at Poplar and Ilford. My wife's mother—a dear old lady over eighty years of age—answered the telephone. He said he had a lovely bag of fish for me, and would she mind being on the platform at Malden station at twelve o'clock at night when he passed through in the train on his way to Thames Ditton? She of course was there—though she generally goes to bed at seven o'clock—waiting for the lovely bag of wonderful smoked haddocks. As the electric train drew in George Gunnup handed her the bag of fish with his compliments. Dick Burge, Sam Mayo, and a lot of the lads were in the same compartment. When she got home and opened the bag it contained a rabbit skin, a pair of old boots, and a couple of bananas. Of course George Gunnup did not know anything about it. He had bought the fish, and told them at The Ring that it was for Carlton. Dick Burge and Sam Mayo, I believe, rang the changes on me, but I, of course, was not there, so the joke fell flat. The old lady took it in good part, but George Gunnup never forgave Sam Mayo and Dick Burge.

I have now come to the end of my story. I hope you have been amused by these rambling recollections of a strolling player and trust that we shall meet again. You as my audience, and myself, as always, yours to entertain.

"Carlton"